Our Sisters' Promised Land

Women and Culture Series

The Women and Culture Series is dedicated to books that illuminate the lives, roles, achievements, and status of women, past or present.

Fran Leeper Buss
Dignity: Lower Income Women Tell of Their Lives and Struggles
Forged under the Sun / Forjada bajo el sol: The Life of María Elena Lucas
La Partera: Story of a Midwife

Valerie Kossew Pichanick
Harriet Martineau: The Woman and Her Work, 1802–76

Estelle B. Freedman
Their Sisters' Keepers: Women's Prison Reform in America, 1830–1930

Susan C. Bourque and Kay Barbara Warren
Women of the Andes: Patriarchy and Social Change in Two Peruvian Towns

Marion S. Goldman
Gold Diggers and Silver Miners: Prostitution and Social Life on the Comstock Lode

Page duBois
Centaurs and Amazons: Women and the Pre-History of the Great Chain of Being

Mary Kinnear
Daughters of Time: Women in the Western Tradition

Sally Price
Co-wives and Calabashes

Diane Wood Middlebrook and Marilyn Yalom, editors
Coming to Light: American Women Poets in the Twentieth Century

E. Frances White
Sierra Leone's Settler Women Traders: Women on the Afro-European Frontier

Lynda Hart, editor
Making a Spectacle: Feminist Essays on Contemporary Women's Theatre

Verena Martinez-Alier
Marriage, Class and Colour in Nineteenth-Century Cuba: A Study of Racial Attitudes and Sexual Values in a Slave Society

Kathryn Strother Ratcliff et al., editors
Healing Technology: Feminist Perspectives

Mary S. Gossy
The Untold Story: Women and Theory in Golden Age Texts

Jocelyn Linnekin
Sacred Queens and Women of Consequence: Rank, Gender, and Colonialism in the Hawaiian Islands

Glenda McLeod
Virtue and Venom: Catalogs of Women from Antiquity to the Renaissance

Jill Ker Conway and Susan C. Bourque, editors
The Politics of Women's Education: Perspectives from Asia, Africa, and Latin America

Lynn Keller and Cristanne Miller, editors
Feminist Measures: Soundings in Poetry and Theory

Domna C. Stanton and Abigail J. Stewart, editors
Feminisms in the Academy

Ayala Emmett
Our Sisters' Promised Land: Women, Politics, and Israeli-Palestinian Coexistence

Our Sisters' Promised Land

Women, Politics, and Israeli-Palestinian Coexistence

Ayala Emmett

THE UNIVERSITY OF MICHIGAN PRESS

Ann Arbor

First paperback edition 2003

Copyright © by the University of Michigan 1996, 2003

All rights reserved

Published in the United States of America by

The University of Michigan Press

Manufactured in the United States of America

⊗ Printed on acid-free paper

2006   2005   2004   2003   4   3   2   1

A CIP catalog record for this book is available
from the British Library.

Library of Congress Cataloging-in-Publication Data

Emmett, Ayala

   Our sisters' promised land: women, politics, and Israeli-
  Palestinian coexistence / Ayala Emmett.

     p. cm.

   Includes bibliographical references and index.

   ISBN 0-472-10733-X (hardcover : acid-free paper)

    1. Jewish-Arab relations—1973–   2. Peace movements—Israel.
  3. Women and peace—Israel. 4. Israel—Politics and government.
  I. Title.

  DS119.7.E565   1996

  327.1'72'095694—dc20   96-9949

                                                                     CIP

ISBN 0-472-08930-7 (pbk. : alk. paper)

Preface

For most Americans, violence, anger, and revenge have become the daily face of the Middle East on their television screens. The Promised Land, in national and local newspapers, has become synonymous with severe occupation and horrific suicide bombings. It is not surprising that as I write the preface for this paperback edition, people ask me the same question that I often heard seven years ago when the book was first published: Why do most Americans know so little about women's peace groups in Israel?

In 1990, when I began my fieldwork for the book, and now in the new millennium, media reports have been replete with stories of constantly hardening political positions, inflamed nationalisms, and shrill calls for revenge, as extremes on both sides shamelessly exploit religious sentiments. What, then, is wrong with these reports when they do in fact, as I show in this book, represent real events as they happen on the ground?

The problem then and now has been that to make sense of political violence requires a meaningful cultural context. A single social fact, as anthropologists insist, is incomprehensible unless it is firmly placed in its local cultural context and seen in relationship to other social and political events. Instead, in the case of the Middle East, a single social aspect, albeit a heartbreakingly tragic one, now characterizes two nations as senselessly brutal. Many Americans have come to see two nations and a region as nothing but pointlessly vengeful and hopeless.

Sorely missing from this depiction, then and now, is a context of real social life that includes not only violence, not only the official version that discounts coexistence, but also contesting grassroots groups and individuals that promote peace, believe in reconciliation, and work across national conflicts.

Missing, for example, is media attention to women's peace groups such as the Jerusalem Link, a joint Israeli and Palestinian endeavor that actively encourages peace and promotes coexistence. In a city often described as holy, yet so bitterly divided, The Jerusalem Link, established in 1994, brings together Bat Shalom (Daughter of Peace), an Israeli women's group located in West Jerusalem, and the Palestinian group Marcaz al-Quds la l-Nissha, the Jerusalem Center for Women, located in East Jerusalem. Together they state:

"We are women who are unalterably opposed to both suicide bombings as well as to the violence of political assassinations. We are women who insist that our humanity and commitment to justice not only connect us, but impel us to continue to jointly struggle to end Israel's inhumane occupation of Palestinian people and their land" (Bat Shalom—The Jerusalem Link, <http://www.batshalom.org/2002/1.htm>, accessed December 25, 2001).

The Jerusalem Link women, like other peace activists, know that they lack the government's easy access to the media and understand its power to shape public opinion. Women want, as they told me in 1990, to challenge the official Israeli version that still dominates media reports that "there are no partners for peace on the other side."

On June 5, 2002, Amneh Badran of the Palestinian Jerusalem Center for Women addressed this very issue and spoke of the Jerusalem Link's goal of bringing joint voices to public attention in both nations: "Together we aim to create a public atmosphere of dialoguing through speaking/addressing each other by newspapers, radio and if possible TV. We will do it because we believe that we should tell each other that there are people who care about and feel for each other, there are people to speak to and there is a partner on the other side" (Bat Shalom—The Jerusalem Link, <http://www.bat-shalom.org/2002/1.htm>, accessed June 5, 2002).

Americans deserve to know that the "no partner on the other side" official position is challenged by the presence not only of women's groups but of numerous grassroots peace organizations that I describe in the book. These challenges, as I show, take different forms. The founders of the Jerusalem Link, for example, contradicted the official version in 1989 when Palestinian and Israeli women met in Brussels to promote coexistence. From then on they continued to work together and eventually founded The Jerusalem Link.

It would be easy to dismiss women's peace groups as marginal and out of touch with the rest of their communities. Since I make an argument for understanding facts within their own cultural context and because this book focuses on Israel, where I carried out my fieldwork, it is important to note that women's peace groups are part of ongoing passionate debates and intense and at times bitter disagreements. These fervent debates, as I show in the book, are one of the distinguishing features of Israel's social life. Debates take place daily in the Israeli parliament, in street vigils and demonstrations, in the media, in literature, in films, and around kitchen tables.

One could argue that there is no need to give Americans meaningful and insightful information about women's groups, or for that matter other peace groups, because they constitute a fringe minority in a country that is solidly behind occupation, settlements, and conflict. In the Israeli cultural context of heated deliberations in which both ordinary citizens and career politicians participate, it is important to address the question: Are women's peace groups simply out of step with the rest of the country?

Let me begin with an American political favorite, looking at polls and numbers, to see what Israelis say. According to the Zemach June 2002 poll, "74 percent said that Sharon was doing a good job and 60 percent believe that the Israeli army should be allowed to attack the refugee camps in Gaza" (Israelinsider, <http://www.israelinsider.com>, accessed July 15, 2002). At first glance the answer would seem to be that the women are not standing with the rest of the country because they, like other peace groups, oppose Prime Minister Ariel Sharon's policies. But to look at poll results means to examine not just one question but the rest as well. To do so means to face social life with its inevitable messy confusions and contradictions because most Israelis, who may or may not regard the occupation as unjust, say, like the women, that they want to end it: "According to the June 2002 findings by Mina Zemach, Israel's foremost pollster, 63 percent of Israelis are in favor of 'unilateral withdrawal.' In fact 69 percent call for the evacuation of 'all' or 'most of' the settlements" (Israelinsider, <http://www.israelinsider.com>, accessed July 15, 2002).

These are indeed contradictory poll results, which approve Sharon's job performance but challenge his long political ambition of a Greater Israel, a state that would include the West Bank and Gaza, and his well-known dedication to supporting settlements that are a must in making his political ambition a reality. Occupation, thus, supports settlements, and these, as I note in the book, give substance, meaning, and hope to the idea of a Greater Israel. To relinquish occupation, to dismantle settlements, is to give up the idea of a Greater Israel. Clearly 69 percent of Israelis, who call for the evacuation of "all" or "most of" the settlements, like the women, do not support Sharon's building settlements or the Greater Israel idea.

Americans who want to know the settlers' position on the question of evacuating the settlements may be surprised. In a July 2002 poll conducted by Peace Now, and contrary to the claim of ultra-right groups that should the Israeli government call for withdrawal there will be a bloody fight, a "large majority of Jews living in the settlements would be prepared to obey withdrawal orders" (*Forward,* August 2, 2002, p. 7). The poll results may not come as a surprise to most Israelis, but the numbers can serve to affirm what they have been sensing all along: "If Israel decided to withdraw from the West Bank and Gaza, Peace Now found, 59 percent of settlers would consider suitable financial compensation as the best solution, while another 10 percent would prefer moving to a community inside the Green Line as sufficient compensation. Around 23 percent of settlers would prefer moving as a community to another settlement in the territories. Just 9 percent would refuse any solution" (*Forward*, August 2, 2002, p. 7).

For Americans to have an informed opinion on the Middle East, it is vital for them to know the kinds of contradictions and shifting alliances that mark Israel's social life. These include the fact that the settlers do not present a unified position and the fact that the majority of the settlers said that if asked by the government, they would take financial compensation and come back to live within what is called the Green Line, the 1967 border.

For Americans to have a better understanding of what they see daily on the television screen, it is essential that they pay attention to grassroots views in Israel that differ from the government's position that there is no alternative to occupation. It is important not to miss critical information such as these two recent 2002 polls or the fact that the Zemach June 2002 poll finds that 60 percent of Israelis, like women's peace groups, support a Palestinian state as part of a peace agreement (Israelinsider, <http://www.israelinsider.com>, accessed July 15, 2002).

It is important, as I show in this book, to question the notion that all Jewish peace activists are secular and that religious Jews in Israel support the occupation or are all committed to a Greater Israel ideology. Very few Americans know, for example, of Oz Veshalom (Strength and Peace), a religious Jewish peace organization that opposes using religious sentiment to justify occupation and injustice to Palestinians. Like women's groups, Oz VeShalom emphasizes justice, peace, and human rights. But, as I show in the book, the group deliberately distinguishes itself from Jewish religious fundamentalists on the question of what takes precedence, land or human life. Oz VeShalom states, "We are in the unique position to counter fundamentalist and extremist political arguments that have erroneously placed the value of the Land of Israel ahead of human life, justice, and peace—concepts which have always been central to Jewish Law and tradition" (Oz VeShalom, <http://www.netivot-shalom.org.il>, accessed July 15, 2002). Yet the religious sentiments that get the most media attention are those of ultra-right groups that have little regard for the paramount Jewish values of life, justice, and peace.

Clearly, an almost exclusive attention to violence offers Americans a flat, unflattering, inhuman, and inhumane view of Israelis and Palestinians as either all brutal occupiers or all murdering terrorists.

Surely Americans, who see a caricature of themselves portrayed by others, know how easy it is to turn a complex social reality into a convenient stereotype of Americans as selfish, greedy, hedonistic, materialistic, godless, and so on. This kind of portrayal of Americans has prompted the White House to create an Office on Global Communications to improve what it calls America's image. And "the Council on Foreign Relations task force [has] urged Bush to fix 'America's shaky image abroad'" (*Rochester Democrat and Chronicle,* July 31, 2002). It is not only that Americans resent being reduced to a parody. After September 11, Americans recognize the relationship between image and political consequences. Thus, the task force concludes, "We must come to understand and accept that 'image problems' and 'foreign policy' are not things apart: They are both part of an integrated whole" (*Rochester Democrat and Chronicle,* July 31, 2002).

In the Israeli case, an image of endless violence has its own dire political consequences because it lends support to those who for years have been promoting the view—in Israel, in the Middle East, and in the international community—that conflict is "in" and peace is out. The danger is that the official version that the turmoil is endemic will not merely dominate local Israeli political decisions but will seriously affect international policies in the Middle East to the detriment of peace efforts.

In 1990 and in 1993, when I did fieldwork in Israel, peace activists agreed to talk to me for this book because they understood that the media's focus on the official story ignored, overlooked, or dismissed peace efforts. Then and now women ask, "Why is it that when 100,000 people demonstrate in Israel for peace, as they just did recently in Tel Aviv, on May 11, 2002, television cameras turn suddenly shy, silent, or perhaps uninterested in news without blood?" The women want Americans to know that Israeli society is not monolithic and is far from solidly supporting the occupation or the idea that there is no partner on the other side. They want Americans to know about ongoing efforts by people of two nations to promote peace and coexistence between Israelis and Palestinians.

Various groups, as I describe in the book, have made serious attempts to take the women's local message to the international community—not only by linking with other similar women's peace groups around the world but also, as Bat Shalom has recently done, by addressing the United Nations Security Council.

Representing Bat Shalom, Terry Greenblatt spoke to the Security Council on May 7, 2002, just a few days before that large peace demonstration in Tel Aviv. She said: "I stand here as an ally and advocate of those women in Israel, Jewish and Arab, who ask of you to use your power wisely and with a moral compass whose needle is uncompromisingly pointed toward justice. We ask of you just this—that you fulfill your responsibility as set out in the United Nations Charter."

Greenblatt brings together the local tragic political impasse and global human rights concerns as United Nations obligations that should not be lightly shirked: "You are mandated to reaffirm faith in fundamental human rights—for until you do, the soul of our society will never heal, neither from our fear of global anti-Semitism, nor from the inhumanity of our 35-year subjugation and dehumanization of the Palestinian people. For until you do, the extremists on both sides will rejoice, both those who talk of the transfer of indigenous populations and an eternal occupation, as well as those who walk into coffeehouses or a supermarket to blow themselves and others up, leaving our joint future smoldering in the rubble" (<http://www.bat-shalom.org/2002/1.htm>, accessed May 7, 2002).

The reality is that the international community, including the United Nations and the White House, is always ready to deplore and condemn one side or another, or both. But none, including the United States, is currently engaged in any consistent, committed way or politically devoted to bringing about peace. Women's peace groups are well aware of, at best, a passive international position. Representing Israeli women peace activists, Terry Greenblatt reminded the Security Council that it has duties and obligations upon which it must act: "You are mandated to establish conditions under which justice and respect for international law can be maintained. This includes ensuring the security and well being of Israelis. But it also includes insisting on a standard of behavior and compliance to international law on the part of Israel" (<http://www.batshalom.org/2002/1.htm>, accessed May 7, 2002).

Bat Shalom's call for a peace that is indivisible from justice marks, as I note in this book, the women's peace position and distinguishes it not only from the Likud government policy but from Yitzhak Rabin's 1993 Labor government position as well. Readers will want to know that almost ten years later, the women's dedication to the same principle of justice has not diminished even in the midst of unimaginable grief.

On November 8, 2000, for example, the Coalition of Women for a Just Peace, an umbrella organization of ten different women's peace groups, was founded. Most of these groups, including the Women in Black, were on the ground when I did fieldwork in 1990 and 1993. I describe them in the book in great detail to allow readers to see the ways in which grassroots groups seriously challenge the official government position that there are no partners on the other side. While several new women's groups have emerged since my fieldwork in 1993, such as Bat Shalom, their principles have remained steadfastly devoted to a call for a peace that is indivisible from justice and human rights and that includes an end to occupations and promotes coexistence—two states side by side living in peace and security. The various groups' commitment to a just peace is also reflected in the Coalition of Women for a Just Peace official statement: "We Jewish and Palestinian women, citizens of Israel—representatives of various women's organizations and individuals—have agreed to coordinate and organize in order to work together for a just peace" (Coalition of Women for a Just Peace, <http://www.coalitionofwomen4peace.org>, accessed April 4, 2002).

The more recent groups that have become part of the coalition include "Machsom Watch, a group of women who monitor and prevent human rights violations at checkpoints"; "Women Engendering Peace, a group promoting a culture of peace in Israel"; and "New Profile, a Movement of the Civil-ization of Israeli Society, addressing the issues of militarism and giving support to conscientious objectors in Israel" (Coalition of Women for a Just Peace, <http://www.coalitionofwomen4peace.org>, accessed April 4, 2002).

It is always easy to dismiss women's position on peace as sadly naive and accuse women of lacking a more profound understanding of security matters. So it will be helpful to just briefly mention here other peace groups that readers will encounter in the book, such as Peace Now, "which was founded in 1978 by 348 reserve officers and soldiers of the Israel Defense Forces," and now includes both women and men (Peace Now, <http://www.peacenow.org>, accessed July 14, 2002). With these military credentials, and like The Jerusalem Link and other groups, Peace Now has always contested the idea that there are no partners for peace: "From the mid-1980s Peace Now conducted dialogues with the Palestinian leaders in the territories and abroad in order to develop understanding of each side's needs and interests" (Peace Now, <http://www.peacenow.org>, accessed July 14, 2002).

Peace Now argues that its consistent joint activism contributed to the Oslo Accords; the organization has since shifted to grassroots dialogue linking Palestinian and Israeli towns and villages to promote coexistence: "The dialogue project today involves hundreds of people, with groups paired between, for example, Ramallah and Jerusalem, Tulkarm and Kfar Saba, Haifa and Nablus, Beersheva and Gaza men" (Peace Now, <http://www .peacenow.org>, accessed July 14, 2002).

In times of turmoil Peace Now, like the women's peace camp, continues to support coexistence and claims that occupation and settlements contribute to the growing violence: "Even the tragic scourge of terrorism can best be combated by a realistic and just peace based on mutual agreements." Contrary to those who would like to put a belated "security" face on the early territorial ambitions of a Greater Israel, Peace Now argues that "only peace will bring security to Israel and ensure the future of our people" (Peace Now, <http://www.peacenow.org>, accessed July 14, 2002).

One could easily conclude that peace groups' position on security would be contradicted by the settlers. The latter, readers might assume, would claim that they chose to live in Gaza and the West Bank to safeguard Israel's security. Americans may be surprised, however, to know that according to the recent July 2002 Peace Now poll, a large majority of the settlers, 77 percent, were attracted to the occupied territories not for security or ideology but by extraordinary government funding, subsidies, loans, and other conveniences. Those who settled for national reasons (Greater Israel) or religious sentiments (biblical promises) constituted 20 percent. But only 3 percent of settlers said that they were motivated by security considerations (*Forward,* August 2, 2002, p. 7).

Peace Now, like women's groups, claims that the settlements created a security problem, not the other way around: "The building of settlements in the occupied territories constitutes the major obstacle to peace, designed by successive Likud governments to prevent the return of land and the creation of a viable Palestinian state" (Peace Now, <http://www.peacenow.org>, accessed July 14, 2002).

Despite the military credentials of many founding and current Peace Now activists, it would still be easy to question their intimate knowledge of security matters and to argue that even military officers would not necessarily have all the information regarding security. So it is appropriate here to enlarge the cultural context and include the view of Ami Ayalon, who was head of the Israeli Shin Bet, Israeli Internal Security, during the governments of both Benjamin Netanyahahu (Likud) and Ehud Barak (Labor). In an interview published in the French *Le Monde* on December 22, 2001, Ayalon questioned Sharon's policy of occupation. He said: "There are today more Palestinian terrorists than a year ago . . . and there will be even more tomorrow! If we are winning, how come the terrorists are multiplying?" (Mid-East Realities, <http://www.middleeast.org>, accessed January 3, 2002). And on the failure of the last round of peace talks during the Clinton administration, Ayalon challenged the previous Israeli and American leaders, Prime Minister Barak and President Bill Clinton, and their version that "there was no partner on the other [Palestinian] side." This version has since been often repeated in the American media, but Ayalon denied it: "'We have been generous and they refused!' is ridiculous, and everything that follows from this misperception is skewed." Ayalon contended that September 11 had been detrimental to the peace process because it gave support to the current government's occupation policy: "Since September 11, our leaders have been euphoric. With no international pressure on Israel, they think, the way is open. This obscures the consequences of our holding onto the Palestinian Territories" (Mid-East Realities, <http://www.middleeast.org>, accessed January 3, 2002).

But Ayalon also challenged the current Israeli-American official position that getting rid of Arafat is the solution: "If we kill Arafat, the Palestinian people will continue to want its independence. We say that Palestinians behave like 'madmen,' but it is not madness but a bottomless despair. As long there was a peace process—the prospect to end the occupation—Arafat could maneuver, incite or repress violence to negotiate. When there is no more peace process, the more terrorists one kills the more strength their camp gains" (Mid-East Realities, <http://www.middleeast .org>, accessed January 3, 2002).

To the question in *Le Monde* of whether Israel had missed an opportunity for peace in Camp David, Aylaon replied: "Yes. It is not all the Israelis' fault. The Palestinians, the International Community, bear some responsibility" (Mid-East Realities, <http://www.middleeast.org>, accessed January 3, 2002).

Contrary to the official version that occupation is the only means to ensure Israel's security, Ayalon argued that creating a state in the West Bank and Gaza is vital not only for the Palestinians but for the whole Middle East, not least for the political and spiritual well-being of Israel: "As long as the Palestinian question is not resolved, the region will not know stability. Only a Palestinian state will preserve the Jewish and democratic character of Israel" (Mid-East Realities, <http://www.middleeast.org>, accessed January 3, 2002).

For Americans who want to place violence in a meaningful wider context, I present a detailed cultural discussion in the book. But even in this short preface it is clear that women peace activists' position is not out of step with 60 percent of the country, in the call for a two-state solution, or with Ayalon's clear position that ending the occupation, creating a state side by side with the state of Israel, is an essential first step for peace. A similar view is also expressed by a number of bereaved parents who have lost their children in the violence.

It is hard to imagine a sorrow greater than that of parents burying their children. So it is of the utmost importance for Americans to know that this indescribable tragedy prompts some bereaved parents, women and men, Israelis and Palestinians, to reject the cycle of revenge on both sides and to work for peace, reconciliation, and coexistence.

Malka Tzemach, from Kibbutz Hulda, an active member of Women in Black, is a bereaved mother whose son Tal, a soldier, was killed in March 2002. In an interview with reporters after her son's funeral, Malka Tzemach said: "The death of my son, like the death of hundreds of boys, is senseless. There is no justification for all the young people being killed every day in the territories. The occupation not only corrupts, it also kills" (Israelinsider, <http://www.israelinsider.com>, accessed March 21, 2002).

Americans will also like to know that just recently, in March 2002, Galilee residents, some of whom were former Mothers for Peace activists, "staged a demonstration in the north . . . calling for Israel to evacuate Palestinian areas to break the cycle of Israeli-Palestinian violence. 'We feel that the concept of a military solution is a failed policy,' Arhmelle Lehman, one of the demonstration's organizers, told the *Jerusalem Post*. 'The number of attacks inside Israel and in the territories has increased along with the number of fatalities and wounded'" (Israelinsider, <http://www.israelinsider.com>, accessed March 21, 2002).

Readers will also undoubtedly want to know that "mothers like Tzemach and Lehman hope that their attempts to bring an end to the violence will lead to a lasting peace in the region." The mothers also address the issue of a partner on the other side. Partnership, they believe, is not automatic, is not self-evident, and is not easy in the midst of violence. Partnership has to be created, nurtured, and encouraged if people are asked to believe in coexistence: "If the Palestinians start to hear a different voice being sounded in Israel it may help motivate them to opt for an end to the violence and seek a political solution" (Israelinsider, <http://www.israelinsider.com>, accessed March 21, 2002).

Also challenging the government's position that "there are no partners on the other side" is the Bereaved Families Forum for Peace. This joint group of families in Israel, the West Bank, and Gaza who have lost their children and loved ones in the violence has come together to promote peace and coexistence. Two bereaved men from both sides of conflict, Ghazi Brigit and Yitzhak Frankenthal, wrote the following joint statement:

> We have every reason to despise each other, to be mortal enemies. One of us is an Israeli whose son was kidnapped and killed five years ago by Hamas. The other is a Palestinian whose brother was killed by Israeli troops at a checkpoint in his village. But our grief has united us behind the same goal.
>
> As part of a delegation representing 350 Palestinian and Israeli families whose loved ones were killed in the blood feud between our peoples, we will travel to the United States next week. Together, all of us will plead with the Bush administration, the UN and the European Union to stop the insane violence that our leaders are unable—or willing—to prevent. Many parents who have lost sons and daughters in this conflict are angry and demand revenge. We are no less angry at those who took our loved ones away, but we demand peace and reconciliation. (Bereaved Families for Peace, <http://www.mideastweb.org>, accessed March 29, 2002)

Not only women's peace groups, bereaved families for peace, and other grassroots peace groups challenge the government's version that "there are no partners for peace on the other side." Israeli newspapers, as readers will see in the following chapters, are also a vital part of the intense political debates. Since I raised the question of whether women's peace groups are out of step with the rest of the country, it will be helpful to note briefly two examples of criticism of government policies that have been printed in Israeli newspapers.

Orit Shochat, a senior member of the editorial board of Israel's most prestigious newspaper, *Haaretz,* questioned, for example, the government's "no partner for peace" position. In an article she published in the Tel Aviv *Ha'Ir* newspaper on January 17, 2001, she reminded readers of Sharon's long history as a supporter of a vengeance policy: "The commander of the notorious Unit 101 is now Prime Minister, and it is he who dictates the policy of revenge attacks like those of the 1950s. When there are no terror attacks to revenge, the cabinet fabricates excuses for revenge. When there is no excuse, it makes provocation. When there isn't even a provocation, we revenge *assumed* intentions to kill Jews. . . . Revenge has now become the spice of our life, the unifying factor, the basis of consensus, and also a permanent working order to the IDF and the Secret Service. The strategic goal is to prevent a cease-fire at all costs."

Since Shochat published her article in *Ha'Ir,* the question, for Americans, might be whether *Haaretz* would publish articles critical of the government. It will be helpful to offer here at least one example from *Haaretz.*

Recently, a year and half after the publication of Shochat's article, on Thursday, July 25, 2002, Ari Shavit wrote in *Haaretz:* "On July 23, 2002, just after midnight, the State of Israel deployed an F-16 fighter plane and a one-ton bomb in order to carry out the first terrorist attack it has perpetrated in years."

Like Shochat, Shavit reminded Israelis of Sharon's history and his part in and support of the politics of vengeance and violence: "With his election as prime minister in early 2001, Ariel Sharon was handed an opportunity that few have had—the opportunity for rehabilitation." And for a while, in Shavit's view, Sharon seemed to be taking advantage of just that. "However," Shavit continued, "the decision to bomb that Sharon made this week gives rise to concerns that he may be abusing the credit he received. Along with a series of additional racist and brutal decisions he has made in the past month, this latest one raises serious questions about the mental world of the man who is in charge of our fate. This week Sharon plunged us deep down the slippery slope of bestiality. He sullied the justice of our war and blurred beyond recognition the moral image of the country he was called upon to protect."

Our Sisters' Promised Land describes how in good times and in bad times, the women's peace camp has been steadfast, unwavering, and consistent in peace politics. Now is a very bad time. It is a time of a cycle of violence and counterviolence, of bloodshed, and of existential fear of both sides. Yet women and other peace groups, such as the Bereaved Families

Forum for Peace, insist that peace is the only way and that the alternative to coexistence is a tragic codestruction. But I want to prepare readers for the fact that the peace activism that I describe here is not without severe obstacles, obvious hardships, and serious problems.

Americans will easily recognize that cooperation needs to take place despite and because of social strife, power differentials, discrimination, and exclusions both political and economic. These are all, in their own way, part of the American experience. Yet how to produce the necessary working together, as a community, across these divisions is not simple or self-evident.

Because I have often wondered how women manage in painfully trying times to remain consistent in their activism, in the following chapters I want to give readers a sense of how they work around and through tragic attacks and heartbreaking funerals on both sides. I do not want to minimize, ignore, or deny the difficulties in joint activism. I pay close attention in the book to the ways that Israeli and Palestinian women continue—despite anger and pain, national borders, and power differentials—to promote coexistence.

At the same time it is equally important to see how peace groups succeed in speaking and acting in coexistence. It is helpful to see how, on the string of a messy social life, activists thread, one by one, moments of compassion and shared common humanity. Americans will recognize such moments of transcending solidarity because many have described experiencing one after September 11. I want to include in this preface one account of a recent Israeli event that offers a glimpse of the kind of transcending solidarity that I describe in the book and that can serve as a reminder of its immense promise for coexistence.

Gila Svirsky, one of Israel's most prominent women peace activists, wrote about a peace rally that offers a vision of hope stretching across divisions and differences:

In a recent pro-peace rally, on February 9, 2002, about 10,000 Jews and Arabs citizens of Israel gathered in Tel Aviv. . . . It was a rally in which the stage was shared by Arabs and Jews, women and men, Mizrahim and Ashkenazim, young and old, religious and secular. . . . There was the transformation of a beloved Zionist song "Ein li eretz aheret," I have no other country to go to.

Reciting this song in two languages, Hebrew and Arabic, suddenly infused it with a new meaning. The song says, "I have no other country to go to. And even if the land is burning under my feet, this is my home." For the Arabs in the crowd, the song suddenly became theirs too, and for the Jews, it meant a land we both love deeply. I hope that someday you will join us, and the world will be one. (Coalition of Women for a Just Peace, <http://www.coalitionofwomen4peace.org>, accessed February 10, 2002)

Americans deserve to know about peace activism for many reasons, not least because the Middle East conflict is in the news in the United States every day. It is Americans' right, as consumers of news, to get the full picture, to see the complex cultural context of violence, and to get to know the ways in which women and men resist the official policy of codestruction.

Moreover, grassroots peace activists of two nations, as women note in the following chapters, can offer career politicians an example of how to work together in turbulent times. Peace groups can be a model of and for cooperation not just when things are easy but also in bad times, in the midst of tragic, senseless violence, and after such violence is over.

Readers will easily see how women's intricate and dedicated joint hard work can offer a blueprint and a map for the road ahead, when serious peace negotiations will resume. When two states, coexistence, and reconciliation take their inevitable turn, they will take root in the seeds of peace put in the political soil of the promised land by women and men in both nations who then and now have refused to give up.

—A. E.
August 13, 2002

Author's Note

Yitzhak Rabin, Israel's prime minister, was assassinated on November 4, 1995, at a public event, a peace rally, in Tel Aviv. He was killed by an ultra-Right Israeli Jew who opposed Rabin's peace politics. As prime minister since 1992, Rabin was a key leader in changing the state's official policy from one of conflict to one of coexistence. Rabin transformed mere talk about coexistence into a political fact as he signed peace agreements with the PLO in 1993 and with Jordan in 1994. Shimon Peres, Israel's new prime minister, was determined, as he declared after Rabin's death, to implement the peace process. In a political act designed to give substance to peace agreements, Peres ordered the withdrawal of the Israeli army from seven major Palestinian cities and some 400 villages.

This book, which focuses on women's peace activism, was written in 1994. I drew on my fieldwork in Israel in 1990, two years before the labor party won the elections, and in 1993, several months after Rabin became Israel's prime minister. A political transformation that seemed inconceivable during the Likud government took place in Israel after the 1992 elections. The women's peace and coexistence position shifted from the political margins of protest groups to official government policy. While women's peace activism faced strong and at times violent opposition from ultra-Right groups, it seemed implausible that Israeli Jews would turn political disagreements into political assassinations of elected leaders. These two events are closely intertwined yet are vastly different in their understanding of the relationship between nation and state. While the elected government is shifting the policy from conflict to coexistence, ultra-Right Israelis who oppose the state policy invoke the nation to legitimate violence against elected officials. This book describes the ways that the evocation of the nation to transgress state laws brings to the fore fierce disagreements about the relations between the nation and the state in Israel. I hope that the book will provide a comprehensive context for the profound political turnabout that is taking place during the 1990s in Israel and in the region.

Acknowledgments

I am most grateful to all the women peace activists in Israel and in the Occupied Territories who made this book possible.

I want to thank the Department of Anthropology at the University of Manchester and Marilyn Strathern, the Center for Middle Eastern Studies at Harvard University and Mary-Jo DelVecchio Good, and the Susan B. Anthony Center at the University of Rochester for inviting me to present earlier versions of the chapters.

For their support and encouragement I thank the Rochester Jewish Women Feminist Study Group, the Song of Songs group, and the Saturday group.

For their friendship, collegiality, and comments I thank Laura Perez and Karen Fields.

The Lucius N. Littauer Foundation gave me a generous grant to write this book.

Portions of chapter 1 appeared in *Culture, Medicine, and Psychiatry* 16 (1992).

Contents

Introduction

In 1990, when I went to Israel to do an ethnographic project on women's peace activism, words like *peace, coexistence,* and *Palestinians* were silenced in official public discourse. Three years later, after the display of two internationally legitimated Middle East peace agreements, it was hard to recall just how much official resistance to coexistence there had been in Israel only three years earlier. The audience present at the White House for the two ceremonies in Washington in 1993 and 1994—and the rest of the world—linked to the center of international power via television, all could see the handshakes between former enemies, as a reluctant Rabin took Arafat's hand or enthusiastically shook hands with King Hussein. Reluctant or joyous, the official agreements were a turning point from the Likud government's view that the state of Israel is destined to live on the sword and the Middle East is doomed to exist in perpetual conflict. During the Likud government, from 1977 until 1992, it was difficult to pierce the wall of silence for those who, like women peace activists, held a coexistence position. Consequently, local and international media paid little attention to struggles for peace and focused instead on the center of political power.

Attention to the margins—in this case women peace activists—is indispensable to a comprehension of the changes that swept the region and altered official politics, of Israelis, Palestinians, and Jordanians, from conflict to coexistence. When I started my fieldwork in Israel in 1990, the Likud Party was in power. In June 1992 Israel experienced a major political transformation, when Labor won the elections after fifteen years of political exile. In September 1993 Israelis and Palestinians made a historic gesture of mutual recognition; in July 1994 another agreement was made between Israel and Jordan. The peace politics of the margins have become the legitimate politics of the state: the Labor government embraced an official policy of coexistence with the Palestine Liberation Organization (PLO) and with Arab countries. The 1992 change in the Israeli government was vital in shaping the transformation from a state policy that denied Palestinian nationhood to one of coexistence with Palestinians.

Because women peace activists had advocated coexistence with Palestinians during the Likud government, they were regarded as outside the national consensus. Until 1992 the women's peace and coexistence position seemed utopian, if not simply politically foolish and naive. Women were seen by their more benign opponents as bleeding hearts, in Hebrew *yefei nefesh,* "beautiful souls," and by the extreme right wing as traitors and whores. At the time their peace politics was seen as nothing more than a fringe protest, a minuscule dot on what the government portrayed as a broad national consensus. Local and outside observers of Israeli politics mirrored the official position and ignored or marginalized the peace movement. During my initial fieldwork in 1990, political predictions made by various experts about the Middle East in 1990–91 did not include agreements between Israelis and the PLO. The Israeli official position was one of an ongoing conflict with Palestinians and Arab countries, a conflict endless and eternal as far as the eye of the Right could see.

The Margins Illuminate Political Life

Much has been written about women's marginalization in political systems all over the world. This book, however, is not about the global phenomenon of women's inequality in organized politics, nor does it argue that the Israeli case is different in this regard. Instead, it shows that to place women peace activists at the center of a discussion is to illuminate significantly Israel's political life itself. Most studies on politics are silent about women, and those that do focus on women are either concerned with their marginalization or argue that women have more power than is acknowledged by researchers or by local men. In turning the spotlight on women, I show instead how attention to the margins—where women peace activists are—reveals aspects of political life that, despite their significance, have been ignored. Moreover, to spotlight the margins exposes political issues that the center would like to conceal.

To attend to the margins is more than a mere shift in focus: the margins in fact reveal what, after Freud, I call political denials by those in power, who would like to conceal or suppress what is at odds with their ideas and actions.[1] Studies on politics often focus on the center and ignore the margins and thus fail to locate the dissent simmering on the margins that permeates political life and eventually threatens the status quo. The collapse of the Soviet Union, the war in Bosnia, and the signing of the peace agreement between Israel and the Palestinians provide some of the more recent and startling cases of concealed political simmerings that burst to the surface.

Such political simmering often goes undetected worldwide, however, because much of the focus (by the media, political analysts, scholars, and others) is on the center of power, on the government, and on the ruling political parties that control access to information. In both democracies and in socialist countries, governments have the means to draw attention to the official version of social reality and the power to conceal serious political smoldering. In global politics, for example, attention to the center of power in the Soviet Union offered few clues to the demise of socialism and to an impending major political transformation in world politics. In the local Israeli context attention to the Likud in Israel in 1990–1991 would have provided little indication that a peace agreement would be possible in 1993. Women's peace activism reveals this kind of simmering under the official political surface. Beyond the exposure of government silencing, attention to women's discontent with the center provides insights into recent political changes and reveals the ground on which drastic agreements have taken place in the Middle East since 1992.

In the international political game of the rise and fall of superpowers, locals are often seen as pawns. This view, however, ignores the power of locals to take advantage of global transitions for their own regional purposes. Recent changes in the Middle East came about by the locals (Israelis, Palestinians, and Jordanians), who seized global political shifts and used international emphasis on a new world order to bring about regional political transformations. A local political turnabout—the change in the Israeli government—uses the emergence of the United States as the sole superpower to bring about further regional changes. President Asad of Syria may use the peace process to get legitimation from Washington; he may also use the United States' new global status to persuade his own people that Syria must move to a peace agreement with Israel. In Israel the Labor government now deploys Washington to deal with homegrown opposition to its peace initiative.

Meanings of Peace: Women Face a Labor Government

Despite the fact that the government is moving toward coexistence with Palestinians, there is strong opposition from the Right and the extreme Right to the peace process. Moreover, there is no consensus on the meaning of peace among those who support the peace process.[2] In 1993, women activists still acted from the political margins because their concept of peace differed from the government's. Of the three political goals that women's peace activism struggled to achieve—end to the occupation, two states for two nations, and direct talks with the PLO—only the last goal has materialized as a result of the government's peace approach.

Women's peace activism objected to the partial nature of the government's peace agenda, which agreed to a limited autonomy to Jericho and Gaza but excluded the West Bank from the 1993 agreement. A concept of justice emerged as a crucial element in the women's disagreement with the government. Rabin's government spoke of peace that was good for Israel; women activists attended to justice to Palestinians as well. The disagreement focused on the question of whether those who support peace include or ignore considerations of justice. Those who advocate peace can argue, for example, that it is beneficial for Israelis or that it redresses injustice to Palestinians or both. Women's activism inserted the issue of justice at the heart of the peace and coexistence policy; facing a Labor government, they insisted that justice for Palestinians must be included in the concept of peace between the two nations. Because of the opposition of right-wing political parties even to a partial peace, the women had to situate themselves between the rock of supporting the government's peace efforts (against the Right) and the hard place of challenging a government that initiated a peace process. Challenging the Labor government was also harder because a number of activists from the peace camp who became government officials were at the forefront of peace protests and demonstrations during the Likud years.

Producing Women's Peace

During the Likud government the major opposition to its political position regarding Palestinians and to its policy of annexation and settlements in the Occupied Territories came from the Israel Peace Camp, a broad category that included more than one hundred joint groups of both women and men. Women's peace activism, which consisted of more than ten women's organizations, was part of the Israeli Peace Camp yet was distinct from it. Women's activism mobilized gender structurally, in creating women-only groups and in weaving gender into a peace position (*Alternative Directory* 1991; Chazan 1991). Many women belonged both to women's peace organizations and to joint groups; some began their political activism in the Peace Camp and then became prime movers in forming women's peace groups.

Women's groups were galvanized after the 1982 Lebanon War. Groups such as Women against the War and other groups such as Parents against Silence (also called Mothers against Silence) mobilized mothers to protest the war (Gillath 1991). Other women's peace groups were founded after the onset of the Intifada, the Palestinian uprising in the West Bank and the Gaza Strip in 1987. They include Nashim Beshahor (Women in Black) (1987); Shani (Israel Women's Alliance against the Occupation) (1988); Reshet (Women's Network for the Advancement of Peace) (1989); and Nashim Veshalom (Women and Peace Movement) (Chazan 1991). All groups emphasized a women's perspective of peace, which they considered different from the broader position of the Peace Camp. Gender was seen as the ground on which women could stand together despite differences; gender was also mobilized when women took a more radical peace position than the Peace Camp regarding justice for Palestinians.

Official documents issued by the various women's peace groups focused on the three political aims cited earlier: end the occupation, talks with the PLO, and two states for two nations.[3] Women's groups noted, however, that, though their members agree on ending the occupation, they differ on the ways to achieve a lasting peace. Thus, there was broad support—for example, in Women in Black in Jerusalem—on the urgency to end the occupation but less unity regarding the PLO or the establishment of a Palestinian state; the Women in Black in Haifa, however, held all three goals as its official position. Women's peace groups were simultaneously at work on related agendas. The Women's Organization for Political Prisoners, for example, provided legal and other kinds of aid to Palestinian women prisoners in Israeli jails; the Women in Black held a weekly vigil to protest the occupation, and Shani promoted activities that advocate close interaction and cooperation with Palestinians (*Alternative Directory* 1991).

In this book I use the terms *women's peace activism* and *women's peace camp* interchangeably and as a broad category for women's peace groups. When I note a women's peace position on particular issues, I refer to a political position that is broadly shared by women. I use not only my conversations with women but also, more significantly, official documents as well as public events in which statements were collectively agreed upon by women from different groups. Identifying a shared position does not mean ignoring disagreements and power differentials among women. Indeed, gender was often enlisted by women when various divisions threatened solidarity.

Peace activism reveals the ways that gender is mobilized to forge solidarity in and around divides and inequalities; at the same time, it sheds light on the limits of gender unity.

Some Fieldwork Considerations

When I began my project I planned to talk to women and to record their personal accounts on their peace activism. Together these individual stories would, I hoped, provide a solid ground for understanding how in a local context the politics of peace and gender politics coalesce in women's activism. But why would most women peace activists, who were already extremely busy, spend time, a scarce resource, to talk to an anthropologist? It seems to me that the women and I engaged in a kind of bartering: I wanted to write about their peace activism, and they wanted their story to be recorded and told. Beyond the personal (I knew some women or knew someone who knew them), the women were politically motivated to talk to me. In 1990 women peace activists were well aware of the prominently displayed Likud government's position of perpetual conflict. Accordingly, both local and outside media paid little attention to peace efforts in Israel. Women peace activists were willing to speak to people like me, who were writing about peace efforts in Israel. In 1994 women kept reminding me that, despite major political changes, little had been written about their peace activism. Women activists were not part of the official peace celebration in Washington, D.C., and their struggle for peace was not acknowledged by local or global media.

During my fieldwork I talked with peace activists, both women and men, in a variety of groups and with elected government officials as well. While some with whom I spoke were not concerned, a number of people— Israeli (Jewish and Palestinian) and Palestinian women and men from the Occupied Territories—saw anonymity as essential. Accordingly, the names of the people I talked with have been altered; I use people's real names only when I quote from published material. While I have retained the actual dates and titles of the women's peace conferences, to preserve privacy, in quoting conference panelists, I have sometimes attributed more than one name to a particular panelist's statements. I transcribed and translated my tapes. All tapes of Israeli-Jewish and Israeli-Palestinian women were translated from the Hebrew. Palestinian women from the Occupied Territories spoke in English in public events as well as in our private conversations. When I use Hebrew sources in this book, the English translations are mine. A number of official documents issued by women's groups were written in English and in Hebrew; I use the English version of these documents.

In translating from the Hebrew, while I was concerned with preserving a cultural context of the accounts, I also was aware of the political implications of language for women. In my conversations with women, and in women's peace conferences, language was more than an obvious form of communication: it was a site of power differentials. For Palestinian women from the Occupied Territories, Hebrew was the language of the occupier; since many Israeli-Jewish women did not speak Arabic, Palestinian women used English as an international language. English was a reminder that the occupation separated women, but, like the issue of gender, it also provided a ground on which women could come together. Hebrew was used by Israeli-Jewish women and by Israeli-Palestinian women in interviews and in the conferences. The use of one local language (Hebrew) but not Arabic was another reminder of inequality within the state. Israeli-Palestinian women often said that, as citizens, they had to learn Hebrew but that Jewish women who belonged to the majority community and did not speak Arabic did not feel compelled to do so.

I came to Israel to do fieldwork after fourteen years of living and doing research in the United States. During six months of fieldwork in 1990 and in a brief visit in 1993, while my focus was on women's activism, I talked to women and men and attended peace demonstrations and conferences. My ties widened to include women from the various women's peace organizations. I had conversations with Israeli-Jewish peace activists, Israeli Palestinians, and Palestinians from the Occupied Territories. Being an Israeli Jew, I had different relations with women peace activists from the three communities. As a native daughter temporarily returning home, I had immediate and easy access to Israeli-Jewish peace activists and enjoyed obvious advantages, including close ties to some Jewish peace activists. Among them I was recognized as someone who chose to live in the United States. I was often questioned about my life in the United States and my relationship to Israel.

My meetings with Palestinian women from the Occupied Territories were more complicated. Because I will not go to Gaza and the West Bank during Israeli occupation, we often met in East Jerusalem in a public place, a café or a restaurant, but the occupation was always there—physically, emotionally, and politically. It pressed on all our conversations; despite much political agreement, neither the women nor I could get around the fact of occupation and our differential positions.

I also got to know a number of Israeli Palestinians and had special ties with several families in one Israeli-Palestinian town. These friendships, however, had their own complications. Since I visited my friends often, I wanted to know, for example, if I would compromise them within their own community. Israeli Palestinians introduced me to people as a Jewish woman associated with peace activism—yet I was a member of the majority community. When I asked Israeli Palestinians about it, their response was that, as long as they were not selling me land, all was well. Land in Israel and in the Occupied Territories is more than property; in all three communities it symbolizes nationhood and patriotism. To sell land is to be a traitor. I did not come to buy land; they did not sell land.

My encounters with Israeli Palestinians were also marked by the fact that they knew that I lived in the United States and planned to write a book. People wanted me to bring attention to their plight. Israeli Palestinians, women and men, would often talk to me about what it meant to be second-class citizens in one's own state. Many stories of discrimination and racism were recounted by Israeli Palestinians on my visits to the towns and when some of them came to visit me in Tel Aviv, where I had rented an apartment. The accounts that I heard in the Israeli-Palestinian town and in women's peace events resonated with collective hardships, not merely individual experiences. Inequality between citizens of two communities emerged as a critical issue not only in women's peace activism but in Israel's political life.

Palestinian Citizens of Israel: A State of Two Nations

Israeli Palestinians constitute about 18 percent of Israel's total population; some of the prominent leaders in the women's peace camp are Israeli-Palestinian women. They are citizens of the state of Israel who see themselves as Palestinian by nationality. They describe their position on the Israeli-Palestinian issue in a phrase I heard often: "My country and my nation are at war." Women's peace activism that includes women of two nations challenges a historical attempt to deny that the country that Jews claimed as their homeland was not empty space; it is a constant reminder of an indigenous population with equal attachment to the very same land (Morris 1991; Grossman 1992; Kimerling 1992).

Women's peace activism brings into focus state policies regarding Israeli Palestinians. The women's transnational peace activism goes against a historical ideological grain of many of the state's founders. While the founders of the state expressed different views, some, like Israel's first prime minister, David Ben-Gurion, attempted to forge an unbroken link between the state and a Jewish nation in a way that left little room for a Palestinian nation.[4] In the early years after its independence Israel put the "hidden question" (Kimerling 1992, 61) of another national claim within the state on the back burner. Within the last few years the Israeli consensus on the history of the birth of the state has begun to unravel.[5] A revisionist history, or a new history, *historia hadasha,* has emerged, challenging the traditional Israeli historiography of the birth of the state. It has generated a heated debate, particularly around another birth, "the birth of the Palestinian refugee problem" (Morris 1991), and has raised a question: "Was the birth of the state of Israel conceived in sin?" (Selah 1991). In contrast to the assertion that the Palestinians who fled between 1947 and 1949 left of their own accord, scholars such as Morris offer a more complex account of voluntary and forced exile and ask: Was the justified birth of the state compromised in acts of injustice to Palestinians?

Women's peace activism reflects this emerging attention to injustice to Palestinians and calls into question some of the fundamental assumptions that have informed Israeli politics regarding the Middle East conflict. The women's peace actions question an entrenched "perception of a ubiquitous threat against the survival of the State of Israel" (Yaniv 1993, 87) and an assumption that the "Arab-Israeli conflict is inherently and unalterably asymmetrical and that the Jewish state is and will always remain the weaker party" (87–88). While the Labor government began a political course of coexistence and abandoned the Likud's politics of conflict, the government, as Rabin's statement to the Knesset in May 1994 reveals, still gives great political weight to security.[6] Women challenge what they see as the government overemphasis on what it calls security considerations in its dealings with Palestinians. The women see some of these acts as inflicting further injustice on Palestinians.[7]

What the Locals Tell the Anthropologist

Women in all three communities knew, as I noted earlier, that I am an anthropologist interested in their peace activism and that I was planning to write a book. We discussed how I would use the material; I told them that my project would represent my understanding of women's peace activism and Israeli politics. I would tape their accounts and participate in public events, vigils, and demonstrations and would write about my understanding of their actions—the book would be my version of their story. The decision to structure the book around women's public events came, however, from the women themselves and originated in what I experienced in 1990 as extreme frustration.

My research in the United States dealt with individualism and self-reliance as the foundations of American social life. This emphasis on the individual as the locus of social action, and the endless self-disclosures that mark media culture in the United States, disposed me to plan interviews with individual women, thinking that out of these personal accounts I would understand women's peace activism. Yet, when I talked to women about their life histories, they constantly turned attention away from their own stories to speak about collective actions and public events. I was interested in a biographical account that would shed light on a woman's choice to become a peace activist, but at some point she would shift the conversation from *I* to *we.* Or, I would ask questions about individual acts, and at some stage in the conversation women would bring up public events and ask me if I had participated in this conference or that demonstration. If my answer was no, the women responded by saying something like: "Too bad. That was a great conference. You really missed something." My heart would sink with a sense of lost, vital information regarding peace activism.

While it was never made clear to me what I had missed, I felt frustrated because I was absent from events in which something important had happened. If I asked the women for details so that I could retrieve the event by getting accounts from those who were there, I was told that I had to be there to get a sense of it. If I looked upset that I had missed what seemed to be the most critical event in women's peace activism, I was told not to mind it too much; next week, I was reassured, there would be a conference that I could attend. So I would check my calendar, only to discover that I was already committed to be at another conference or demonstration or that I had scheduled interviews in another part of the country. I asked myself: How could I possibly do this project when I cannot even redeem a past absence (the event I missed) through a future presence (the event I will have to miss) because I have to be somewhere else? It often seemed that the event at which I was *not* present was where I should have been.

I did not realize at the time that the women were telling me not that I needed to be everywhere at once (which is what I initially thought they were telling me) but, rather, that I should shift my focus from their individual stories, which they insisted were not that important, to public events and to collective activism. I had been intent on finding individual heroes; I had been so sure that personal accounts would tell it all. The women, however, would interrupt the personal account initiated by my questions and refer instead to conferences and vigils. Listening to our taped conversations and attending as many public events as I could, I began to comprehend what the women were telling me. Their insistence that I attend public events contributed to my decision to organize my account of women's peace activism around five public events, a weekly Friday vigil, four conferences in 1990, and a conference in 1993. I chose these specific events because each one, while focusing on peace and coexistence, drew public attention to acute simmerings within Israeli society. Each event is not only about the relations of margins and center in women's peace activism but about a shifting political center, from Right to Left, and tensions among groups on the margins. Facing the center (the government), women peace activists recreate unity and solidarity. When women face one another, various conflicts surface and indicate the limits of solidarities on the margins. Together these five events capture major social (class, "nation-ness," gender) and cultural (West-East, Left-Right, Religious-Secular) conflicts that Israelis confront as they struggle to engage in a peace process.

The Production of Politics: Transforming "Mere Talk" into Political Action

Attention to women's peace activism thus sheds light on the production of politics in Israel. More specifically, it reveals how politics (or what constitutes politics) is made and how citizens are able to engage in debates with the government and to contest state politics. Women's activism reveals fundamental elements of Israel's political life: the salience of public events and the overriding concept of the collective. Politics is made in public events; to negotiate with the government people have to speak from within a "we" collective. Collectives rather than individuals enter into political discussions with the state. Political discourse between those on the margins and the center of power takes place in public events such as conferences, demonstrations, and vigils. Irrespective of changing governments, untouched by the rise and fall of political parties, these basic political features, public events and collectives, unfailingly and forcefully come forth. Despite their powerful persistence, however, they are not as immediately obvious as, say, the number of political parties and thus have not been explored in a sustained way in discussions on politics. Women's peace activism in Israel turns its own dramatic light upon those elemental aspects of political life in Israel.

Women's peace activism brings to the fore the significance of an Israeli distinction between the realms of "talk" and of "action." In Israel public events, or organized public activities such as demonstrations and conferences, *are* politics, because they transform insubstantial talk into solid *uvdot bashetach* (facts on the ground). Politics *means* to act and to create facts. Linguistically and conceptually, therefore, politics is something other than just talks, promises, and ideas.[8] Political ideologies remain "mere talk," *rak diburim,* until they are transformed into political action through the conduit of public events. Public events give substance to the two major competing political ideologies regarding the Israeli-Palestinian conflict: the Left's insistence on "peace and coexistence" and territorial compromise and the Right's wish to create a "Greater Israel" through settlements in and annexation of the West Bank, the Gaza Strip, and the Golan Heights. Ideologies become significant only when they are perceived not as mere talk but as facts and acts. Accordingly, women peace activists transform talk about equality and peace into political action by stepping into the public space, forming vigils, organizing conferences, and linking with Palestinian women to construct women's public events.

Each side on the political divide, the Right and the Left, firmly believes that its ideology best ensures Israel's survival. Both sides fear that following the other side's agenda courts disaster, using words such as *ason* (disaster) and, more significantly, *shoa,* which is the Hebrew word for the Holocaust. Each side carefully chooses the location of the public events they so often stage, because in the political realm what happens may not matter as much as *where* it happens. The space of appearance, the symbolic qualities of the site, infuses the event with the appropriate political meaning.

Building settlements—that is, the fact of putting up houses on the ground—is a significant public event; the very act of putting up buildings transforms "mere talk" about Israel's right to settle in the Occupied Territories into a political fact and a sign of power.[9] Similarly, the Labor government chooses its space to give the state's official policy substance; the ground of the Israeli Knesset and of the White House in Washington, D.C., provide that official public space. On May 11, 1994, in a statement to the Knesset (the Israeli Parliament) regarding Israel's agreement, Rabin displayed the distinction between mere talk and political acts: "The current government, headed by the Labor Party, went to the elections and emerged with the upper hand—promising to make a serious effort, not merely paying lip service, to achieving peace; to put an end to wars; to try and end 100 years of hostility" (Rabin 1994, 8). In that public event in the Knesset building, among peers, Rabin transformed mere talk about peace into a fact on the ground.

The 1993 and the 1994 agreements in Washington, beyond their ceremonial display, have taken on a local Israeli meaning of the construction of politics. In the White House public event the Israeli government has turned mere talk of coexistence and peace into a political act in full view of locals and the international community. In the 1994 ceremony in Washington, Rabin addressed Israelis in Hebrew to display at home that peace is not mere talk in English for global consumption but a political act in the local context. On July 12, 1994, the Women's Organization for Political Prisoners demonstrated outside an Israeli prison, calling on the government to release all Palestinian prisoners.[10] The women's vigil is intended to call on the state to transform talk about peace into political action in which justice and peace are indivisible.

Reproducing Collectives

Public events also highlight the importance of the collective in Israeli social life. What Strathern (1981) calls the "social good" looms larger than "self-interest" or individual wishes. When Israelis speak about the "collective" they are referring to the nation and "national unity" and often invoke the word *consensus*. Women peace activists are seen by their political opponents as challenging that unity, breaking the consensus, and placing themselves "outside of the boundaries of the collective" (Benziman 1989, 38). Women also contest the boundaries of the national collective when they forge a transnational solidarity with Palestinian women. The national collective is easily identified, yet there is a constant proliferation and formation of other collectives as well. To speak of, and for, the social good in the political arena is to speak from within a collective.

Whereas in countries such as the United States individualism and self-reliance mark exemplary citizenship, in Israel communal approval and collective legitimation are socially, culturally, and psychologically crucial for the individual. While this is not a startling observation to those familiar with Israel, the women's peace camp unveils the significance of public events as powerful productions of collectives from which individuals can act politically with a sense of legitimacy. In public events every act of challenging the larger collective necessarily, therefore, brings forth other kinds of unities.

Women's activism does not challenge collectives as political entities that can speak for the social good. Far from rejecting the idea of a collective by replacing it, for example, with a concept of individualism or self-interest, the women's camp and other protest groups in Israel actually reproduce collectives that claim to speak for the social good. Collectives such as women's peace groups produce their version of the social good, which challenges the official version. Women use phrases such as "one of us"[11] to cast themselves as a solidarity group and allude to a collective that is mindful of the social good. Women's groups' official documents frequently use the words *we women* to inscribe a collective that is concerned with a just solution to the Middle East conflict.

Gendered Transnational Collectives

Since the women's peace camp includes women citizens of the state of Israel who belong to two nations, women create different kinds of collectives depending on the context. In facing the state, women produce a transnational collective of Jewish and Palestinian peace activists.[12] The women's peace camp reinterprets the notion of "we," recasting it as a collective in which gender is the raw material for producing a community of women of two nations. Women's groups implicitly and explicitly declare the possibilities of producing collectives on the basis of gender and across various social and national divisions. These groups unveil a construction of gendered transnational collectives absent in the wider Peace Camp. Although the women's groups are part of the larger Peace Camp and though their peace ideology in the Israeli-Palestinian conflict parallels that of the Peace Camp, the women's camp constructs a distinct peace ideology that insists that justice and peace are indivisible.

In the women's vision of justice, gender comes to the fore but in complex and intricate ways. In some contexts gender is mobilized to forge solidarity, but in other contexts it is seen as shaky ground for unity. Power differentials among women, issues of occupation, and ethnic and class divisions provide grist for the mill of disunity. These divisions and power differentials that have emerged and reemerged in women's public events illuminate the broader simmerings within Israeli society and between Israelis and Palestinians that accompany and continue to challenge the government's official coexistence policy. The peace process on which the government embarked in 1993 did not immediately convince women that their work was done. Women peace activists have altered political culture by making public space for peace and coexistence, but this act has politicized women in a new direction.

From Silence to Political (Public) Engagement with the State

For the first time in the history of the state of Israel women have chosen to take a public position regarding the Middle East conflict in organized women's protest groups, thus establishing a women's peace camp.[13] It is not simply that women's groups add an "edge" of gender to politics. More important, the fusion of gender equality and peace ideologies that distinguish these groups represents a different kind of politics from those of the wider peace camp, producing something that is more than the sum of its parts. Women's peace activism is not the mirror image of men's peace activism; the difference between them is linked to women's secondary position in Israeli society. Various gender discriminations, particularly exclusions in the army, allow Israeli women to create a different peace link with Palestinian women, because men, not women, are identified with the image of soldiers in the Occupied Territories.

Women have moved from political silence to speaking out in heated public debates regarding borders, marginalities, and the relationship between women and the state.[14] New women's groups, such as the Israel Women's Network, and well-established groups that have in recent years radicalized their positions, openly support the notion of the struggle for gender equality in all spheres of social life. In 1990, for example, *Naamat,* the working women's organization affiliated with the *Histadrut,* the trade union federation, has established its own Committee on the Status of Women. At a 1990 conference Masha Lubelski, *Naamat*'s general secretary, said that women's position was one of the most critical issues in Israeli society. She turned to hundreds of female delegates from all over the country, Jewish and Palestinian, and asked them to fight for equality.[15] More significant is that *Naamat,* which traditionally confined itself to women workers' concerns, is now taking a much stronger peace position on the Israeli-Palestinian issue: "Lubelski declared that 75 percent of the members of *Naamat* voted in favor of keeping the issue of peace on its agenda until a just solution for the Palestinian nation is found" (*Hadashot,* December 31, 1989).

The politicization of women in response to the Middle East conflict signals another change in Israel's political life from a policy of conflict to a policy of peace. Women peace activists brought this change to the public sphere long before the 1993 peace agreements.[16] During public events women engaged in a dialogue with the state, contesting government policies. While the women's dissent during the Likud government was diametrically opposed to the official policy, women's position in 1993, united on ending the occupation, did not match the government's Jericho-Gaza agreement. The women's position of two states for two nations was in contradiction to the Labor Party's policy, since "Prime Minister Rabin and the Labor party have officially gone on record numerous times as opposing the creation of a Palestinian state" (Golan 1994, 65). To place women at the center of the discussion, however, goes beyond a focus on political dissent from government policies. Women's peace activism provides insights to the complexities of negotiating coexistence. Events in the region threaten coexistence, and the process requires constant tending and mending. Women's peace groups illustrate that coexistence is not a "quick fix" to years of conflict and mistrust and that to be successful political leaders will have to work through and around differences, inequalities, and animosities within and between national communities.

About Women's Public Events and Israel's Political Life

Beyond the Left and Right divisions regarding the peace process, women's public events, presented in this book, expose serious conflicts within the Israeli-Jewish community, such as conflicts between religious and secular people and between Israelis who have immigrated from Arab countries (mizrahi Jews) and those who came from Europe (ashkenazi Jews). Women's public events bring to light these simmering disunities, which the center would like to deny, silence, or ignore. Women's public events, however, are politically disturbing in more than one way; beyond revelations of disharmony within the nation, they also do not tell a simple, linear, or cozy story of peace and gender equality; in each public event organized by women these local conflicts give different kinds of meanings to issues of peace and gender. Each conflict tests the limits of peace and of gender solidarity in different ways; thus, in each public event, peace and gender equality appear both familiar and unfamiliar, stable and shifting. Together, however, public events display the possibilities that peace and gender equality positions offer for coexistence within Israel, between Israelis and Palestinians, and between Israel and its neighbors.

Following the women's (indirect) suggestion, I framed the chapters in this book around their public events. Each chapter, however, offers material that I chose to include because I believe that it gives a crucial and meaningful context to the women's insights on Israel's political life and public events. In each chapter I discuss some historical and contemporary political events that were raised in the women's public events; I draw from Israeli scholarship, documents, popular literature, and the media. I consider all of these, including ideas expressed by past and present political leaders, as I view women peace activists as sources of local culture and as part of what the locals have to say about crucial political issues. Beyond providing a necessary local framework, the inclusion of these various sources, events, and people has to do with the fact that center and margins are linked in dialogues, struggles, and revelations. The book is therefore as much about Israel's political life as it is about women's peace activists and their struggle for coexistence with Palestinians and for equality within the state. At the same time, the book discusses, indirectly (all along) and directly (in the last two chapters) issues that are at the heart of political life not only in Israel but in the United States as well. Readers will easily draw some analogies (as well as differences) regarding major social and cultural conflicts in the United States. In the last two chapters I offer, more directly, some thoughts about global/local relations as the United States as a global political power and Israelis and Palestinians negotiate (and use) these relations. I also provide a brief discussion on the ways that the Israeli case offers new insights on how scholars think about the political wisdom of groups on the margins regarding international events (e.g., the collapse of socialism) or domestic issues such as multiculturalism in our campus life.

CHAPTER 1 · Citizens of the State and Political Women

This is not a war
It is only a chapter in the history
Of the powerless
Against themselves
Who cannot see
The rainbow from above
Stretching with abundance of color
Across borders.
　　　　—*Esther Yerushalem, 1990*

A Women's Public Event: Making Peace Politics on a Friday Afternoon

Friday afternoon is a time in Israel when the public domain, stores, businesses, and offices, close down in preparation for the Sabbath, and roads teem with cars heading home, making their way through narrow streets and overcrowded highways. The Women in Black—Nashim Beshahor, as they are known in Hebrew—headed in the opposite direction, not toward home and domesticity but to the public square to gather between 1 and 2 P.M. for a protest against the state's occupation of Palestinian territories.

The Women in Black in Jerusalem chose Paris Square as a site to transform talks about peace and coexistence into political acts. Paris Square is one of several squares intended by architects to grace the city. Once a week this stagelike square, which was elevated above street level, looked like a theatrical performance. A group of women dressed in black, holding signs that say "Stop the Occupation" in Hebrew, Arabic, and English, stood silently around the square. In the strong yellow and orange hues of early afternoon in Jerusalem, the women's deliberate silence was answered by a raucous and aggressive counter-demonstration that displayed the national colors of white and blue. The Women in Black were surrounded by pedestrians dressed in bright colors and by cars whose drivers shouted insults, curses, and obscenities. Even just passing through this busy intersection, it was impossible to miss the vigil. Standing in the vigil, it was hard to ignore the hostility of the opposition.[1]

Every Friday the women displayed a fact on the ground—a vigil—a citizen's call to their government to end the occupation. The women's silent Friday vigil, which originated in Jerusalem in 1987, shortly after the onset of the Intifada, quickly spread to other parts of Israel. In 1990 there were about twenty-six places around the country where the Women in Black kept a Friday vigil (*Women in Black National Newsletter*, no. 1 [January 1992]). During my fieldwork in 1990 I spent almost every Friday with the Women in Black. I was often in Jerusalem but have also been to various other vigils. The vigils spread from Eilat in the south to Rosh Pina in the north. They took place in major cities such as Jerusalem and Tel Aviv and in cities such as Haifa, Nazareth, and Acre with large numbers of Israeli-Palestinians. Though I will pay closest attention here to the vigil in Jerusalem, I also draw on material from a number of other vigils around the country.

On any given Friday the groups varied in size from under ten in some places to over one hundred in others. Women of all ages joined, from young girls in their early teens to women in their eighties. Often mothers and daughters stood together, and occasionally three generations of women joined the vigil. While a number of the women in each vigil in 1990 were Israeli-Jewish ashkenazi (of European descent) and educated women, it was still a varied group. There were religious and secular women, young and old, urban and rural; the vigils differed from one location to another. Thus, in some places most of the women in the vigil were Israeli born and from kibbutzim, while in others, such as Jerusalem, there were also a number of women who were born in other countries but have been in Israel for most of their adult lives. In the Haifa vigil, for example, there was an active and vocal feminist core that included *ashkenaziot, mizrahiot* (of Middle Eastern descent), and Israeli-Palestinian women. On special occasions, such as Women's International Day, Palestinian women from the Occupied Territories have joined the Israeli women.

Each group of women was autonomous and decided locally on procedures. Whether women were prepared to advocate in a vigil all three principles of peace—end the occupation, talk to the PLO, and two states for two nations—would depend on how far from the national consensus forged by the Likud government the women wanted to move. In Jerusalem, the largest and most stable vigil in 1990, the women have agreed to display only a hand-shaped sign saying "Stop the Occupation"; in other locations women carried signs like "Talks with the PLO" and "Two States for Two Nations." In May 1990 the Jerusalem Women in Black produced a document to outline their political position that stated: "We are women of different political convictions, but the call 'End the Occupation' unites us. We all demand that our government take immediate action to begin negotiations for a peace settlement. Many of us are of the opinion that the PLO is the partner for peace negotiations based on the principle of two states for two people—while others are of the opinion that it is not for us to decide who the Palestinian partner for negotiations is nor the exact solution on which peace will be based. We are unified in our belief that our message is powerful and just and will eventually bring peace."

Drastic Political Shifts but Continuing Divisions

It seems that the women's call for a peace process in 1990 has become the Labor government's policy. Since the change of government in 1992, Israel has experienced an extremely rapid official shift from the politics of the Right, which denies Palestinian nationhood, to the peace policies of the Left. The shift of official policy, however, did not eliminate, nor did it diminish, the division between those who support a peace process that includes Palestinians and those who oppose it. Because of these deep and continuing disagreements, a peace process that includes Palestinians (and ultimately the future of the Jewish settlements) is still controversial in Israel and is threatened by those who oppose it. In its far-reaching progress (the two agreements signed in Washington, D.C., and one in Israel in the presence of the United States president) the peace process has already drastically altered political conventions in the Middle East. Yet within Israel the Right's opposition to the peace process regarding Palestinians, Jewish settlements, and the Golan Heights persists. When violent acts take place between Jews and Palestinians (the killing of Palestinians in Hebron by Jewish settlers, the kidnapping and killing of an Israeli soldier by the Islamic Hamas, the bombing of a bus in Tel Aviv—all in 1994) opposition to the peace process is publicly rekindled.[2] Whenever the peace process encounters problems, particularly when killings take place, this divide takes on sharper turns; the Likud, which opposed a comprehensive peace policy when the Right controlled the government, still objects to it.[3]

The women's Friday vigils and the counter-demonstrations of those who oppose the Women in Black provide one expression of these acrimonious political divisions among Israelis.[4] Opposition to the vigils displays the scope of the divide and the emotions that surround it. The counter-demonstration also foreshadows the uphill struggle for Israelis (leaders and ordinary citizens) who continue to seek peace with Palestinians. The violence expressed by the opposition in 1990 indicates how difficult it has been to take a public peace position. Not too many people on the Left chose to do it collectively and consistently. Women in Black has been the most visible group within the Peace Camp. In 1990 it was also the most steady public challenge to the Likud government's official policy regarding Palestinians. Women in Black was the single peace group that, every week, publicly transformed talks for peace and for an end to Israel's occupation of the West Bank and the Gaza Strip into a consistent political act. In the Jerusalem document the women stated: "We, Women in Black, citizens of Israel, have been holding a weekly protest since the beginning of the Intifada. This protest vigil is an expression of Israeli society and expresses our need to actively and strongly oppose the occupation."

This statement, in which the women evoke their citizenship as the ground for political protest, is more than a gesture to address the state collectively. In this deliberate insistence on citizenship the Women in Black lift the veil of democratic rhetoric that proclaims citizens' equality in the state and reveal an ongoing and heated Israeli debate on the nature of citizenship. In forging gendered peace vigils, the Women in Black address several issues. They question whether all citizens (Israeli Jews and Israeli Palestinians, women and men) are equal. The vigils also test the right of citizens to dissent from a national consensus in a society that places high value on the collective. Moreover, the women raise questions about citizens' relationship to the law—specifically, whether political citizens can break the law or whether they should stay within its bounds. In the Friday vigils the women offer their view in this critical debate on citizenship; those who oppose them present a very different one.

The Counter-Demonstrations: Questioning Women's Citizenship

The counter-demonstrations were not organized independently but came into being in reaction to the Women in Black. They therefore entered a discourse on peace with Palestinians and on gender already framed by the vigils, and they responded to both themes. They called into question the women's loyalty as citizens and cast them as (female) traitors. Accordingly, they took on the mantle of patriotism and appropriated key national symbols, such as the Israeli flag, and made much use of the national colors of blue and white to deny the need for black. The counter-demonstration, which represented the Likud government's vision of a "Greater Israel" (a state that includes the West Bank and the Gaza Strip) and an "only-by-force" political approach to the Middle East conflict, expressed vehement opposition not only to the call to end the occupation but also to the women's very right to make a political statement as female citizens. The women in the vigil were well aware of this double objection; even a fourteen-year-old girl, such as Roni, recognizes what is at stake: "They don't want us to stand here. They are angry because we are women. They think that women should not interfere in politics."

In 1990 the counter-demonstrations were organized by people from the ultra-Right political fringe, including Kahane's Kach group and small, extreme Right political parties, such as Tchiya and Moledet. While most, though not all, of their participants were ashkenazi males (predominantly boys), the counter-demonstrations, like the vigils, do not fall into a tidy category; differences exist across the country. In Jerusalem, for example, at the time of my fieldwork the counter-demonstrations included Kach supporters (many wearing Kach shirts or carrying identifying posters) and religious boys. In other places, such as Raanana in the center of Israel, the counter-demonstrations were composed of ashkenazi and secular adults and youngsters, male and female, who identified themselves as Tchiya and Moledet supporters.

To deny the women's political act, physical and verbal threats were quite common; in most locations attempts were made by the opposition to either force the women to leave or to obscure the vigil by standing in front of them. In Jerusalem this opposition took on a struggle over "territory," when the counter-demonstrators forced the women to leave Paris Square for several weeks and stand on the street while the counter-demonstrators occupied the square. In occupying the square and forcing the women out, there was a covert threat that those who strayed from the national consensus could be "exiled," sent away. National vulnerabilities such as the Holocaust were invoked against the women to mark the fact that they were betraying the Jewish collective: "The Women in Black are longing for Auschwitz" (Galili 1989), and more direct accusations of treachery were made; for example, "The Women in Black—A Knife in the Back of the Nation" on a poster that shows a knife dripping with blood. Women as killers are portrayed in a statement handed out by the counter-demonstrators, such as "We 'recognize' Black Widows. We recognize that they can kill, and we recognize that they are insects."

Going against an Official Consensus

Only two years before the signing of a peace agreement between Israel and the PLO, the vigils of the Women in Black were a dangerous business; women felt vulnerable and outsiders recognized that the women were exposed to violence. Even Israelis who were not necessarily sympathetic to the vigil acknowledged that for women to take an extremely unpopular political position and to call for an end to the occupation required courage and determination. Around the country the Women in Black stood perilously close to the traffic at extremely busy and highly congested intersections, protesting the Likud government's occupation of the West Bank and the Gaza Strip. In summer the blazing sun was beating down on them; in winter the cold chilled them. In every season they faced an aggressive ultra-Right counter-demonstration. Because the vigils publicly questioned a consensus on the issue of occupation, there was an ever-present violent response.

The women's political act in a public event was also clear to those who did not join the organized counter-demonstration but who opposed the vigils' peace position. Opposition to the vigils was thus displayed by drivers and pedestrians who were predominantly, but not exclusively, male. They hurled verbal abuse, curses and sexual insults, and made physical threats, such as pushing, spitting, and throwing food. The response to the Women in Black in 1990 indicates not only the degree of opposition to peace and coexistence by the Likud government but also the extent to which citizens' dissent in a public event was perceived as a threat. The ultra-Right counter-demonstration expressed, and was joined by, a disapproval of the women by the more moderate right wing, which supported the government's settlement and occupation of the West Bank and the Gaza Strip.

The encounter between the vigil and the counter-demonstration brings forth tensions between the Likud government's insistence on a national consensus and peace groups, who in 1990 opposed the state Middle East policies. The degree to which the Peace Camp departed from the state's policies in 1990 was made visible every week in the women's vigils; their distance from official politics could be measured by the fact that the ultra-Right groups were empowered, at least covertly, by the Likud to speak for the government's policies of occupation. The counter-demonstrations, which were composed of members of these groups, were aligned ideologically with the Likud government's position of a Greater Israel. The alliance between the Likud and ultra-Right groups was expressed in the fact that members of these groups who were found guilty of crimes against Palestinians, including murder, received light sentences and favorable terms of imprisonment and were pardoned by Israel's president.[5] Since these facts were well-known in Israel, the ultra-Right's opposition to the Women in Black in the form of threats of verbal and physical violence was meant to warn women peace activists that their stepping outside the national consensus could have detrimental consequences.

Gendered Contentions

Within each local vigil women had to decide on how far they, as a collective, were willing to place themselves outside or opposite the national consensus. The vigils of Women in Black around the country displayed differences in the degree to which a local group was willing to be contentious, reflected in the signs ("End the Occupation," "Two States for Two Nations," "Talk to the PLO") that groups chose to display. For the Women in Black, as for all women peace groups in Israel, activism is forged in social spaces between adherence to the consensus, to traditional gender roles (convention), and forging new roles, shifting domestic/public boundaries, and distancing from state policies (contention). The vigils as public events become sites in which cultural conventions are employed by women to create political facts of contention. Women defied convention by choosing Friday afternoon (domestic time) to protest as citizens (in a public space); at the same time, they used conventional roles (of wives, mothers) as the ground for their defiance as political demonstrators.

It would be easy to assume that the Women in Black's gendered defiance was a statement on women's position in the state but not on their position in the Peace Camp. It would, however, be a hasty assumption. In challenging gendered roles, women faced not only the state, the Right, and the ultra-Right but the Peace Camp as well. A Left position on peace with Palestinians did not necessarily mean support for women's equality. The Women in Black challenged a position that peace politics is not gendered (or egalitarian) and formed their own independent peace group. As the women tell it, the conception of the vigil happened almost by accident, but it struck an immediate chord for the women who were there. Sarit, one of the founders of the Women in Black, noted the vigil's roots in the joint (male and female) peace organization End the Occupation, *Dai Lakibush,* and described an event that in her view was the launching point for a women's peace vigil.

"We had a man in Dai Lakibush who was a theater director and he and one of the women, who was a graphic artist, had decided that we should have a group of men in white and women in black and we would stand there to dramatize the situation. Well, the women showed up in black but the men never got together to come in white. It was very dramatic. Not a car went by without stopping and looking. So we decided to have it as a separate women's demonstration. At the beginning there were eight of us. We stood in a different place every Friday between 1 and 2. At that stage the men from the group were around giving out leaflets but not demonstrating. And then it became a separate entity; other women started joining and eventually it separated off from Dai Lakibush and became what it is now, a national and international women's peace group."

Within the Peace Camp, Women in Black insisted on their right to participate in political debates as an autonomous group and to engage with the state as a collective of women. To insist on women's groups goes beyond a demand that women participate equally in the Peace Camp. Women claimed their own collective voice (the vigils and other women's groups) as female citizens in speaking to other collectives (the state, the Peace Camp). Sarit offered her view of a conjunction of the politics of peace (demonstrators as citizens) and the politics of gender in the vigils (demonstrators as female citizens): "Some of the women who joined the Women in Black in the beginning, not from the Dai Lakibush days but once it got a little bit beyond that, were politically active in the feminist movement here and they very much wanted it to be a women's thing. And it seemed to us logical that it would be. Part of the vigil's attraction and part of the reason why it has kept up the impetus is that it is women. We decided on the name Women in Black. So that was it. It was done for dramatic purposes; we did know the symbolism of black."

The vigils weave conventional female roles of wife and mother into a fabric of political peace protest. By embracing, yet subverting, customary gender roles, the vigils define women citizens at the confluence of the politics of peace and the politics of gender. The social good is invoked as members of the vigil say that they are fulfilling their social duty to guard the well-being of husbands, brothers, and children. Gender is mobilized to forge a peace position as women self-consciously remove conventional boundaries between the domestic and the larger social good; the domestic, rather than being merely enfolded by the political, contains and encompasses political concerns. Rachel, one of the women in the Jerusalem vigil, said: "Some of the accusations and the nastiness that we get thrown against us are, 'How can we, as women, possibly spend time on Friday afternoon demonstrating when we should be home, we should be cooking, we should take care of the children?' Yet I am here taking care of my child."

Women citizens mobilize conventional gender expectations for political contention. Culturally encoded gender elements such as femaleness, motherhood, and domesticity were deployed by women in the vigils to shift the relationship between themselves (as politically passive or powerless citizens) and the state and between the political and the domestic. In the women's version the political and the domestic were closely linked. Sarah, a religious Jewish woman who stood in the Jerusalem vigil, said: "We get ready for the Sabbath. We are under the same pressures as everyone else. But we say that it is not possible to forget at any moment, including our busy preparation for the Sabbath, what is going on around us. And it is important enough to us that we try to be heard and do something about it and make a difference." Women like Sarah reconstituted traditional Jewish roles as compelling elements in the politics of peace. Domestic roles entailed political obligations and compelled women to act politically—the kitchen spilled over to the public square, to the vigil; conventional domesticity, the women seemed to argue, now pointed toward public spaces.

While the Jerusalem Women in Black accommodated different political views on the details of the peace process, the women saw themselves as unified on ending the occupation. Gender provided the glue of the vigil, which was marked by the color of the black clothes, the structure of a vigil (a weekly protest), and the time of Friday afternoon. The only requirements for joining a vigil were gender and dress code: any female, young or old, dressed in black could become part of the group. When men joined, they did so as guests, on special occasions, and did not necessarily observe a dress code. Some wore black; others did not.

Collective and Transnational Grief

While Jewish mourning customs do not require women to wear black, the women in the vigil did refer to black as a symbol of grief. Those who saw their weekly vigil recognized it as a symbol of mourning. At the same time, black is a sign of mourning in much of the Middle East, where black clothes are gender specific and highlight mourning customs that apply to women but not to men; gender, therefore, is emphasized in the black of the dress.

The Women in Black were aware of women's groups around the world who use black in their respective protests, such as Black Sash in South Africa and the Madres of Plaza de Mayo in Argentina, but they claimed that their use of black was conceived locally.

The significance of Black thus was self-consciously and readily articulated by the vigils' participants. The official statement of the Women in Black in Jerusalem (1990) says, "The Black clothing symbolizes the tragedy of both nations, the Israeli and Palestinian." Daphna, an Israeli-Jewish woman, offers her understanding of it: "The black symbolizes our sadness and mourning. We have lost many, many Israelis in the war. But the other side has also lost, and so the black is a sign of mourning. We want this to stop. That is why we wear black." A woman at a vigil in the Gilat intersection emphasizes the tragedy of the conflict for women and men: "I have a husband who is in the military reserve and two sons in the Israeli army. How long will they have to go to wars and the women will have to wear black?" (Bar Meir 1989).

The women's frequent use, in conversation and official statements, of the plurals *we, they,* and *women* is important. Citizens in Israel are expected to be concerned with the social good. An emphasis on a women's collective signifies that the grief articulated in the vigil concerns the larger collective; this concern is displayed in their emphasis on their mourning for the nation and is anchored in a tradition of mourning concerning collective grief.[6] The grief expressed in the women's black clothes is collective and transnational, concerned with both Jewish and Palestinian national suffering.

At the same time, the vigils reveal the ways in which the collective is also concerned with the loss of individual life. The grief that marks the vigils is also consonant with the high value that Jewish tradition places on each person's life.[7] It is precisely because the women extend this Jewish value to Palestinians—because they construct it to have universalistic, transnational applications to include Palestinians—that their vigil is strongly contested by the counter-demonstrators. The vigils' expression of grief enraged the ultra-Right opposition, which cast itself as the guardian of the Jewish nation, precisely because the symbolic implications of the women's mourning are anchored in Jewish tradition but cross national and gender boundaries.

In the discourse on citizenship and who has a right to act as a political citizen, those who opposed the Women in Black attempted to challenge their right to act as citizens and to diminish the collective nature of their actions. To undermine the vigil as a political entity (a collective) to deny that the women (female citizens) can put demands to the state, the opposition deliberately addressed individual (domestic) women and used the singular when talking to them. The counter-demonstrators recognized the political significance of the women's clothes as a transnational sign of mourning and made mocking references to the black clothes to deny the grief articulated by the vigils in comments such as "Tell me who are you mourning for?" and by using the singular pronoun in Hebrew in angry curses, as, for example, "May your husband die so that you will really be a widow, *almana.*" Using the singular was meant to indicate that women were "mere" individuals; evoking their domestic roles meant to delegitimate them as political citizens and to cast them as "just" women. Since public events in Israel are political spaces in which collectives transform ideologies (talk) into political facts on the ground, the use of singular pronouns was meant to deny that the women were there as a collective. The implication of the use of the singular was that individual women lacked the necessary attributes to act as political citizens.

Collective Emotions: Grief and Rage

The vigils and the counter-demonstrations display tensions not only between two political positions but also between two groups, each expressing collective emotions surrounding these political positions. The women's vigil expresses grief for tragedies in both nations; its ultra-Right opposition expresses rage toward Palestinians and by extension toward the women, who are seen as representing them. In the Friday vigils grief and rage represent neither individual sadness or anger, nor are they about the mourning of individual deaths; instead, they are the collective emotions that represent political relations between two groups.[8] These two emotions are each expressed by a political collective, grief by the Women in Black and rage by ultra-Right groups. Rage and grief in the Friday vigils are about politics and are located in a social interaction between women peace activists and ultra-Right opposition. These collective emotions articulate two drastically different political positions about Palestinian nationhood. While the Women in Black's grief recognizes and embraces a Palestinian nation and its entailed rights, the opposition's rage denies such an entity for either Israeli Palestinians or for Palestinians in the Occupied Territories.

In 1990 Israelis were fiercely divided on the question of the Occupied Territories; no peace demonstration that included men, however, elicited such violent reactions as the all-women vigil of the Women in Black.

Though some demonstrations expressed much sharper political messages, such as the call to refuse military service in the Occupied Territories, none elicited the kind of violent response that the Women in Black have faced. The intense response to the vigil has to do with the intersection of the politics of gender and the politics of peace and the particular discourse that it creates about *gvulot,* a Hebrew word meaning, among other things, borders, boundaries, and limits. In the Friday confrontations, collective emotions of rage and grief articulate the divisions over the borders of the state of Israel (with or without the Occupied Territories), over the boundaries between Israeli Palestinians and Israeli Jews, and over the relationship between women and the state. The rage and grief are about all of these.

The vigils displayed an Israeli debate on the state's borders, and the grief and rage were about the presence or absence of political boundaries and borders. In the Friday public event, collective emotions displayed a dramatic reconstruction of boundaries: grief-mourning (the Women in Black) stood on one side of the street (representing Israeli borders without the Occupied Territories) and rage-violence (the counter-demonstration representing the borders of a Greater Israel) stood on the other; they faced each other, spatially divided and in fierce political contestation.

Given the close links between gender and peace in women's groups, grief and rage, as collective emotions that accompany the vigils, may seem to be articulations of gender. Given the attribution of emotions to women and rationality to men that has dominated Western philosophical ideas from the Greeks to Freud, it would be easy to assume that the vigils reveal that men are associated with vengeance and rage and women with peace and grief. This is not the case, however: on the side of the counter-demonstration there are women, albeit few, and the right-wing parties include women; the Tchiya Party had a prominent, active, and vocal woman leader in 1990.

As for the vigil, men periodically join the Women in Black. There are men who would do so on a regular basis but for the women's insistence on keeping it a gendered vigil. While it is obvious that the women choose to emphasize mourning in a way that joint peace demonstrations do not, when men join the vigil they become part of the collective grief. The incorporation of men in grief can be seen in a notice issued by the Women and Peace Movement that called on women and men to wear black and join in a silent memorial service for Palestinians who were killed by Israeli police in October 1990 in Jerusalem.

Women, as the vigils make clear, are not associated with emotions any more than men are associated with rationality, and in this political confrontation both women and men articulate emotions.[9] Insults leveled at the women do not imply the absence of female rationality. Emotions in the Friday vigils are about politics: grief in this context is a political statement about two national rights of Jews and Palestinians, while rage is about exclusive nationalism.

Rage Politics and Mourning Customs

The confrontation between the women's vigils and the counter-demonstrations reflects a larger political dispute in Israel regarding both the law of the state and Jewish laws of mourning. It became prominent in the last decade as ultra-right-wing groups publicly defied state laws and Jewish mourning customs. These ultra-Right groups, for example, have invaded funerals of soldiers and civilians killed by Palestinians, calling for revenge and randomly attacking Palestinians who happened to be on the street on the day of the funeral. These groups, who see themselves as guardians of the nation, claim that Jewish national interests supersede state laws and override notions of democracy (Gal-Or 1990). Yet bringing rage into grief is considered by bereaved families to be a breach of customary Jewish rules of mourning and a violation of proper behavior at funerals. Rage is not part of Jewish mourning customs, and the Kaddish, the mourner's prayer, is recited in public to signify the bereaved's acceptance of death and the justification of God's will in the midst of grief. A number of Israelis, among them family members of the victims, express their dismay that the extreme Right's call for violence toward Palestinians has invaded the families' mourning and have politicized their grief. An Israeli-Jewish widow whose husband, a taxi driver, was killed in retaliation for the killing of Muslims at the Temple Mount area on October 8, 1990, noted the rules for proper mourning conduct and rejected the politicization of grief by those on the extreme Right who call for revenge: "While the murder of my husband was motivated by revenge I don't want revenge visited on Arabs. I have not changed my views after my husband was murdered. I am glad that his funeral was peaceful, without the participation of extremists, like Kahane's people and others. We did not want them. I have never thought of, and will not think of, taking revenge on all Arabs" (*Al Hamishmar,* October 14, 1990).

The opposition to the women's Friday vigil reveals this politicization of rage by ultra-Right groups. It also reveals that in the discourse on convention and contention, the opposition breaks conventions, such as the law, that the women uphold. In this context grief can be seen as a representation of convention, while rage represents the defiance of religious and legal conventions. A letter to the editor speaks to politically motivated intrusions at funerals, which disregard the law and mourning customs: "Whenever there is an attack, one immediately notices the political gamblers, the variety of 'blood consumers,' those who never allow the mourners to be with their sorrow in a quiet and dignified fashion" (*Al Hamishmar,* October 31, 1990).

While the women's grief certainly takes on some gendered traditional properties, like the black of mourning, in other respects it stretches the bounds of customary rules of mourning in several ways. The vigils have shifted the focus of mourning from that of the particular (the death of an individual) to the collective (many deaths) and from the specificity of nationality (Israeli or Palestinian) to a transnational, inclusive one (both). The intensity that in traditional mourning diminishes with time here remains unabated. Where it is usually time bound (for Israeli Jews it is marked by the funeral—seven days, one month, one year, etc.), it is here politically bound: the women intend to mourn for as long as the occupation lasts.

What Kinds of Citizens Are Women?

The vigils display different positions on the relationship between citizens and the law of the state. The Women in Black represent a political position that promoted protest within the bounds of the law; the counter-demonstrators challenge the law of the state in their threats, which at times border on the dangerous. The extreme Right position, which regards Palestinians as outside the protection of the law, is also evoked in the threats made against the Women in Black, threats that disregard their civil rights. In some locations drivers have tried to run over the women (Keshet 1989). In Jerusalem a soldier pointed a gun from a car window toward the women, and a young man in army uniform went from one woman to the next cursing each one of them. The threat shouted in a number of vigils, "We will transfer you first," refers to the threat of Right extremists to transfer all Israeli Palestinians and Palestinians from the Occupied Territories to Arab countries. A middle-aged man in Jerusalem kept shouting, "We will visit Der Yassin on you," and made a throat cutting gesture. Der Yassin was a village in which Palestinians were massacred by Jews; by invoking the village, the threat could not be clearer. Placing the Women in Black outside the state and the community is also expressed in politicized threats such as "Go to Iraq" and "Saddam will take care of you," and in curses such as "I hope you die of cancer, slow, Palestinian cancer."

The Women in Black challenged the government's occupation of Palestinian territories, but, unlike the opposition, upheld the law. To underscore this position and in response to the violence of the counter-demonstration, the Women in Black's vigils have called for and receive police presence and protection. Calling for police presence is also the women's statement that they are citizens of the state. While the opposition casts the Women in Black outside the state by accusing group members of being disloyal ("You are all PLO"), the women chose to highlight their position as citizens who speak for the social good.

The women's vigils are one way in which citizens forge a collective to challenge the government's policy of occupation in a public event. Moreover, it uncovers how gender matters in this kind of a political challenge. As Women in Black insist on their right as citizens to make a claim that they are an expression of Israeli society, they uncover a contested understanding of citizenship. They provide their version to a question about the politics of gender in Israel: What kinds of citizens are women? Women's peace groups such as Women in Black position themselves against a more conventional version of Israeli women as nonpolitical citizens. This version can be seen, for example, in a newspaper cartoon featuring a couple: the woman wears an apron, holds a cooking spoon, and has tears in her eyes; the man holds a pistol and grins mischievously. The woman asks him: "Why are you grinning?" and the man replies: "Next week it is our turn" (*Hadashot,* October 22, 1990). Like the vigils, the cartoon alludes to the themes of violence and counter-violence and brings to the fore a conjunction of Middle East conflict and the politics of gender. But, unlike the vigils, the cartoon constructs different social identities for women and men regarding this conflict: men are the warriors, the fighters, and the protectors; women are the domestic, the protected, worried, and distressed. This conventional version presents Israeli women as passive, domestic, and protected citizens.

The vigils and the opposition bring forth a discourse on women's roles. While the women insist on their right to challenge domestic and political convention, the opposition deligitimates this very right. It links peace politics to both female domesticity and sexuality; women's peace position is equated with domestic negligence and sexual transgression. Verbal assaults on the group's legitimacy included inserting conventional domesticity into the discourse to depoliticize the vigil in comments such as "Go back to the kitchen," reminding the women of traditional definitions of the "good" mother. Personalized questions in the singular were often asked: "Why don't you go home? My mother is home right now, and she is cooking. How come you have time to stand here?" And some hecklers attempted to flatter individual women as objects of desire: "Not all of you are ugly. Some of you are really beautiful. So why are you standing here?" Female indecency and a peace position (contra the government) were joined in insults that sexualize not only the women but Palestinians as well: "Whores," "You like to fuck Arabs," "Arafat's whores," "Saddam's whores," and, since at that time the Right dominated the government, "This government will fuck you."

Struggles for Women's (Equal) Citizenship

The women's vigils contest this construction of women as domestic and protected beings. The Women in Black's insistence that they are political citizens concerned with the social good is grounded in political debates on gender equality in Israel. These contemporary debates on women's relationship to the social good have critical local antecedents; they are home-grown products, so to speak. The roots of these indigenous debates go back to the very early days of the Yishuv, the early settlement prestate period of 1880–1947. Struggles for women's equal citizenship, such as that of the Women in Black, were sown on the native ground of the Yishuv. Despite the promise of equality made by Theodore Herzl and the Jewish liberation movement, women time and again fought to be equal citizens of the Zionist collective and struggled for political representation in Palestine (Friedman, Shrift, and Izraeli 1982). Women's accounts from the prestate period reveal that they objected to what they saw as a systematic exclusion from organized politics within the prestate structure (Azaryahu 1980; Trager 1984). Documents written by women pioneers about women's efforts to become full members of organized politics as it existed in the prestate structure reveal a gap between the ideology of equality for women and its implementation in social reality. Women of the First Aliya (the first wave of Jewish immigration to Palestine) demanded the right to vote in local elections in an effort to define themselves as equal citizens in the collective.[10] Women demanded to share political power because they had shared in social projects, working equally and side by side with men in building the community, and had shared the hardships of the early settlements. In using phrases such as "We the daughters of this settlement" and "We take part in building a new society," they created a female collective that could claim political equality and engage in a dialogue with the Yishuv official collective because of their work for the social good.[11]

The vigils of the Women in Black express similar concerns with the relationship between the state and its female citizens. The vigils reveal the scope of the marginalization of women peace activists. Women are on the political margins not only because they distance themselves from state politics; they are mostly absent from organized politics and from positions of power in Israeli society. The difference between mere talk (an ideological position) and a fact on the ground is reflected in the state's position regarding women's equality. In its Declaration of Independence the state of Israel espoused gender equality; in 1951 it reaffirmed its commitment in a Women's Equal Rights Law, which proscribed discrimination against women and introduced a number of laws to correct inequitable practices (Bowes 1989; Karp 1989). Women's peace groups came into being because, among other things, the reality of organized politics does not reflect equality for women. The birth of groups like Women in Black takes place alongside, and in response to, women's negligible representation in organized politics. While there are 120 seats in the Knesset, women have held no more than 11 of them in any one term.[12] The change in government and in Middle East politics is not matched by a similar gender change. The current Knesset, elected in June of 1992, has 11 women, the exact same number of women as in the first Knesset. While the present government includes 2 women ministers and 2 elected women who are members of the Foreign Affairs and Security Committee, Israeli women by and large are not part of the political decision-making process. Moreover, their domestic roles as wives and mothers are used to exclude women from public and political positions of power and authority (Sharfman 1988). The absence of women from Israel's organized politics is so pervasive that it is perceived by many Israelis as a natural phenomenon rather than as a cultural product of the politics of gender.[13] While the women's vigils take place in a political context that excludes women from organized politics, they also indicate an increasing politicization of women beyond and around organized politics. The vigils provide one way in which Israeli women establish themselves as citizens/protectors and political persons.

Women as Protectors of Collectives

The Women in Black establish themselves as protectors against the conventional exclusion of women from positions of authority in the Israeli army; this exclusion means that women are treated as protected citizens. Israeli-Jewish women are excluded from combat units and, in effect, from reserve duty. Consequently, they are shut out of most positions of power and authority in the Israeli army and thus disadvantaged in later careers. The social difference between women and men soldiers has been noted in many conversations I had with women like Rachel, who in 1990 had two daughters in the army: "Men learn to relate to women as something to defend, and to relate to everything, to all relationships, as competitive situations: everyone is either a friend or an enemy. All men here are fighters or pseudofighters, and all the women are not. And it changes everything; it affects women's lives. Every man has something important to do in the army. He can be a total physical wreck, a *kaliker,* but yet be considered to have something important to contribute. Not so women. I have two daughters in the army, and they do worthwhile things, but they realize that they do not have responsibility. They work for someone (male: *mishehu*), and while they acquire many skills they have no responsibility, and they feel less important. They learn in the army that women are less important, that their tasks are less important, and that the relationship between men and women is unequal. Women soldiers have less responsible jobs despite the fact that things have changed in the army."[14]

This exclusion from combat units has serious political implications for women because there are intimate links in Israel between army careers and political leadership, the former providing powerful and almost essential credentials for the latter (Sharfman 1988; Chazan 1989; Ben Eliezer 1990). Some women speak clearly on this issue. Judy, who is a longtime activist in the peace movement and one of the founders of the Women in Black, says: "If you look at the position of the army in the culture of this country, women are almost totally excluded from that. There are women in Keva [the regular army], and there are women who are high officers, but they don't even figure in it. And the army is such a vital part of the culture in this country for nepotism, *protekzia,* or everything, and women are excluded totally." Exclusion from combat and reserve duty has created not only political inequality but also a very different social reality for women that spills over to other, seemingly unrelated, areas, such as literature. Esther, who positions herself in the

Peace Camp and has written protest poetry, says: "The war affects writing as well. How can I write about war in the same way as men poets who have been in the war? I do write about the war, but my authority is less than the male voice who was there. It is seen that I have less legitimacy to write about the war."

A Nonmilitary Woman Warrior

The Women in Black question the warrior image, which is linked with a wide range of social entitlements, and insert instead one with women as protectors of the social good. In claiming to act for the social good, the vigil challenges military characteristics, such as warrior-hero-protector, which are expected of males; these in turn become requirements for full male adulthood and success in organized politics. The vigils contest a conventional cultural version of Israeli-Jewish women, who are defined as actual or potential wives-mothers-protected and apolitical persons. The Friday protests go against the idea that "the division of labor in [Israeli] society is clear and unequivocal. Men defend women and children. Women, like children and the elderly, are seen as helpless in times of war" (Lieblich 1988, 221). To be the protected rather than the protectors has political consequence in Israel, because it constructs two kinds of citizens within the state.[15] In this sense the Women in Black have appropriated the role of safeguards of the nation when they claim to take care of their traditional defenders—husbands, sons, lovers, and brothers. Ruth, a Jewish woman, noted: "We say that as women, and out of concern for our husbands, our brothers, and our sons, we want to stop it. We have a consensus on that."

The Women in Black embrace gender difference to create a nonmilitary collective from which they reclaim their right to share in major political decisions in Israel. The women present themselves as full citizens in the vigil, as nonmilitary protectors. Yael, who regularly attended the Friday vigil, said: "We feel that, though some of us are soldiers, we as women have a different statement to make. In this country women are not in active combat, and we feel that our call for peace comes from a different perspective. There are a number of women's peace movements in this country, and we have a stake here and a way to express it in a different fashion." This different fashion of women's nonmilitary status as protectors is an important element in creating a transnational female community.

A Women's Transnational Collective

To speak in a political voice about a way to ensure survival in Israel requires women to speak from within a collective and to stake some claims to the role of protector. Yet, paradoxically, women's marginal role in the army becomes an asset for women trying to construct grounds for solidarity with Israeli-Palestinian women who do not serve in the army and particularly with Palestinian women from the Occupied Territories. Since women are mostly excluded from duty in the Occupied Territories, a semi-combat situation, and since they do not act as military occupiers, they can, literally and metaphorically, stand side by side Palestinian women in the vigils in which military occupation is the key issue of protest. By contrast, there are obvious complications for Jewish men in the Peace Camp who wish to demonstrate against the occupation, because they have to serve in the Occupied Territories. Tamar, a member of the Women in Black, offered her perception: "I think that on the personal psychological level if you are not the one who has to make the decision 'Should I serve in the Occupied Territories or should I not,' it is much easier to be a protester because there is no schizophrenic break between what you are standing out there doing and what you might have to do one month in a year doing reserve duty."

Women's noncombat status in the army opens a way for women to dislocate nationalism as militant (only by force), exclusionary (there is no Palestinian nation), and confrontational ("The whole world is against us"). The women construct a transnational women's community that both affirms each nation and momentarily transcends national boundaries. Moreover, the vigil structurally includes Israeli-Palestinian women and in its statements acknowledges the Palestinian nation. To construct a nonmilitary status allows the vigil to shift national boundaries and to universalize and transnationalize grief so that traditionally competing Palestinian and Jewish national vulnerabilities are both acknowledged. The Women in Black's document states: "We are protesting against the occupation and against all its manifestations: destruction of homes, expulsions, administrative arrests, collective punishment, extended curfews, killings and bloodshed" (May 1990). Aliza, a woman from the vigil at Tzomet Gilat in southern Israel, explained: "We are standing here wearing black because we mourn the situation, the killing that is taking place in both nations." Nadia, an Israeli-Palestinian woman from a vigil in northern Israel, said to a young Jewish male counter-demonstrator: "I stand here so that young men like you don't have to die. So that your mother's son and my son can live." The women's emphasis on gender and the reiteration of "We are all women" and their uniformity in black clothes shift national boundaries and stake a political position that the value of the lives of sons of both nations is the same.

Occupation and Oppressions

Five years after the inception of the vigil, in June 1992, when a peace position became state policy, the Women in Black debated on how the group should reconstitute itself and what kinds of peace activities it should engage in. The fundamental debates have been whether the women should sustain a weekly vigil as an act of support for the Labor government's peace position. In some places the women decided not to continue with the Friday vigils; in a few places they came back convinced that, despite the change in Israel's official peace policy, the occupation did not come to an end. Since 1992 other activities, such as a few large national demonstrations and conferences, have been considered as alternatives to weekly vigils.

The peace process initiated by the Labor government thus did not bring an end to women's peace groups. Women in Black, like other women's peace organizations, while going through changes, are still active in Israel, following the Labor government's signing of two peace agreements with the PLO and Jordan. The fact that women's peace groups such as Women in Black have neither disbanded nor disappeared highlights the intricate links between peace and gender politics. The persistence of these groups illuminates both the complexity of the swift political transformation in Israel and a recent burgeoning of women's acts toward gender equality. The peace process has brought about questions of reconstituting women's peace activism; it includes setting new goals and maintaining previous political commitments such as social justice for women and for Palestinians.

The Women in Black's striving to redistribute power between Israel and the Palestinians is linked to the group's striving to share power within the state. Discrimination against women, its members say, makes them sensitive to other forms of oppression; their de facto exclusion from political power enables them to empathize with other marginalized groups, including the Palestinians. Chazan, a political scientist and a peace activist, notes: "If we oppose the oppression of women, how can we fail to oppose the suppression of another people? In reality, many Israeli women's rights activists merge their feminism with the quest for equal rights for the Palestinians" (1989, 13). This link between these two kinds of injustices is clearly and self-consciously articulated by women. But it is also quite apparent to the counter-demonstrators and an irritant to those who oppose the vigil.

The struggle of groups such as Women in Black to redistribute power at two levels is linked to their objection to violence. In its 1990 document the Women in Black in Jerusalem denounced violence against Palestinians: "We have had enough of the legitimization of brutality, of violence," and declared, "We call on all women to join us in our staunch, persistent and non-violent protest." The women's document is located in a broader discourse of violence as a women's concern. It links violence against Palestinians and against women. Various women's groups work to change the state's lack of response to increasing violence against women in Israel. Shifting the boundaries between the domestic and the public spheres in the Friday vigil also parallels other ways in which domestic issues can be brought into the public; the violence that surrounds the vigils has some echoes in domestic violence against women.[16] In 1989, for example, women launched a national project called Bat Adam to coordinate various organizations' activities concerning victims of sexual assault, shelters for battered women, and Naamat's center for victims of domestic violence.[17]

Like the Women in Black, various women's groups in Israel have recently engaged in a dialogue with the state on women's rights. In a parallel way to the Women in Black, they form collectives that transform women into full citizens by allowing them to take on the role of protectors of women in public demonstrations. Thus, when in 1990 the Likud government promised an ultraorthodox political party, Agudat Yisrael, to restrict severely abortion laws, several women's groups demonstrated to protest the proposed restrictions. These groups issued a written statement (November 1990) in which they took on the role of protectors of women's lives. The statement said: "We will oppose this threat to our health and our lives. This male government will not expand (to include Agudat Yisrael) at the expense of women's health. This male government will not endanger women's lives."

Groups that fight for women's rights all engage in gender politics, because they strive to redistribute power between women and the state and between women and men. The vigils of the Women in Black are one articulation of the various attempts to bring to public attention violations of human rights. At one level the women's vigils are political because they call for an end to the occupation, which means, in reality, changing the distribution of power between Palestinians and Israelis. At another level the vigils, like other women's groups, engage in the politics of gender as they actively reallocate power between women and men by stepping into the public arena and by taking on the role of protectors traditionally allocated to men.

The Women in Black's rejection of violence is a key element in the politics of peace and of gender. The women's statement against violence and their sign "End the Occupation" can be seen as metaphors for other kinds of violence and occupations; the word *occupation* can be read as a symbol of a number of injustices: an absence of human rights, oppression, and violence. In the vigils "End the Occupation" is an expression of the politics of gender: it is a statement by women about women, by women peace activists about the position of women in Israeli society as citizens of the state. The very presence of the vigils is a statement about the politics of gender because they display, in full view of the public, women who constitute themselves as female protesters/protectors and ultimately as full citizens of the state. Yet gender unity is partial—women peace activism moves between unity and power differentials of the occupation and various forms of discrimination (Israeli Palestinians, mizrahi Jews) within the state that cut across gender. The Friday vigils are public events in which women peace activists face the state and in which gender unity, rather than difference, was emphasized. Women's public events, which, unlike the vigils, are not designed as direct encounters with the state, reveal both the potentials and the limits of gender as the ground for coexistence within and between nations.

CHAPTER 2 · On the Borders of Nations: Sororal Transnational Territory

I publicly declare before the nation and the world
that I too am occupied and enslaved territory,
  the West Bank in me
and the East Bank
Struggle within me each according to its ability
                    —Bracha Serri

Love for a homeland [moledet] is natural
But why does love stop at the border?
We are all one family
We are all responsible for the other
We are all leaves on a tree
The tree of humanity
Love for a homeland is natural
But why does love stop at the border?
              —Chava Alberstein

Women Transgressing Borders: Legitimating Palestinian Nation-ness

On November 18, 1991, the newspaper *Hadashot* published a striking photograph of an exuberant group of Israeli-Jewish women peace activists holding hands with Hannan Ashrawi, a member of the Palestinian delegation to the 1991 Middle East peace talks in Madrid, where she had been instrumental in placing Palestinian nation-ness in the international community. Hannan Ashrawi's circle of female supporters and well-wishers included prominent leaders among the Israeli Left whose names were quite well-known in the country, such as Shulamit Aloni, who was a member of Knesset and is now a minister in the government; Alice Shalvi, the chairwoman of the Israel Women's Network; Yael Dayan, a well-known writer and now a member of the Knesset; Naomi Chazan, a professor of political science and now a member of the Knesset; and many others. The women were making a political statement regarding Palestinians. Publicly, they broke Israel's official denial of Palestinian nation-ness: they defied the Likud government's position that there were no longer any 1967 borders, that the Occupied Territories (including the city of Ramallah) were part of a Greater Israel, and that there was no Palestinian nation.

In holding hands with Hannan Ashrawi and through other public events, Israeli and Palestinian women created transnational spaces for both nations several years before Norway offered such a space for Israelis and Palestinians in 1993 and before Washington provided a transnational ceremony in 1993 that would publicly establish new political facts in the Middle East in the historic handshake between the leaders of Israel and the PLO. The women's journey to the town of Ramallah in the Occupied Territories entailed crossing the 1967 borders, the so-called green line, to honor a Palestinian woman who had been outspoken in her criticism of the Israeli occupation. Women clasped hands across national boundaries in a local event, and, according to *Hadashot,* when Hannan Ashrawi returned from the Madrid conference the Israeli women went to her home in Ramallah on a *bikur hizdahut* (solidarity visit)—a transgressive act in 1991 because its purpose was to honor a Palestinian leader. The Hebrew word *hizdahut* means both "solidarity" and "identification with," and this dual meaning suggests that the women's visit was in fact a double transgression: it both supported Ashrawi as a leader and suggested their identification with her political positions and against their own government regarding the nation-ness of Palestinians.

For a number of years before the signing of an agreement between official representatives of Israel and the Palestinians, women of both nations were steeped in a peace activism that demanded innovative approaches to three complex questions: How can they work together toward peace from within their respective communities, and from within their own nation-ness, yet recognize the rights of the other nation? How can they create a transnational space (across nations) in which they can act jointly? How can they sustain dialogues and actions when differences have to be confronted and when periodic crises seriously threaten their solidarity? The Gulf Crisis, for example, brought dissent into the Peace Camp and challenged its solidarity with Palestinians. Yet the members of Shani, Women against the Occupation, remained firm in their support for Palestinian nation-ness. They published a position statement in February 1991, during the Gulf War. The Shani document argued that Israel must take three steps in order to begin a resolution of conflict: first, it must recognize the Palestinian nation and its aspiration for a state of its own; second, it must negotiate with the legitimate representative of the Palestinians, the PLO; and, third, it must support the establishment of a Palestinian state side by side with the state of Israel, because this is the only solution for both nations if they wish to coexist in peace and security (Shani 1990).[1] It took courage to reiterate this position in 1991 when the Iraqi scud missiles threatened Israel and the Likud was still in power. But the Shani document demonstrates the degree to which women peace activists were, for many years, adamant that their political peace position would ensure Israel's survival and would allow the state to do the only viable political act: recognize the nation-ness of the Palestinians.

Women's transgression of boundaries takes on both metaphoric and literal, geographic and political, forms. The visit to Ramallah signifies this double transgression. Geographically, women redrew borders that the Likud government had attempted to eradicate. The government ignored the 1967 border between Israel and the Occupied Territories, while the women put the border in place by visiting a national Palestinian leader who insisted on reinstituting the 1967 boundary. Politically, the women crossed the political boundaries that the Likud had made between those who have a national identity and those who do not—between Israelis, who have a nation-state, and the Palestinians, who are regarded by the Likud and the right-wing parties as "Arabs" who have no local national identity and who could, according to this position, live in *any* Arab country.[2] The visit, like the many public events initiated by the women's peace camp, took place on what Appadurai and Breckenridge (1988, 6) call "a zone of cultural debate" in Israel on the question of Palestinian nation-ness. In this debate the Likud viewed, and still views, the Occupied Territories as ancient patrimony of and for the Jewish nation. In their visit to Ramallah the women literally took their action to the very terrain of contest and debate, a town in the Occupied Territories. By displaying solidarity and identification with a Palestinian leader, the women's visit was a political fact and a show of power precisely because the Jewish-Israeli women went to the Occupied Territories not to *settle* but to *unsettle* a dominant, right-wing ideology that denied Palestinian nation-ness. Under the circumstances their act was tantamount to a public recognition of Palestinian nationalism that was anathema to the right-wing government. In visiting a Palestinian leader, the women reconstituted boundaries between Israel and the Occupied Territories that the Likud government's ideology of a Greater Israel vehemently opposed.

The photograph in a major Hebrew paper featured iconographically and metaphorically an act of Israeli women's inscribing boundaries along the green line, which the government's policy denied. The visit to Ramallah by Israeli-Jewish peace activists was a statement about Palestinians' right to self-determination and a refutation of the Likud government's attempts to delegitimate this right by treating the Madrid delegation, in general, and Hannan Ashrawi in particular, as a *local* representation only and as part of a Jordanian delegation—in short, a delegation stripped of its Palestinian nation-ness.

Though women peace activists on the political margins tackled these complicated, prickly questions, the Likud government consistently avoided them, even as it reluctantly participated in the 1991 Madrid peace talks. With the change in government in Israel, the task of confronting these questions has now shifted from the margins (women peace activists) to the political center, from rank-and-file activists to the official politicians of both nations. The women's joint struggle is nevertheless illuminating, because the struggle in which they engaged belongs to their respective nations, which have been locked together in a violent relationship for so long. The women's struggles and dilemmas mirror what was—and will continue to be—a difficult, risky, and unpredictable process, yet the women, who are firmly anchored in their respective communities, were adamant in their determination to forge a transnational territory in which they could act together.

Printing Women's Acts: How the Media Participates in Female Transgression

Like other women's public events, the visit to Hannan Ashrawi in Ramallah reveals the ways in which Israeli and Palestinian women have addressed competing national agendas, different collective anxieties and fears, rivaling claims, and cycles of violence and counter-violence. It also shows how the media has occasionally participated in the women's transgressive acts by providing public space for their agenda. On November 22, 1991, for example, several days after the photograph appeared in *Hadashot,* the Hebrew newspaper *Yediot Ahronot* published an interview with Hannan Ashrawi entitled "Israel Is Negotiating with the PLO." The title itself was subversive because it stated what the Likud government had vehemently denied in its insistence on total exclusion of the PLO from any negotiations.

Dan Shilon, the *Yediot Ahronot* journalist who interviewed Hannan

Ashrawi, added textual substance to the political message of the photo-graph in *Hadashot* by referring to Ashrawi as the "spokeswoman for the Palestinian delegation." Shilon participated in this political mapping as he spoke of a Palestinian state not as a questionable possibility, an "if," but as a matter of time, so that such a state was taken for granted. When he asked, "Despite your declarations that you want to go back to academic life, is it possible that I have met today with the prime minister of the future Pales-tinian state?" he gave further support to the idea of the birth of a Palestin-ian state.

Through its reporting and publicity the media has reinscribed a fact on the ground of a gendered, transnational territory that women of two nations have publicly sketched on the political map. Shilon reconstructed women's sororal unity and their transgression of political boundaries by asking Ashrawi: "What did you feel regarding the Israeli women who earlier this week came to your house in Ramallah to express solidarity [identify] with you?" Ashrawi inserted feminism into her response: "It was wonderful. It was a genuine demonstration of solidarity not only on a political basis but on a feminist one as well. They demonstrated a true commitment to the peace process." The Israeli women's solidarity visit was thus a public event that took place in the town of Ramallah in the Occupied Territories and was reperformed in the media—in *Hadashot* and *Yediot Ahronot*—for a larger audience of Israelis who were not present as witnesses.

An event in private has very different implications when it takes place in public, and it is in public events that political facts are established in Israel. What is seen as mere talk about solidarity with Palestinian women when it takes place in private is transformed into a display of action and power in a performative event. A "mere" women's visit to another woman, in her home, was transformed into a political event, by an act of alliance and identification with a Palestinian national leader; the visit also transformed women's powerlessness to end the occupation into a defiant crossing of the government's position regarding Palestinians. *Hadashot* and *Yediot Ahronot* thus participated in constructing the women's visit to Hannan Ashrawi as a public event that transformed an ideology of national coexistence and of female identification, *hizdahut,* into a transnational political territory. The media thus gave substance to women's recognition of Palestinian nation-ness by publicizing the Israeli women's visit to Ramallah to honor a Pales-tinian woman.

A Paradox: Accommodating Gender Unity and
Confronting Inequalities

The women create a transnational territory—a sororal community of "we women for peace"—from within their respective nations. This sororal territory is complex; it embraces a paradox of female solidarity, on the one hand, and inequalities between Israeli-Jewish and Israeli-Palestinian women and power differences between Israeli women and Palestinian women from the Occupied Territories, on the other. While these inequalities threaten joint activism, female solidarity makes it prevail. Circumstances (such as intercommunal violence) and choice (what the women decide to say and do when they face opposition) determine when women confront inequalities and when they emphasize solidarity.

Forging transnational territory means that in the midst of the Israeli-Palestinian conflict these women step outside their respective national consensus to create an alliance and recognize the national aspirations of the other. It takes courage and fortitude to stand against one's community even in normal times; it requires even more in places like the Middle East, where every political outburst calls on primordial group loyalties. In every public event, such as the women's visit to Ramallah, women peace activists constantly faced complicated negotiations between competing duties and different resistances. For Israeli-Palestinian women transnational territory involves an accommodation of power inequality in the relationship with Israeli-Jewish women, on the one hand, and a difference with Palestinians from the Occupied Territories, on the other; while they identify with the struggle for a Palestinian state in the Occupied Territories, they are citizens of the state of Israel and enjoy privileges denied to Palestinians who live under occupation. Palestinian women in the Occupied Territories who work for peace also need to take a stand against those in their nation who reject peaceful coexistence and, in times of political crises, to be willing to continue to engage with Israeli-Jewish women—who, despite their peace position and unanimous opposition to the occupation, are part of the occupying state. For Israeli-Jewish women transnational territory meant in 1990 both acknowledging their privileged position compared to Palestinian women and pursuing their dissenting stand, which publicly opposed the Israeli right-wing government's pervasive efforts to silence Palestinian nationalism. The epigraphic poems by Serri and Alberstein at the beginning of this chapter reflect the problematic relations of occupied and occupier that women's peace activists face. Serri's poem expresses the pain of the struggle between women of two nations and alludes to the power differential between them. Alberstein, who views love for the nation as a natural sentiment, refers to a wider transnational love that could, but does not, stretch across borders.

How do women peace activists from two nations in the thick of a bitter and violent conflict balance this paradox, in which they simultaneously juggle two kinds of "we" communities—how do they both affirm (different) nation-ness and create (same-gender) transnationalism? How do they confront inequality and occupation? To explore the intricacies of this process I examine two public events that were organized by women for peace in 1990. The first was a conference in Kufir Yasif, an Israeli-Palestinian village, which took place in July, shortly before the Gulf Crisis. The second conference met in October in Haifa, a mixed city of a majority of Israeli Jews and a minority of Israeli Palestinians.

The two conferences took place in two different political periods. The one at Kufir Yasif was in a relatively peaceful month. Events happen quickly in Israel, and a relative tranquillity can easily turn into violence, rage, and grief; the one at Haifa came at a time of political turmoil and violence. What do women peace activists do in times of crisis, when national loyalties are pressing hard on sororal solidarity and seem to question their transnational unity? At the Haifa conference women of two nations tried together to make sense of what was fundamentally senseless: the terror that accompanies violence. The periodic eruptions of violence and terror test the relationship between members from the two nations, Israeli Jewish and Israeli Palestinian. At the Haifa conference nation-ness openly collided with the transnational sororal territory. Yet even at the peaceful Kufir Yasif conference competing national claims had to be faced. These competing claims have global and local antecedents and have shaped and continue to shape relationships between Israelis and Palestinians. An attempt to solve the global problem of Jewish nation-ness known as "the Jewish Question" is now confronting Palestinian nation-ness in the Middle East.

Women peace activists are aware of these global and local historiographies of nation-ness. In the conferences in Kufir Yasif and Haifa, Jewish and Palestinian women referred to these competing claims. Palestinian women spoke of their people's suffering, of the Arab Question in Israel, in ways that resonate a Jewish discourse on the Jewish Question in Europe. They often stated that given Jewish-European experience, Israeli Jews should be particularly sensitive to Palestinian national aspirations. Jewish women confront the meaning of Zionism and nation-ness in their peace activism. Women peace activists propose a politics of coexistence; to do so they, as well as the leaders of both nations, constantly confront local and global historiographies of competing aspirations. Women's peace activism provides a perspective on the unfolding (past and present) political struggles of minorities (Jews in Europe, Palestinians in Israel) on the margins of nations.

Local and Global Historiographies

The women's public events in Kufir Yasif and Haifa underscore that at the heart of the Israeli-Palestinian conflict is the issue of people's right to define their nation-ness and to live in a state that they see as their Promised Land. The two conferences are part of a discourse on nation-ness; along with other political acts such as the women's visit to Ramallah, they resonate a familiar but critical question: Who has a right to define a group's nation-ness? The question is critical; it still haunts the agreement between Israelis and Palestinians. It is familiar because it was precisely this question that the founders of the Zionist movement, at the end of the nineteenth century, put forth to their own nation in Europe and to the international community: then (in Europe) as now for Palestinians in the Occupied Territories (even after the signing of the agreement in 1993, which does not include the West Bank and East Jerusalem), there was and is a question of a people's right to self-determination. Within the state the issue of Israeli Palestinians' nation-ness is still unresolved; the state still claims nation-ness solely for the Jewish majority population. The majority, defining itself as "the nation," sees other groups as minorities, mere "ethnic groups," or as just "local groups" or "religious communities"—giving the other groups within its borders any possible identity except that of nation. The founders of Zionism, particularly Theodore Herzl, were well aware that groups that are defined as minorities do nonetheless insist on imagining themselves as nations, as the Jews did in Europe, but that these groups live in states that have the power to define them otherwise. While semantics are also political—that is, it is easier for the majority population to push "minorities" around than nations—the founders of Israel realized that the difference between being a nation and being a minority was beyond linguistic nuances (Dominguez 1989); it was about the political reality of the power of the majority nation and the powerlessness of minorities.

Benedict Anderson's concept of the nation is useful for exploring the process by which people have come to see themselves as such an entity.

Anderson proposes the following definition: a nation is "an imagined community—and imagined as both inherently limited and sovereign. It is *imagined* because the members of even the smallest nation will never know most of their fellow-members, meet them, or even hear of them, yet in the minds of each lives the image of their communion" (1983, 15). The question that emerged forcefully for Jews in Europe and for Palestinians in the Middle East is: Who has the right to imagine themselves as a limited and sovereign community? Is it an inalienable right of any group of people, or does this kind of imagining require some outside international legitimacy? Is the very right to imagine a nation the privilege of international organizations? Or is the right to imagine a community a dual process, an interplay between a people's auto-imagination and global legitimation? Anderson does not take a position on the issue of who has the right to imagine the nation, but he does note a direct link between nation and the state: "Nationalism was, and is . . . *official*—i.e., something emanating from the state, and serving the interests of the state first and foremost" (145). This direct but far from simple link between state and nation characterizes both the status of Jews in Europe and the status of Palestinians inside the Jewish state and in the Occupied Territories.

Anderson argues that "nationality, or, as one might prefer to put it in view of the word's multiple significations, nation-ness, as well as nationalism, are cultural artefacts of a particular kind." He provides a temporal and spatial context as he argues that "the creation of these artefacts towards the end of the eighteenth century was the spontaneous distillation of a complex 'crossing' of discrete historical forces; but that, once created, they became 'modular,' capable of being transplanted, with varying degrees of self-consciousness, to a great variety of social terrains, to merge and be merged with a correspondingly wide variety of political and ideological constellations" (ibid., 14). Anderson proposes that "since the end of the eighteenth century nationalism has undergone a process of modulation and adaptation, according to different eras, political regimes, economies and social structures. The 'imagined community' has, as a result, spread out to every conceivable contemporary society" (143).

What kind of "modulation" did imagined communities take in nineteenth-century Europe? Often, despite lofty democratic rhetoric, states saw themselves as indivisible from the nation of the majority population in ways that had detrimental consequences for minorities such as the Jews. Then, as now, minority groups that did not belong to the dominant nation have been—and still are—between a rock and a hard place. They could either be invisible and complicitous with the majority and not challenge the state, or they could resist and become like Quebec now or the Jews then, a "problem" for the nation-state. At the heart of the peace process is still the Palestinian Question confronting the Israeli government, which denied the nation-ness of any other group as it framed the issue of nation-ness as one of accommodating "minorities" (Dominguez 1989). Israel's decision to regard Palestinians as minorities is politically ironic because the so-called Jewish Question, which the founders of Zionism clearly understood, was essentially: how to accommodate this "different, other" group, or community, such as the Jews, within European nation-states. In women's public events, as I will note, global issues (past and present) of the relationship between nationalism and minority populations receive local expression. Then in Europe and now in Israel, issues of racism emerge as part of states' forging nation-ness for the majority populations only.

Made in Europe: A Modern Nation and a Modern Racism

Europe is part of local historiography precisely because the Middle East (Zion) was seen by Jews as a solution to their problem within European nation-states. With the emergence of what Anderson identifies as the modern nation, the Jewish Question in Europe took on a new and ominous racial twist. A modern racism of nation-ness of the ruling majority directed toward "minorities" spurred a Jewish migration from Europe to the Middle East. Anderson observes that "in the last decade of the fifteenth century Dom Manuel I [of Spain] could still 'solve' his 'Jewish question' by mass, forcible *conversion*—possibly the last European ruler to find this solution both satisfactory and 'natural'" (Anderson 1983, 60). Anderson argues that until the fifteenth century people believed that assimilation by religious conversion was possible, that a minority community could be absorbed into the majority population by renouncing one set of beliefs, its "misguided" notions (in the case of Dom Manuel I, it was Jewish beliefs), and take on another's "true" beliefs, and so eventually become part of the dominant group.

Colonialism and the encounter with many new societies, however, have among other things contributed to major transformations in European cultural beliefs—beliefs that have come to inscribe an insurmountable divide between the European "self" and the other (in the colonies), who was seen as inherently and genetically different and inferior. These cultural changes had political consequences, because they had given birth to a new kind of racist relationship with minorities, not only in the colonies but in the European home countries as well. This new racism, in the form of beliefs in biological inferiority, appeared as a major element in relation to others and made their assimilation into the ruling class virtually impossible. For Europeans, in fact, the other has come to incorporate an unalterable demonized identity—unalterable because it has become a product not of culture, such as religious beliefs, but of nature, of genetics and heredity, doomed forever to an inferior "separateness" marked by racial, innate flaws. These innate failings would make any absorption by conversion or similar processes impossible, as any other was seen as by nature different from, and inferior to, the dominant group.

Hannah Arendt (1974) makes a similar observation about why the efforts of Jews in Germany to assimilate into the wider German society were inevitably and tragically doomed. The Jews' blindness to Euro-German racism, which precluded any form of assimilation, was detrimental to their very existence. Arendt notes that conversion to Christianity in Germany or marriage to Christian spouses—a route that seemed particularly attractive to some Jewish women—no longer provided insurance against racism in Germany. The arms of German spouses were never culturally long enough, and often not morally strong enough, to ward off racist attacks on their Jewish spouses. In hindsight Anderson's and Arendt's somewhat similar understandings of European racism (the events of World War II served tragically to underscore its consequences) make it clear that, in the eyes of many if not most nineteenth-century European countries, no act on the part of Jews could have altered the fact of their otherness. The wish to assimilate in Germany was, as Arendt notes, as detrimental to individuals as it was to communities; it was dangerous socially and psychologically and at times physically as well. In some important ways this racism, not only of Germany but of nation-states in Europe, produced ideas about Zion in the Middle East as a solution to the Jewish Question. It gave a modern birth to the idea of a Jewish Promised Land.

Migrating to the Local: Seeking a Jewish Homeland in the Middle East

The Middle East began to take hold of European-Jewish imagination as the experience of being the other convinced them of the racism within the growing rhetoric on liberty in Europe; the message to them as minorities was loud and clear. To some Jews the contradiction between the talk of equality that drifted in and out of nineteenth-century European rhetoric and the reality of their disenfranchised status was glaringly evident. The widening gap between the ruling nation and its "otherized" minorities became a galvanizing force in the founding of Zionism. As the early Zionists saw it, Jews lived on the borderlands of European states, a nation in desperate need of what Herzl identified as a Promised Land. The nation needed a safe haven, one that welcomed the stigmatizing stereotyped characteristics of Jews, which had become the whetstone for racist anti-Semitic ideas. To some extent Herzl, himself a product of European culture, accepted the European biological racism when he said, "the Promised Land [is] where we can have hooked noses, black or red beards, and bow legs, without being despised for it; where we can live at last as free men on our own soil, and where we can die peacefully in our own fatherland. There we can expect the award of honor for great deeds, so that the offensive cry of 'Jew!' may become an honorable appellation, like German, Englishman, Frenchman—in brief, like all civilized peoples; so that we may be able to form our state to educate our people for the tasks which at present still lie beyond our vision" ([1896] 1988, 39).[3]

The Promised Land was a place that would join nation and state, a place where the imagined nation could be sovereign like other European nations, which Herzl still insisted on calling "civilized people." In the European patriarchal context, however, Herzl paid little attention to women. Using terms that Europeans would understand, Herzl wanted the Jews to have a "fatherland," a (male) soil, where the Jews could live from cradle to grave, a place in which they would be able not only to live but to die in peace as well. In short, they would create for themselves a new history in which they would no longer be a minority living endangered and terrorized in the land of another nation. Herzl, who grew up in a family that hoped for assimilation, turned his back on what he considered its false promise and became a European-Jewish Zionist leader. He had come to realize that assimilation was a fiction of European liberalism: "In vain are we loyal patriots, our loyalty in some places running to extreme; in vain do we make the same sacrifices of life and property as our fellow-citizens; in vain do we strive to increase the fame of our native land in science and art, or her wealth by trade and commerce. In countries where we have lived for centuries we are still cried down as strangers, and often by those whose ancestors were not yet domiciled in the land where Jews had already had experience of suffering. The majority decides which are the strangers; for this, as indeed every point which arises in the relations between nations, is a question of might" (77). As Herzl saw it, even as Jews made substantial efforts to be loyal citizens and contribute to the states in which they lived, they could still at the slightest pretext be branded as dangerous strangers and subjected to death threats and pogroms.[4] This sense of constant threat to their very existence impelled Herzl to find a political solution for the stateless nation.[5]

While the Promised Land was for Herzl, at least initially, any place that would offer Jews a state of their own, he always saw the Jewish Question in national terms. He realized that the question that had to be sorted out was a national one: Could a group of people, in this case European Jews, imagine themselves a nation in order to *be* a nation, or was something external to the group required as well? Herzl recognized that self-determination was a necessary but insufficient step toward becoming a nation. He concluded that for the Jews the "national question . . . can only be solved by making it a political world-question to be discussed and settled by the civilized nations of the world in council" (ibid., 76). An internal "imagining" of the nation required an external imagining—a sanctioning by an international organization. This international legitimation that was necessary then was also dramatically displayed almost a century later in the signing of the agreement in Washington in 1993.

The Jewish quest for a homeland for the nation did not sound as wild an idea in the European or the global historical context. "By the second decade of the nineteenth century, if not earlier, a 'model' of 'the' independent national state was available for pirating" (Anderson 1983, 78). Herzl understood that the modern birth of the Jewish nation would require the official benediction of an international organization. Nations could not simply come into being; they had to be recognized by such an organization. At the end of World War I the nation, as Anderson notes, was inscribed into an international body. "In the place of the Congress of Berlin came the League of Nations from which non-Europeans were not excluded. From this time on, the legitimate international norm was the nation-state, so that in the League even the surviving imperial powers came dressed in national costume rather than imperial uniform. After the cataclysm of World War II the nation-state tide reached full flood" (78). For Herzl, then, it was necessary not only to imagine oneself as a nation but also to be affirmed as such by what he called "the civilized nations," despite evidence of their blatant uncivilized behavior. For the newly emerging nation-states, God as a source of legitimacy of the European kings had been replaced by a new international secular creator of political sanctity.

The crucial question of who has the right to imagine the nation was, and still is, a major global problem. It is as central in the Israeli-Palestinian conflict as it was for Herzl and the founders of Israel. The Madrid Peace Conference, in which Hannan Ashrawi, a Palestinian spokeswoman, played a key role, parallels the process that Herzl proposed: an international council to resolve the dilemma of minorities-turned-nations. At the same time, Israel has to confront another question of legitimating the nation-ness of its own Palestinian minority. Legitimation of nation-ness, forged in Europe's Jewish Question, confronts on the local political map the Palestinian Question.

The Birth of the Jewish State Produces New "Minorities"
Some Israeli scholars, such as Elie Rekhess, trace the birth of Israel's relationship to what the state calls minorities in the prestate, Yishuv, years. He argues that "before 1948, little thought had been given to the possibility that the future state of Israel might harbor an Arab minority. The Zionist movement hardly dealt with the matter. Zionist Congresses did no more than pass noncommittal resolutions couched in generalities on the desirable, almost idealistic, future of Jewish-Arab relations. Equality of rights was mentioned in broad terms, but there was no in-depth discussion of its ideological significance or practical implications" (Rekhess 1991, 103). Yet within this "benign neglect" kind of thinking about Jewish-Arab relations, there have been, then as now, publicly dissenting voices. People of considerable stature in the prestate community, such as Martin Buber, called for coexistence between the two nations in the Zionist Congress (September 1921), the first Congress after the Balfour Declaration, but he failed to convince the majority of his peace position. In the Congress in Carlsbad in 1921 Buber put forth a resolution regarding the relationship between Jews and Arabs that, according to Glazer, "affirmed the will of the nucleus of the Jewish people to return to its ancient homeland, to build a life that was to be 'an organic element of a new humanity.' However, this national will was in no way directed against another nationality. 'It turns with horror against the methods of a domineering nationalism.' We wish to build a common home in a 'just covenant.' We trust that a 'deep and lasting solidarity' will manifest itself between ourselves and the working Arab people. 'Mutual respect

and mutual goodwill' will bring about the renewed meeting of the two peoples" (1973, x).

The Zionist Congress, however, did not embrace Buber's position, and for him the experience of the Carlsbad Congress was a political watershed. He felt that his failure to convince the Congress to pass the resolution was a sign of his "ineffectiveness as a political leader and for many years withdrew from official Zionism." Like the women's peace activism, his own protest led him to chart a new and different political path, and "in the fall of 1925 he and a few similarly minded men founded the Brit Shalom (Covenant of Peace) group. Its aim was the creation of a peaceful symbiosis of Jews and Arabs in Palestine as peoples having equal rights in a binational commonwealth" (ibid., x). Brit Shalom's hope for a binational commonwealth did not materialize, and the government of Israel placed the local Palestinian population under military administration from 1948 until 1966 (Peretz 1991). While women's peace activism takes a different national path, because it calls for two states for two nations, its actions are closer to Buber's ideas than to the state's choice to impose military government on Palestinian populated areas.

Eighteen years (from 1948 to 1966) of military administration imposed by Israel on its "minorities" are seen by many as a humiliating and devastating period for Israeli Palestinians. "Nearly all Arab political and community leaders had left Israel for a variety of reasons. Instead of 800,000 Palestinian Arabs, just over 150,000 remained in the new state by 1949. . . . The Arab economy was almost totally demolished. Families were fragmented, with only remnants remaining in Israel, while most members were dispersed and inaccessible across the lines in enemy territory. This, then, was the setting in which the new state began to evolve policy for its Arab minority, a process that emerged and took form between May 1948 and the early 1950s" (ibid., 83). The reasons for the mass exile are at the heart of debates that emerged with the revisionist historical accounts. The major question in the debate is: Was the exile forced, was it voluntary, or was it both? Scholars such as Morris, who have become identified with revisionist history, propose that "the Palestinian refugee problem was born of war, not by design, Jewish or Arab. It was largely a by-product of Arab and Jewish fears and the protracted, bitter fighting that characterized the first Israeli-Arab war. In part, it was the creation of deliberate actions by Jewish military commanders and politicians; in smaller part, it was the result of actions by Arab military commanders and politicians" (1991, 42).

Kufir Yasif, the site of a women's peace conference in 1990, is one of the villages that did not leave, nor was it forced to leave. It became part of what the Israeli government calls the Arab sector in the state. After the 1948 war "the largest concentration of remaining Arabs was in the western, central, and upper Galilee, from Nazareth northward. A smaller number remained in the frontier area acquired through the armistice agreement with Jordan. East of the narrow coastal strip, a few thousand Arabs remained in Ramle, Acre, Haifa, Jaffa, and the Negev, and in several scores of smaller villages. This constituted Israel's new Arab citizenry, which, by the end of 1949, numbered some 160,000, or about 12.5 percent of the population" (Peretz 1991, 85).

But Israeli-Palestinian villages and towns, including Kufir Yasif, are situated on a political "marginal land" within the state. Democracy is not fully extended to them, and in every respect, socially and culturally, they are what Grossman (1992) calls "present absentees." There is a striking parallel between the space behind the divide, *mechitza,* provided to women in the synagogue and the space allocated by the state to what has been known in official government language as "the Arab sector." Women in the synagogue are present absentees in terms of their passive participation in the services. In a similar way Israeli Palestinians are citizens who are not full participants in the state. Equality has been promised to women and to Israeli Palestinians. "The state's commitment to the principle of equality was first expressed in the Declaration of Independence: 'The State of Israel . . . will uphold the full social and political equality of all its citizens, without distinction of religion, race, or sex; [it] will guarantee freedom of religion, conscience, education and culture'" (Rekhess 1991, 104). But the state's commitment, to a large extent, has not been transformed from mere talk into political facts on the ground. Women and Israeli Palestinians are not the same kinds of citizens as Israeli-Jewish men. For Palestinians, however, their secondary position as citizens is intimately linked to their nation-ness; this has serious political ramifications for their daily lives.

The State and the Arab Question

As a sovereign state, Israel has ignored or dismissed Palestinian nationalism not only regarding the population of the West Bank and the Gaza Strip but for the population within the state. Nabila Espanioly, an Israeli-Palestinian peace activist, notes that, "while the Israeli government granted citizenship to Palestinian Arabs, it did not recognize them as a national group. This was clearly reflected in its calling them 'minorities,' 'Israeli Arabs,' 'non-Jews'—anything but Palestinians. Between 1948 and 1967, the question of identity was largely neglected by the majority of Palestinian Arabs. It was only after the 1967 war, when Israeli Arabs met with their brothers and sisters in the occupied West Bank and Gaza, that they began to feel the need to emphasize their identity as Palestinians. For the first time, Arabs living in Israel felt they were members of a larger collective" (1991, 149).[6]

Ironically, though the founders of the state of Israel desperately wanted to solve the Jewish Question, when they had to face the "Arab Question" (i.e., the local Palestinians), many of them, like Ben-Gurion, were reluctant to see some of the national parallels (Teveth 1985, 7). The birth of the Jewish nation in the Promised Land was accompanied by a silencing of another nation for almost half a century. In the age of nation-states, however, both Israel and the Palestinian Question refused to go away. The signing of the agreement in 1993 indicates that both have become issues that need to be legitimated by international and superpower interventions. Herzl's passionate statement that "We are a people—one people" (1988, 76) corresponds to Hannan Ashrawi's equally passionate expression, "We are one nation." Both were made in the face of denials of, respectively, a Jewish and a Palestinian national identity, and both appeal to the international community as a source of legitimation for their national aspirations.

Herzl's firm position on the nation-ness of the Jews and the link he made between land ("old soil"), a state, and the sovereignty of the nation parallel some of the statements that were made by women of both nations in the peace conferences in Kufir Yasif and Haifa. The women's peace groups affirmed their position that land is divisible, so that "two states for two nations will live side by side in peace and security." In Anderson's terms the women accept that the nation is an imagined political community that is both sovereign and limited—limited in the sense of accepting boundaries of a nation "beyond which lie other nations" (1983, 16).

On "Minorities'" Territory: A Women's Conference in Kufir Yasif

In July 1990 about four hundred women peace activists (representing most of the women's groups) gathered in Kufir Yasif (in Hebrew, Kfar Yasif), an Israeli-Palestinian village in the northern part of the country. Kufir Yasif is a place in the state of Israel, but it is also a metaphor for and of the secondary position of Palestinian Israelis. Unlike Ramallah, but like all other Israeli Arab towns and villages, Kufir Yasif is geographically within the state but politically on the borders of Israeli society and is almost invisible, not only to the state's leaders but to most Israeli Jews. The road from Tel Aviv to Kufir Yasif in 1990 was a literal representation of this social invisibility. Israel has excellent road signs, and it is quite easy for travelers to find their way in this small country and to locate even the remotest Jewish city, village, or kibbutz. To find the way to an Israeli-Palestinian village, however, is a different matter. The road signs, or lack of them, reflect iconographically the political marginalization and social silencing of Israeli Palestinians. Driving for the first time to Kufir Yasif, I realized that to find an Israeli-Palestinian place it is necessary to first identify the closest Jewish town, village, or kibbutz and then follow its signs until one is quite close to the destination, where old road signs appear in stark contrast to the newer signs of Jewish places. I was only a few kilometers away from the village before I saw a local road sign saying Kufir Yasif. The boundaries of an Arab village were unmistakable because the state's roads end abruptly at the outskirts of Kufir Yasif, as though to say this is where public services stop. Beyond the different architecture, the minarets, and the churches that characterize Israeli-Palestinian towns and villages, the absence of state support is evident in the inferior quality of public services—roads, sanitation, water, and electricity—which is in stark contrast to the high-quality roads and excellent municipal services in the Jewish settlement in the Occupied Territories.

The choice of an Israeli-Palestinian village as a site for a public event was a rare, perhaps historical, event. In this conference Israeli-Jewish women were the guests in an Israeli-Palestinian village; for many Kufir Yasif women this was their first close contact with Israeli-Jewish women peace activists and the first time that they had Jewish women sleep under their roof. The conference took place in the village schoolyard. As in the vigil of the Women in Black, only women were invited; when men came, they were on the periphery as helpmeets, and their presence as such marked another reversal, this one of gender. In Kufir Yasif men were the ones supplying tables, food, ice, and soft drinks. Hospitality was expressed by these large quantities and in a strong concern to find every woman a home for Friday night.

For a number of Israeli-Jewish women this was their first visit to an Israeli-Palestinian village, and for most it was the first time that they stayed overnight in an Israeli-Palestinian home. Though Israeli-Palestinian towns or villages are not geographically inaccessible, this was the first time that an Israeli-Palestinian village was the site of such a conference. The community of "we women for peace" of Israeli-Palestinian and Israeli-Jewish women is forged in a divided society. Forty-two years of shared Israeli citizenship did not promote close relations between the two communities, and for many years the national divide between Israeli Jews and Israeli Palestinians was so powerful and all-encompassing that it overshadowed any other possible alliances and links between Israeli-Jewish and Israeli-Palestinian women. Issues of inequality permeated all relationships, including the women's peace camp, so that when women peace activists met it seemed almost "natural" that it happened in Israeli-Jewish space. Given this history, the fact that Israeli-Palestinian women in the Kufir Yasif conference were hosts to Israeli-Jewish women was important. At another level, however, the conference was a sharp reminder that Israel is a divided society and that Jewish women's coming to Kufir Yasif entailed a boundary crossing, an anomaly, a suspension of the conventional separation of citizens of the state.

Three communities, stateless Palestinian women and Jewish and Palestinian women citizens of Israel, came to Kufir Yasif. The conference, which started on Friday evening, was celebratory; a bonding ritual of women eating, singing, and dancing together. On a warm and sunny Saturday morning, Amal, an Israeli-Palestinian peace activist and a resident of Kufir Yasif, greeted the women of the three communities. Israeli-Jewish women sat next to Palestinian women from the Occupied Territories; women in jeans talked with women in traditional Palestinian dress, designed for modesty, which revealed little of the body beyond face and hands. Arabic, Hebrew, and English filled the morning air as women greeted one another. The Kufir Yasif community made sure that their houseguests were comfortable and that the festive notes of the previous night suffused preparations for the more serious discussions.

Yet the issue of the occupation permeated the conference. While gender provided the ground of solidarity in Kufir Yasif, the speakers' choice of language marked the differences of occupation. In Kufir Yasif, as in the signing of the agreement in Washington—in which Israelis spoke in English while the Palestinian leaders chose to speak in classical Arabic—the choice of language was made in a political context. Israeli-Palestinian and Israeli-Jewish speakers in Kufir Yasif used Hebrew, a choice that marked a shared citizenship. Palestinian women from the Occupied Territories, however, including some who could speak in Hebrew, chose to speak in Arabic or in English as a politically symbolic act, to distance themselves from the occupier's language. When Israeli-Jewish women chose to speak in English, they also did it in recognition of the power differences and used English to create a transnational linguistic space.

Constructing a female solidarity, Amal welcomed the women. She expressed admiration for all the women who came to experience and explore coexistence and directed her rebuke to the government: "I look around me today and see all these beautiful faces. I look and see the splendor of our integration here. How good it feels that we meet here in an Arab village as we have met in a kibbutzim and in large cities in the past. We all had a great time last night; we sang and we danced together. I would like to invite those in power to come and see how we, Jews and Arabs, can live together. This is a great day, a day of meeting of Jewish and Arab women united in one goal and in one future, and I hope that our activities will spread to the Jewish sector and to the Arab sector and that we will be role models for all women in Israel. We women believe that only together can we take both our nations out of this sad situation. The women's peace movement has organized local and national activities since the Lebanon War [1982] and particularly in the last few years. In spite of all the efforts by the official and nonofficial media to silence us, because they do not want our voices to be heard, our activities have become known to countries everywhere. Many came and heard our cry, and peace movements in Israel and outside of it have come to know us. They see that daily, particularly in the difficult political situation and the Intifada, we are the ones in the country's population who take action. At every crossroads they see us every week, and they hear what effect the Intifada has had on Israeli society. They know that there is a nation here that struggles for its rights and for the creation of its state side by side with the state of Israel. It is a nation hoping for freedom, hoping to have a state like other nations, to have a passport and a flag of its own. It is my greatest hope that history will recognize what we women are doing here today and every day with devotion and courage. We women believe that we can have peace only in working together by overcoming the mutual fears that haunt us. Only together, Jews and Palestinians, can we overcome this right-wing government's attitude of threats of 'transfer' [a euphemism meaning the expulsion of Palestinians]. We are women from different political organizations, but this difference does not divide us. We are united by our desire for peace, and this desire overcomes our differences.

We as mothers must help each other; we must give each other strength. I hope that we will succeed in enlisting more and more Jewish and Arab women."

Amal's account of the suffering of a people, of national aspirations, of the call for a state, have all been addressed by Theodore Herzl. The cry that acknowledges the suffering and oppression, the yearning for national identity that is denied, the need for a state with its attached symbols, a passport and a flag, are all familiar themes in Zionist history. Amal's reference to international recognition is not unlike Herzl's references to the need for external legitimation. Yet Amal's approach differs dramatically from Herzl's because gender, which is absent from his accounts, is paramount for her. Not only are women the political agents in this conference, but gender provides a sororal transnational territory. Because women have displayed unity, they can be those who can dislodge their nations from a history of competing claims. In Amal's account gender itself is turned on its head: being a mother not only means being a protector but also a political leader. In 1990 women's groups, as Amal noted, were the ones that took action, that took to the streets and struggled to draw international attention to the need to recognize another nation and for the creation of a state side by side with the state of Israel.[7]

Unveiling a Minority Identity: Palestinian Nation-ness

Israeli-Palestinian women who spoke at the Kufir Yasif conference gave brief glimpses of what it is like to live as minority citizens in Israel, where they are denied nation-ness, where they are citizens yet are forever seen an enemy of the state. Samira, an Israeli-Palestinian woman poet, highlighted the Janus-like dilemma of Israeli Palestinians, who when they act have to look simultaneously in two directions; they have to worry about reactions from two communities—their nation on the one hand and the state on the other. Samira said: "I was born in Nazareth, and I have lived there all my life. In the past I was afraid to speak of anything relating to Palestinians, despite the fact that they are our people, our nation. We are Arabs living in Israel, but before we began to live as Arabs in Israel we were Palestinians. My husband was a school principal in a school outside of Nazareth for thirty-one years. Over the years he has applied many times for a position in Nazareth and was told that as soon as he agreed to work for the Israeli security he would be transferred. All he would need to do is go to Room 17 and tell what every teacher is doing. He never got transferred. I was afraid to work as a teacher. I was afraid to speak. I am a writer who has written under an assumed name. I have written for television, radio, and the newspapers. I was also afraid that if people in Arab countries would see my real name they would say: 'Traitor.' I was afraid of so many things. Until the beginning of the Intifada I wrote love poems. But my pen has refused to write any more love poems. Now I write poetry with tears as I feel my brothers' pain, as I sense their lives on the other side, in the West Bank and in Gaza."

Samira's account unveils not only inequality but also issues of a politically suspect minority that requires surveillance; requests for job transfers depended on Israeli Palestinians' willingness to become an informant for Israeli security.[8] Dilemmas of how to live: whether to take on a minority identity as a citizen of the state and in this status write "love poetry" that is nonpolitical or to speak openly for Palestinians and write political poetry at great risk. For many years Samira, like many Israeli Palestinians, took on the identity that was given to her by the state and wrote nonpolitical poems. The Intifada for her, and for a number of women—including Israeli-Jewish women—was a political watershed, similar to Herzl's experience after the Dreyfus Affair; like him, the women also have been galvanized to take political action.

Twenty-six years after the end of military administration, Huzeima, an Israeli-Palestinian schoolteacher and a resident of Kufir Yasif, said to the women gathered in the village for the conference: "Since the establishment of the state we have gone through military rule and a widespread state effort to eradicate our national Palestinian identity. We suffer discrimination in government funds for municipalities and in other areas as well. The occupation has served to sharpen issues. All of this has created great fears in both nations, and meetings such as this peace conference are therefore crucial. Only getting together will provide rational dimensions to this reality." Huzeima's statements unveil ways in which women face and deal with the paradox of their relationship. The Israeli-Palestinian women, who are well aware of their inequality in the state, turn to the privileged Israeli-Jewish women and in so doing begin to craft a transnational female community that will provide the ground to solve the conflict. The nation itself is not cast out by Huzeima but, rather, is reaffirmed as a position from which to fashion a transnational community.

Invisible Citizens

Yet this transnational community did not allow women to ignore or deny the inequality between Israeli-Jewish and Israeli-Palestinian citizens. It was there in the first encounter with the village and in women's accounts. While often living in physical proximity, Jewish and Palestinian communities in Israel lead separate, unequal lives and "seem to be in two different worlds" (Espanioly 1991, 148). Beyond a generalized lack of interest, there is a whole array of explicit and implicit expressions that demonize Israeli Palestinians as the threatening other. Shahira, an Israeli-Palestinian singer and a native of the village, described what she experienced growing up in Kufir Yasif as she began to encounter the larger society: "Until I was in high school I was not aware of the inequality. But in high school we started meeting with Israeli-Jewish schools. We went over there, and I realized the difference between the two schools. The discrepancy was in every sense, from the building itself to the contents of the building." Shahira talked about her experience as an Israeli-Palestinian woman from Kufir Yasif who moved to a large city in Israel to pursue her education. She said: "When I came to study in Tel Aviv I rented an apartment owned by a woman peace activist who lived next door. She knew how difficult it was for Arab women and men to rent an apartment. But the people in the neighborhood were Likud voters and kept writing on her door: 'Communist Chicken.' She was not a communist, but they hated her because she had let her apartment to me. After a while they found out that I was a singer. So they said to me: 'You are a singer, you are OK. We see you on television.' All of a sudden I was acceptable. To be recognized as a woman who appears on television made me a 'somebody' in their eyes, and that 'somebody' was a good one. A Jewish woman who lived across the street had a birthday party. She had an Arab boyfriend who invited two Arab men. It was a nice friendly party, not too noisy. All of a sudden there were knocks on the door; some neighbors entered and began screaming: 'Whore, you sleep with Arabs. You are PLO, *ashafistim,* using this apartment for [political] meetings.' The police came and, rather than arrest the people who invaded the party, they took away the woman and her Arab friend. I was very scared. Next thing we know Kahane [who until his death in 1990 was a leader of the extreme right-wing Kach group] decided to demonstrate in front of the house. Why? because I lived there, and an Arab man lived there with a Jewish woman. During my first weeks in Tel Aviv I was very frightened and very nervous. When people found out that I was an Arab they always reacted, sometimes in funny ways. 'You are an Arab? You must be joking.' Taxi drivers, thinking I was a *mizrahi* woman, would say: 'So what are you, Persian? Are you from Iraq?' and I would say, 'No, I am a cousin.' 'A cousin? What do you mean?' I would say: 'A cousin. Don't you know what a cousin is? An Arab.' 'No! You don't say! You really don't look like one.' 'What should an Arab look like?' I would ask. 'So, they let you come and study here?' is all they would say. Sometimes it ended amicably; other times it turned into a tense political discussion. It was very difficult.

"One day as I was sitting in the [neighborhood] health clinic I was having a very friendly conversation with an older woman. Her landlady came in, and the woman said to her: 'What do you mean sticking us with a terrorist right in front of my house? Every morning I have to wake up and see an Arab. I have a terrorist in my house.' She did not know that I was an Arab, but all of a sudden I had terrible pains, and I thought that I was about to lose the baby. A few minutes ago we spoke in the friendliest way, and now she speaks in this way. So I said to her: 'What has he done to upset you?' and she said: 'I don't know. He brings home friends. I don't want to see Arabs in front of my house. I want my kids to grow up without seeing Arabs.' I told her: 'For the last thirty minutes you have been talking with an Arab. I am sitting across from you.' She was in shock. The room was full of women, and I was not feeling heroic at all. But I felt that I must do it. She said something incoherent and then said, 'He is a drug addict.' All of a sudden he turns into a drug addict. So I asked her: 'A drug addict? Because he is an Arab?' And the landlady said: 'What do you mean, a drug addict? He has lived here for twenty years, and he has never been an addict.' So the woman says, 'Well, he is not, but his girlfriend is,' and continued to fabricate stories. The other women, I am sorry to say, were silent. I met them every day in the street, and not one of them challenged the woman."

A Question of Racism in Israel

Batya, an Israeli-Jewish woman and a teacher, used the word *racism* in Israel when she told the women at Kufir Yasif of an incident in her school: "One of the teachers said to me that there were many racist students, *talmidim gizanim,* in our school and asked me what to do. I did not have an immediate answer. I am against moralizing and preaching, because I don't believe that it works. I went into the classroom and wrote on the board: 'Arabs are racists, Arabs are dirty, Arabs are ugly, Arabs are cheaters, Arabs are thieves,

Arabs are murderers.' The class seemed satisfied with what I had written and said, 'Yes, you are with us.' I then showed the class that these were statements from anti-Semitic literature made about Jews, all around the world. The students finally said that they had never thought about the parallels but that it is basically the same thing." Batya's deliberate parallel between the Jewish experience with racism in Europe and what she saw as Israeli-Jewish racism reveals one of the many ways that women activists used Jewish history as a history of others as a context for their political peace position.

As Batya noted, however, Israeli Palestinians have taken on some ominous demonizing qualities. This cannot be attributed just to the folly of youth or the ignorance of children. The process of otherizing Palestinians (or Arabs, the more common Israeli term) is not confined to the classroom. It takes place in daily social relations, as in the following account that I heard from Dr. Nimar, an Israeli-Palestinian physician who practices in a large hospital near Tel Aviv. Of the many experiences that he has told me about, this one is a more benign form of the "otherized," dangerous stranger seen through Israeli-Jewish eyes. One morning, as Dr. Nimar was making his rounds in the hospital, he came to the bed of a new patient, a little boy. The boy's mother, who was in the room, rushed toward Dr. Nimar, shook his hand firmly, and said with great relief in her voice, "I am so glad you came, doctor." Dr. Nimar attributed her behavior to her concern over her son's condition. He checked the boy and concluded that he had a very mild illness and told the mother that the boy could be discharged. The woman said: "I am so glad that it was you, doctor, who gave him such a thorough checkup. I was afraid earlier because they said that my son was assigned to an Arab doctor, *rofeh aravi*. But instead you came. Thank you." Dr. Nimar said to her: "I am the Arab doctor." The woman apologized, saying that she did not mean him personally, and so on. Similar accounts were given by women like Hannan, an Israeli-Palestinian nurse who works in an Israeli hospital. In one instance, she told me, a woman patient said to her: "Nurse, would you please pick up my shoes from under the bed and put them in the drawer? I have heard that many Arabs work here, and they steal everything." Hannan said: "I picked up the shoes and put them in the drawer. What else could I do? I cannot have daily confrontations on my job. I need my job. I have children to feed."

For Israeli Palestinians there is a sense that most Israeli Jews do not regard them as human beings but, instead, see them as demonized, dangerous others. In Israeli-Palestinian accounts irony often underlines the pain of being a stranger in one's own state. What emerges in these stories is the simple fact that Israeli Palestinians do not look any different from Israeli Jews, who cannot tell an "Arab" when they see one, even though they think they can. Any casual observer of Israeli society will notice immediately that, unless either side wears traditional clothes, it is impossible to distinguish them and set them visually apart from each other.

Israeli Palestinians speak about the negative ways in which they are portrayed in the state-controlled media, ranging from the "benign" paternalistic representation to the more dangerous racist expressions. Shahira described the state-controlled Arabic television programs as having "utter contempt for Arab citizens. Israeli Jews are in charge of it, and the news that is intended for the surrounding Arab countries is given as if we, who live here, do not exist. When Arabs are presented, it is mostly as idiots." Nabila Espanioly notes that "the Israeli media rarely report the weekly demonstrations of Women in Black or the daily activities carried out by female peace activists all over Israel. This is especially true when the activities occur in Arab villages, because the Israeli media have no interest in portraying Palestinians as peace seekers. The media cooperate with the government in maintaining the stereotype of the Palestinian as an enemy against whom Jews must defend themselves" (1991, 148).

Forging Transnational Territory within Israeli Jewish Nation-ness

Israeli-Jewish nation-ness was brought into the conference by some women as a ground to forge a transnational territory. Competing national claims were replaced by a vision of coexistence of two national aspirations. Judy, an Israeli-Jewish peace activist, told the women who came to Kufir Yasif of her peace position, which she said was rooted in Zionism. Her comments were framed in her personal experience as an immigrant. She said: "I came to Israel twenty-five years ago from the United States as a proud and idealistic Zionist. I came here loving Israel more than I loved and needed my family and friends, whom I left behind. I am not unusual. Many of you in the peace movement came to Israel as dedicated Zionists. My grasp of what Israel is, and what Zionism means to so many people, has undergone a transformation. I have seen the word *Zionism* being used by Right-wing fanatics and even so-called moderates to oppress others around us, others who are citizens of Israel and Palestinians of the Occupied Territories. I wish to retrieve the word *Zionism* from the racists. The racists have corrupted it—and I declare here that Zionism is a simple belief; it is no more than believing that Israel is the homeland of the Jewish people. I welcome the opportunity to share our belief with others who believe that this is their home in the spirit of equality and tolerance with the many non-Jews who live here. I assert that Zionism has nothing to do with conquest, with occupation, or with oppression. It is a legitimate goal of one people, a legitimate goal of Jews to have a country of their own in the light of anti-Semitism, which happened to be a fact of history throughout Europe. And on those grounds [I believe] in equality and nondiscrimination for all, and on those grounds I believe that the Palestinians deserve their own homeland. I am proud to declare out loud before my Arab and Palestinian sisters that I am a proud Zionist."

Zionism, as women like Judy spoke of it, is a Herzlian idea that Jews needed in order "to have a country of their own in the light of anti-Semitism, which happened to be a fact of history throughout Europe." But Judy's reformulation of Zionism as a concept that includes equality and rejects racism is not necessarily a unanimous view and certainly did not characterize the state's relationship to Israeli Palestinians or to Palestinians in the West Bank and the Gaza Strip. The issue of Israeli-Jewish nation-ness, however, is both taken for granted and problematic. It is taken for granted because it expresses the sentiments of the majority population, yet at the same time it is handled with great care because the concept of Zionism, Herzl's great hope for a liberating Promised Land, has taken on different meanings since 1948.

For many Israeli Jews, Zionism has become a concept not of liberation but of ideological verbosity. In colloquial Hebrew, in fact, it has come to mean taking moralizing positions, and people often say in response to what they perceive as taking a patronizing high moral ground: "Don't give me this Zionist lecture." Women peace activists hold different views on the meaning of Zionism. Some women told me that it is not an issue for them; others said, "I don't consider myself a Zionist; I am an Israeli"; and a few of them linked Zionism with fervent nationalism and with the whole array of right-wing groups from the Likud to the Gush Emunim settlers. Tikva, a dynamic Israeli-Jewish peace activist in a number of women's groups and a forceful woman who likes to rock many political boats, including the ones that she participates in navigating, used humor as she explained her position regarding Zionism: "First of all I consider myself a Marxist, so I don't have much use for the term. Those who say Zionism want a state here of Jews only, with a few non-Jews to do the Sabbath chores. Can you imagine how boring that would be? Who would want to live in such a state? I wouldn't. Right now it is an interesting place in the Middle East. Who wants to live in a ghetto?" But a number of women rescue Zionism from the Right and insist that the women's peace camp and Zionism can live side by side.

Judy's position is not an isolated one now, and it has been voiced in the past as well. Jewish leaders such as Martin Buber, as I noted earlier, brought the question of justice for another nation into the Zionist discourse; his ideas are probably closer to the women's peace camp than to mainstream Zionism. For Buber "'Israel is more than a nation, . . . and Zion is more than a nation.' Zion was once and still is 'the beginning of the Kingdom of God over all mankind.' Zionism is a national fact, but more than that it is 'a supranational mission.' As such, Zionism presages a new type of nationalism which will have overcome the *sacro egoismo* of the current brand. Power politics will be replaced by the power of the spirit that will initiate new kinds of relationships between nations" (quoted in Glazer 1973, xi). According to Glazer, Buber believed that "Zionism aims at 'the creation of a genuine and just community on a voluntary basis.' Such activity 'will show the world the possibility of basing social justice upon voluntary action.' While stressing the Zionist demand for the self-determination of the Jewish community, Buber emphasized that 'independence of one's own must not be gained at the expense of another's independence.' The command of justice refers to the 'future of this country as a whole.' Jewish immigration shall in no way violate 'the fundamental rights of the Arab people'" (quoted in Glazer 1973, xi). The close link between justice and Zionism did not disappear from debates regarding the Israeli-Palestinian conflict and particularly as it concerns the future of the Occupied Territories.

Buber's spirit hovers over women's peace activism; the women's political position parallels his desire that the Jews in the Promised Land will not violate the fundamental rights of the Arab people. In a footnote in his study on the nation Anderson makes a short comment on Israel and Zionism: "The significance of the emergence of Zionism and the birth of Israel is that the former marks the reimagining of an ancient religious community as a nation, down there among the other nations—while the latter charts as alchemic change from wandering devotee to local patriot" (1983, 136). This "local patriot" is undeniably present, yet women peace activists (and men activists), Jewish leaders, and scholars like Buber reveal that for Israelis their nation is a much more complicated political phenomenon than the stereotype of a community of local patriots. The women's peace camp on the Left side of Israeli society and the local patriots on the Right side are clearly at odds and do not share a single imagining of the nation-state. The Israeli-Palestinian conflict, with all its brutality, did not produce a simple unitary Israeli local patriot, either within the Jewish-Israeli or the Palestinian-Israeli community. The "alchemic change" from wandering people to sovereignty also did not, for that matter, produce an uncontested understanding of what exactly are the fundamental rights of Arabs that Buber supported.

The conference at Kufir Yasif brought forth some of the issues of competing fundamental rights. The Israeli-Palestinian women carefully lifted the veil of the violations of their rights as citizens, the violation of the rights of Palestinians in the Occupied Territories, while Israeli-Jewish women talked about the fundamental rights of Jews to a state homeland and expressed concern at what they saw as a threat to democracy from the extreme Right. For women of both nations, though, the desire to forge solidarity and to continue to make public space for a political position of coexistence came forth. The participants at the Kufir Yasif conference would meet again in Haifa, where Israeli-Jewish and Israeli-Palestinian women would face each other in anger and frustration from deeply divided positions.

A Stormy Conference in Haifa: Facing Nation-ness
in Times of Crisis

Just four months after the July 1990 Kufir Yasif weekend, women met in Haifa for another peace conference. The Haifa conference, because it took place in the midst of a cycle of violence and counter-violence that shocked and stunned the two communities, was a dramatic confrontation, revealing that in a time of crisis it takes hard work to sustain the transnational territory on which women can stand together. It also would make explicit the problematics of inequality in the relationship between women of two nations and the ways that the women confront it and at the same time establish a transnational solidarity. At Haifa women juggled divided national anxieties fueled by fears on the one hand and female solidarity on the other.

On Monday, October 8, the Israeli police shot and killed twenty-one Muslims and wounded about two hundred others at the Al Aqsa mosque, on the sacred place in Jerusalem that Muslims call Noble Sanctuary, *al-harem ash-sherif,* and Jews refer to as Temple Mount, *har habayit. Haaretz* published an editorial two days after the killing and wounding: "The events of Monday in Jerusalem, the death of twenty-one people and the wounding of about two hundred—in one spot and in a short time—in a place as sensitive as Temple Mount, mean that things have gone beyond the routine of the *Intifada* even at its peak. The public bloodbath, the blow to Jewish and Muslim holy places, the severe reaction of Israeli Arabs and in the world—all of these have sharpened the significance of the events" (October 10, 1990).

Israeli Palestinians reacted to the killings of Muslim worshipers at the Al Aqsa mosque with shocked anger. In many towns and villages in Israel there were demonstrations, road closings, and sermons in mosques. The bereaved father of one of the victims distanced himself from the violent reactions among Israeli Palestinians; his message was for a transnational humanistic path that will allow both nations to live together. He said about the demonstrations that took place after the killings: "This is not good. Only fools think that this is an Arab, or that one is a Jew. I am a human being and you are a human being. We have to live together in this country. There is no choice. Enough demonstrations, enough daily deaths and injuries. Enough blood. Enough. It should not be this way. Jews and Arabs should live together. Working together and walking together. An Arab has to kill a Jew and a Jew has to kill an Arab? This is no good. We all live in this state, there is no choice" (*Al Hamishmar,* October 14, 1990).

Many Israeli Palestinians (and for that matter some Israeli Jews) did not believe the official version of the event. A government commission was set up, and at the same time B'tselem (the Israeli Information Center for Human Rights in the Territories) conducted its own investigation and seriously questioned the official version. Israeli Jews' view on the shooting on Temple Mount were divided along Left and Right positions, and it was clear that people's interpretations of killings served to confirm their views on the Israeli-Palestinian conflict.

The Women and Peace Movement protested the killings and wanted to express public sympathy for Palestinian families of the victims of October 8. The group planned two vigils in Jerusalem, one at the New Gate and the other at the Russian Compound prison in West Jerusalem, and notified the police. "Inspector-General Yaacov Turner met with the group on Friday and requested that they cancel the vigil in East Jerusalem, saying police had intelligence information that the area was 'overly tense.' The women agreed. . . . However, 20 members of the group set up vigils near the Old City Gates. Those women—all Jewish—felt it was important for Palestinians to know that some Israelis sympathized with them, the spokeswoman said, and the police arrested them 'because they violated the agreement'" (*Jerusalem Post,*

October 21, 1990). The Islamic Movement in Um Al Fahem, an Israeli-Palestinian town, decided to build at the entrance to the town a monument that would inscribe the names of all twenty-one victims (*Al Hamishmar,* October 21, 1990).

There was more violence, this time in retaliation for the killings on Temple Mount. On Sunday, October 21, "a lone Palestinian carrying a 40 cm–long bayonet stabbed three Israelis to death within 10 minutes in the Jerusalem neighborhood of Baka" (*Jerusalem Post,* October 22, 1990). After the killing of Israeli Jews in Baka, several other killings and attempted killings by Palestinians took place in a number of places around the country, and a violence/counter-violence cycle was in full swing. This time the Jewish community went into mourning and displayed anger, including calls for vengeance, retaliation, and acts of violence by extreme groups against innocent Palestinians and Jewish vigilantes shooting at a car and killing one Palestinian. In the Occupied Territories violence was relentless; on October 21 *Hadashot* reported that, according to the United Nations Relief Agency, three hundred Palestinians had been wounded in the Gaza Strip in a Friday demonstration.

The violent events of October 1990 cast an ominous shadow on the prospects of coexistence and put a strain on the relations between Jews and Palestinians within the Peace Camp. Amal's words in Kufir Yasif, "I would like to invite those in power to come and see how we, Jews and Arabs, can live together," sounded utopian in October. Instead of living together, it looked more as if people of both nations were killing each other. Fatina, an author and Israeli-Palestinian peace activist, said after the October events: "Whenever it seems that things could not get worse, in the Middle East they invariably get worse." In October knives and gunshots ignited a political conflict that was already overheated. Regional political acts, such as Saddam Hussein's invasion of Kuwait and the Palestinians' support for Hussein, seemed to pale in comparison to the October events, because the latter were local and immediate and touched not only on fears but on collective existential anxieties as well.

How Stable Is Women's Unity?

The number of women who came to the Haifa conference reflected the deleterious effect on them of the killings: it was a much smaller group than the one that had gathered in Kufir Yasif. The atmosphere in the Haifa conference was tense and somber; the women's accounts revealed anger, fear, anxiety, and frustration. The festive experience of singing and dancing together in Kufir Yasif was almost forgotten. Ruth, the moderator, acknowledged the strain of the times: "The last several weeks in Jerusalem were tough, and I probably sound tired. The reason is that for the last three weeks I have not gone out of Jerusalem, and I must tell you that I feel as though I have come down from a very tense situation, very difficult in every respect." She also proposed to change the structure from four lectures by two women from each nation to a more open discussion for the purpose of "doing in public what we do among ourselves, to try and explore our emotions and our thoughts about the latest events and where we should go from here. We have tonight two Arab and two Jewish speakers who will address one major question: what concerns them most about the latest events and what they think needs to be done at this stage."

The tragic events kept many women away from the conference, but those who came seemed emboldened rather than subdued; because violence has hit so close to home in both nations, the accounts were more explicit, the criticism sharper, and the pain more evident. Galit, one of the conference organizers, noted the small number of participants: "Because of the events that took place last week there are much fewer people here tonight. I too have revised what I was going to say here today because of the pressure-cooker situation in which we find ourselves. We as women who define ourselves as the peace camp, in the sense that it believes in a political solution—two states for two people, side by side, in peace and security—must think of ways to reach people who are not in our camp. There are people out there who, today, for a variety of reasons, say that now more than ever we must find a political solution. The Peace Camp has failed to reach out to this segment of the population, which could potentially join us in putting pressure on our government to sit down at the negotiating table with the other side. The latest events make it clear that we must think of new options."

In addition to the themes of the conference in Kufir Yasif—the power differential between occupied and occupier and the inequality within Israeli society between its citizens of two nations, the discussion was also about trust. More specifically, the issue of mutual trust that shadowed Kufir Yasif was openly expressed in Haifa. Each side in the Israeli-Palestinian conflict is constantly asking itself if the other side is trustworthy, straightforward, and dependable. For many people in each nation the question is: "What are their real intentions?" Fatina highlighted the Israeli-Palestinian fears: "My peace activism takes place now under very strenuous circumstances, as things have become more and more difficult. I had to ask myself some hard questions on October 8, after the incident on the Temple Mount, in the Al Aqsa mosque. What can I now tell Arabs in this country? How can I convince them to come and talk peace with Jews? How can I promise them that there will be peace after what just happened in Jerusalem?"

Tamar, a Jewish woman peace activist, expressed issues of trust and survival that she thought were on the minds of many Israeli Jews: "Many people would like a solution. There are people who want a separation, *hafrada,* from the territories because—let us be honest—both sides are sick of each other. People often ask me: 'Can you trust them? You know that they will not be satisfied with the territories, and then what will happen? I want to say to all of us that, as someone who was born in Kibbutz Daganya, when I was two years old Arab tanks drove by my house. I cannot ignore it. We are facing a difficult decision. I don't know the answer. Will they be content with a state in the territories? It is clear to me that there will be a Palestinian state, but I don't know if they will leave it at that." Hannah, a kibbutz member, offered a practical political reason to support her position: "The moment that the Palestinians have a state of their own they will want and be able to begin and build so that they will no longer engage in a struggle with us."

Palestinians like Samira, who had been at Kufir Yasif, were angered by the constant doubts expressed by Israeli Jews regarding the intentions of the Palestinians: "There is no coexistence from a position of superiority, and the Left, to my great dismay, is doing precisely that and regards the Palestinians with suspicion. The Left expects the Palestinians to constantly prove themselves, prove their willingness, prove their justice. Let us stop it. I say what I mean, so stop asking me to justify myself all the time. Don't ask me or other Palestinians to do it. Not here and not in any other place."

Because the issue of mutual mistrust is so critical, it often comes up in the women's peace camp in publications of various women's groups. In response to this key question, frequently brought up by Israelis: "If we agree to a Palestinian state, can we trust the Palestinians not to continue the state of belligerency?" Shani women argue in their document that "trust—on both sides—is not a necessary condition to begin negotiations. . . . There will always be Palestinians who will go on dreaming of [recovering] Jaffa and Lod [now in the state of Israel], as there will be Israelis who will go on dreaming about a larger Israel. A peace treaty has no control over dreams, but it can advance an understanding between the parties that will mean that

the price of breaking the agreement will be extremely costly. There is nothing to lose in discussions. To enter negotiations will put the PLO to the test"
(*Shani Newsletter,* December 1990, 12). This position was expressed during
the Gulf Crisis and shortly after the Palestinians' support of Saddam Hussein. It was a radical, daring, and very explicit view not only in the face of
the government's objection to the PLO but also because, at the time, even the
larger Peace Camp was quite shaken by this support. Shani women were
aware that "the statements of support for Hussein by Palestinians have complicated the dialogue with the Israeli Left. Yet, the events that took place
since August 1990 do not alter the need for negotiations between the government of Israel and the representatives of the Palestinian nation" (10).

In October 1990 the nagging question of who could be trusted became
most acute and took on personal dimensions because many women peace
activists in both communities knew some of the victims or knew someone
who knew them. The Israeli-Palestinian conflict had taken a familiar turn
from the political to the personal as fear, anger, sorrow, and frustration permeated not only the two communities but women's peace activism as well.
Women's ways of dealing with these respective national tragedies are
diverse, so that anger and empathy, frustration and accusations, may be
expressed by the same person. Batya, who in Kufir Yasif spoke about her students' racism, spoke in Haifa not about prejudices borne of ignorance but,
rather, of chauvinist feelings, including her own, kindled by fear. She said in
the Haifa conference: "I see how with each act of violence, chauvinism
invades the Left. It invades me. Those who deny that it is happening to them
are not speaking the truth. Chauvinism visits me after every murder, after
each attack [against Israeli Jews], and I feel a rebellion inside me that says
'Let's show them,' 'Let's hit them,' despite the fact that I don't usually even
use such language."

Naama, a kibbutz member peace activist, rejects Batya's generalized
sense of revenge: "I want to respond to Batya's comment, 'Let's teach them a
lesson.' Never, never, never would I say such a thing. Why? Because it is not
their fault at all; it is our fault. We are the ones who are destroying a whole
nation under occupation. These are people who have no police, no army, no
government; they are not in charge of anything as we are. They come with
knives, and we go with guns. Why am I angry? Because we need to think
clearly about another problem. We have to think that after two states for two
nations we must live with our Palestinian citizens, and our next struggle
will be equal rights for all the citizens of Israel."

Hannan, one of the Israeli-Palestinian speakers, described her anxiety: "I thought that I would be the last speaker so that I would have time to compose myself. It is very difficult for me, as it is for all of us, to be here today. I want to tell how I felt. Before I came in I had to put some makeup on my face because I needed to change my face. I felt ugly, hard, and depressed. I did not want to come and give you a message of the depression that I feel. I wanted to have a political message that would offer hope, that would identify what we share, to offer what we do share, and to identify some goals."

Challenging the Left

If in Kufir Yasif women were critical of the Likud government, in Haifa they were less concerned with the Likud and more acerbic about the Left. Political events often affect alliances between Israelis and Palestinians, which are already delicate because of the power differential. When Palestinians embraced Saddam Hussein, the Israeli Left expressed disappointment and exposed hurt feelings. After the killings of twenty-one Muslims, Israeli Palestinians expressed similar feelings toward the Israeli-Jewish Left. Hannan said in the Haifa conference: "I think that for us in the Left—and I hesitate to use the word Left; I think of us as the peace movement—this difficult political time is very disappointing. As an Israeli-Palestinian woman who for many years has been active in the Peace Camp, I also see myself as part of the Israeli Left, and I feel extremely let down by the Left. The various peace movements have disappointed me. Now more than ever we have something to say, and we should say it, and yet, despite the gravity of the latest events, when we call for a demonstration in Jerusalem, all we get is 150 or 200 women. I am concerned that the history of the peace movements in this country, and its Left, will be remembered as a desire to be in the middle, at the center, afraid to take a strong position, afraid to express its own position for fear that the Right will move away from us. This fear is already a reality: the Right is further and further away from us and has become much stronger. And we sit and look on and say nothing. Now that they call to cut off the territories, we need to say yes to separate, but to separate on the basis of two states for two nations. Now more than ever our belief in two states for two nations can become a reality. Now is the time to tell those who do not believe in coexistence that there is no coexistence between occupier and occupied. Haim Baram, from the Labor Party, said today that there is no coexistence between occupier and occupied; he is right." Hannan expressed what Israeli-Jewish women have often said about the passivity of the Peace Camp and the absence of public acts to offset the government's policies in the Israeli-Palestinian conflict.

Batya takes up the issue of coexistence, but she does not respond to Hannan's charge that it cannot occur between occupier and occupied. She acknowledges a shift in her position: "I have been a peace activist for years. My activism is based on the worldview that people are characterized by nationalism and religion. The time has come to separate. I used to believe in coexistence. Today it is less important to me. I am less concerned with whether Jews love Arabs or Arabs love Jews. The political act of separation is vital for me. I personally will be very glad if there will be love and understanding between us if that is possible, but it is not the crux of the matter."

Questions about Israel's Commitment to Equality within the State

The occupation was only one of the problematic issues between Israeli Jews and Palestinians in the Haifa conference. Inequality in Israel and the marginalization of Israeli Palestinians was another thorny problem, as it was in the Kufir Yasif conference. While Huzeima delineates both the occupation and discrimination within the state, she is particularly concerned with the discrimination: "I want to know how I, as an Israeli-Palestinian woman, can change people's views, how I can make a political difference. It is hard for me as a school counselor to tell teachers and students in a mixed city that it is possible to talk peace. There is yet another issue. I identify with what happens in the West Bank and in Gaza, and I know that there will be a Palestinian state one day. But I am an Israeli citizen, and as such I am concerned about equality. When there will be peace, and when there will be a Palestinian state, my problems will not be resolved. If there will be peace it will not guarantee that I will enjoy equality in the state. It is a separate issue, and I need to fight hard for equality. I have to fight for equality daily and in every aspect of my life. Twenty-four hours a day I live with the knowledge that I have no equality in anything, in any of my activities. . . . It is hard to convince [Israeli-Palestinian] people to go for peace when the price to pay is so high. There is so much suffering. We need to be fair to both sides, and it is very hard to be fair. I believe that a Palestinian state should come into being, but I also think that we need to struggle for our rights within the state of Israel. I need to fight as a human being who believes in equality, as a woman, as an Arab, but also for the mental health of all of us who live in Israel, Arabs and Jews."

Nation and state become issues in the discussion as women face one another. As Samira said: "I have a serious problem because, when the Palestinian state comes into being, every time that I say that I want equality as a citizen in the state, I will be told to go live in Nablus. I don't want to go live in Nablus [a town in the West Bank]. I was born in Acre. This is my state; Acre is my city. I think that we need to find a solution to my problem before we solve the issue of a Palestinian state. If you will know how to deal with me as an Israeli Palestinian, as an equal citizen, you will also know how to sit at the negotiating table with Palestinians as equals."

At the Haifa conference women like Huzeima and Samira reveal the differences between Israeli-Palestinian and Israeli-Jewish peace activists as the Palestinian women talk about their secondary position to women who belong to the majority nation; in doing so, they expose the cracks that constantly threaten sororal unity, this time the cracks of citizenship and nationness. In these accounts shared citizenship seems not only unequal but, for Israeli Palestinians, extremely tenuous. While Israeli-Jewish women express anxieties about what will happen after the establishment of a Palestinian state in terms of the state's security, Israeli-Palestinian women express different anxieties that stem from their ambiguous position as citizens of the state of Israel. These anxieties underlie the questions that they raise: What will happen to them when there is a Palestinian state? Their fear is that the question of their loyalty, which lurks in the state's discourse, and their right to live as citizens in it will be raised again in full force with what they believe will be dire consequences. The women's accounts reveal fears that the nation-state, after all, is indivisible in Israel and that they will be "transferred" or urged to accept a political position that implies that their proper place is in a Palestinian state.

Threats of "Transfer"

In the Haifa conference Fatina said: "I heard in the last few days, on radio programs, talks about transferring Israeli Arabs. Someone suggested bringing buses to the Dan Hotel and assembling all the Arab villagers, giving them flowers and drinks and putting them on the buses. 'Let them open the windows, let the Arabs make the V sign to their hearts' content and send them over

the bridge [to Jordan].' And people listened, and radio programs allowed people to speak in a classically racist way, and I felt, God Almighty, *ribono shel
olam,* how much can a democracy sustain? If we say that there is a limit to
what people can say even in a democracy, why is it that there is no limit for
Jews?" The Hebrew phrase *ribono shel olam,* which is taken from the Hebrew
prayer book, has become one of the phrases used to indicate states of indignation, disbelief, and irritation, similar to the English expression "for God's sake."
While Israeli Jews know little about Israeli-Palestinian culture, the latter are
well versed in Jewish culture. The use of Hebrew phrases from sacred Jewish
texts, used by women like Fatina, indicate that, along with social marginal-
izations, Israeli Palestinians are steeped in the discourse of the main culture.

The radio call that Fatina described reflects a "transfer" concept that is
seen by fringe Right groups as the solution to what they consider a minority
population in the Jewish nation-state. The ultra-right-wing parties have
inserted into the Israeli-Palestinian conflict the concept of transfer, proposing that the state should in effect get rid of its own "Arab" citizens. Whenever
Jews are killed by Palestinians, the clamor for transfer is heard from this
group. The left-wing daily newspaper *Al Hamishmar* warned in 1990 that "in
the current government there are political parties who call for an extremist
solution regarding both Arabs from the territories and Israeli Arabs . . . several of the Likud members of Knesset are themselves not averse to the idea of
transfer" (October 15, 1990). While these right-wing groups are small, they
make sure that they have public visibility, not only on radio call shows but
also along main roads in the country. On the road from Haifa to Kufir Yasif I
noticed a run of offensive graffiti directed at Israeli Palestinians. Graffiti, usually in red letters, saying the single word *transfer* have been painted on
everything from rocks to billboards by the extreme Right groups and express
their political agenda to evacuate or deport Israeli Arabs. This agenda, which
links nation and state, argues that Israel is only for Jews. These groups
express similar sentiments to those that Herzl identified in Europe: the right
that some people assume both to legitimate their own nation and to delegitimate the nation-ness of others. Those who advocate transfer propose that
Israeli Palestinians do not constitute a nation and that they are Arabs and
part of a larger Arab "nation" that has many states. Those who reside in Israel
should, according to this view, go to any one of those states.

In 1990 the graffiti of transfer was aimed to make "Greater Israel" a political fact of a Jewish state cleansed of any minorities; it was intended to

intimidate both Israeli Palestinians and the Israeli Left. Some Israeli Jews dismissed the graffiti as an expression of an extreme and small minority, but others saw it as an alarming sign of growing intolerance and an indication that democracy had lost some ground in Israel. Israeli Jews who do not even identify themselves as peace activists often found the graffiti quite offensive. Ruth, an Israeli-Jewish member of the Women in Black, told me about a friend of hers who does not describe herself as a peace activist: "The only thing she does is she goes out every few days to some of the places where the extreme groups spray 'transfer' and, using gasoline, wipes it off."

The struggle between the extreme Right and Israelis who disagree with them is mirrored in this one-woman act against racist and exclusionary graffiti. But enfolded in this struggle is also the fact that these groups struck fear and intimidation in 1990 in the Peace Camp when the Likud government was in power and ultra-Right political parties, such as Tchiya, were in the Knesset. Ultra-Right groups and individuals were emboldened by the Likud government, which did little to delegitimate the transfer language of its coalition partners. Tamar, an Israeli woman whose son was killed in 1973 in the Yom Kippur War, said at the Kufir Yasif conference: "I am afraid of Zeevi [the leader of an extreme right-wing party], who says 'transfer,' and I am also afraid of the taxi driver who is ready to kill me if I mention the word *Palestinian*." Israeli Palestinians, the target of the transfer, are daily aware of the threats and view the ideas of transfer with alarm and anguish. As Dr. Nimar phrased it: "The Likud government wants a 'transfer.' But it is impossible to transfer to Kuwait all the Arabs within and beyond the green line. This government treats Israeli Arabs worse than any previous government and has brought about more strain to the relationship. The media distort the image of Arabs, turning them into a stereotype in ways that erase differences between a masked rioter and an ordinary citizen. They are all the same." Huzeima told women at the Kufir Yasif conference of the growing public legitimation for the transfer position. She said: "You will recall Zeevi's declaration in the Knesset? He said that he knows the Arab mentality, and therefore it is imperative to beat down on the Arabs so that they cannot lift their heads up. Or Zeevi's fantasies about transfer, to simply throw all the Arabs out of Israel. You will recall the public panic over the so-called Palestinian demographic threat when we were daily exposed to a discourse about the high Arab fertility rates. The panic was engendered as Arab fertility was described as a deliberate national plot against the existence of the state. And what is happening now with the immigration of Soviet Jews? Has the demographic plot come to an end? Is it possible that the government is going now to let Arabs have sex in peace?"

Like those of other Israeli Palestinians, Huzeima's comments, laced with bitter humor, are framed in the fact that since 1948 the state has treated the Palestinians as unequal citizens and as potential threats, greater if the demographic balance shifts in their favor. This so-called demographic fear, which state officials have been public about, underscores and reminds both communities that Israeli Palestinians are seen as very different kinds of citizens. According to Peretz, "One of the most divisive questions that confronted the government of the new State of Israel was whether to work toward integrating the country's Arabs or maintain a policy of separation. This question has divided those concerned about relations with the Arab minority since the state was established more than forty years ago. The majority, then as now, maintained that Israel cannot be both Jewish and democratic. They argued that if the country's Arabs were integrated into society, it would lead to a binational rather than a Jewish state. . . . The separation made it possible to maintain a democratic regime within the Jewish population alone" (1991, 100).

The Sons of the (Peace) Mothers Are the Soldiers in the Occupied Territories

The issue of differential citizenship became evident in the Haifa conference from yet another perspective. Batya brought up the question of how Israeli-Jewish women for peace can become complicitous in the occupation. Batya's account serves to underline this unequal citizenship when she brings up the issue of soldiers serving in the Occupied Territories. She talks about her fears, but, in contrast to the way in which mothers as a category were used by Amal at Kufir Yasif to cement women's solidarity, Batya's concerns for a soldier son further expose differences between Israeli-Jewish and Israeli-Palestinian women and indicate more ruptures in women's transnational solidarity. As mothers from two nations face each other from two sides of the occupation, motherhood is no longer a stable gender category: it turns from a unifying force into a wedge that separates women. Batya said: "I am afraid of the terror, and I am afraid because I have a son who is a soldier in Gaza, and we all know what it means." Doing military service in the occupation has emerged as one of the thorniest political issues for women peace activists, and the divide that it creates makes it even clearer why it has been much more difficult for Israeli men peace activists to work with Palestinians. The category soldier (male), rightly or wrongly, has become synonymous with the (gendered) brutality of the occupation. While women mostly do not serve in the Occupied Territories, many of them have men in their lives—brothers, sons, lovers, and husbands—who are soldiers. Israeli-Jewish women who do not take a clear position against serving are now seen by Israeli-Palestinian peace activists as complicitous in the occupation against which they protest.

The issue of refusing to serve and a call to join the group of soldiers who refuse to serve in the Occupied Territories, Yesh Gvul (There Is a Limit), came up in the Kufir Yasif conference. At the end of that conference Tikva announced that one of the workshops had arrived at a statement calling for a refusal to serve in the territories. She told the women: "I would like to pass around the document that we have written in our workshop, which states: 'We women, who believe in exchanging territories for peace, call on soldiers to refuse to serve in the Occupied Territories as the appropriate response to the right-wing government's refusal position. I want to encourage you all to sign the statement, but I must remind those of you who sign it that it is an illegal act. I don't want us to have any misunderstanding or that you will claim later on that you did not know. All those who did not sign yet, please sign now. This is not a statement for the press, but I have to tell you that it may get publicized and fall into the hands of all kinds of people. This is not an internal document. I want to also say that this is the first time that a conference, *kenes,* in Israel clearly calls to refuse to serve."

The call at Kufir Yasif for women peace activists to support the political position of groups such as There Is a Limit in refusing military service in the Occupied Territories took on a different perspective in Haifa in October, when so much more seemed to be at stake. The differences between women of two nations on this issue are more evident, as Hannan comes back to Batya's remark about her son, who serves in the Occupied Territories, and takes exception to Batya's endorsement of serving there: "I have to say that many people in the Peace Camp say that they want two states for two nations, but, like Batya, they send their sons to serve or they themselves serve in the territories. Why? To do so is to protect the Greater Israel position. If one holds the position of two states for two nations, it carries with it an obligation of a corresponding act—to refuse to protect the Greater Israel, to refuse to do military duty in the territories. If you do that, then I too will serve the kind of Israel that we want to build together. It will mean to choose equality as our foundation and not to choose the continuation of the occupation."

Fundamentalism Presses on Women's Peace: The Islamic Hamas and the Jewish Gush Emunim Settlers

In the Haifa conference women of two nations also emphasized intranation differences and named the extremes in each community—the Palestinian Hamas, who are seen by Palestinian scholars such as Ziad Abu-Amr (1993) as local Islamic fundamentalists, and the Jewish settlers Gush Emunim, who are identified by Israeli scholars such as Menachem Friedman (1993) as Jewish fundamentalists in Israel. Both groups vehemently oppose coexistence and peaceful negotiations and the idea of two states side by side. Women of both nations have to confront fundamentalism, and it is not surprising that Batya reacts to Hannan's criticism by reminding Palestinian women that Jewish women have to deal with Jewish fundamentalists, such as Gush Emunim: "I have to respond to Hannan's remarks on serving in the Occupied Territories. I am unequivocally against refusing to serve in the territories. I say this openly despite the problems that my saying it will engender. I am not saying that the day may not come when I too will not support it. Today I am totally opposed to refusal because I want a democratic state in which the government must decide. I don't want to play into the hands of Gush Emunim [who settled in the West Bank and the Gaza Strip]. If I do not support refusal on serving in the territories, I can also argue that they cannot refuse to vacate the territories or that they can object to establishing a Palestinian state. I am against the idea that every political group will act out its ideologies. I am sure that there are differences among us here. . . . But I do think that the common ground on which we stand is important, and it is: two states for two nations. On this I do not compromise. It is not easy, but we need to stand together on that common ground."

Fatina links issues of trust and equality to the resurgence of fundamentalism: "How will I convince the Palestinian public within Israel to join the Peace Camp when do they do not trust the Jews? The Palestinian public sees you, a mother, sending your children to the army; it knows that within your terror you speak of peace, but in your broader perspective you do not act in the spirit of equality. You do not treat Arabs as equals. In the educational system there is no equality. On the roads there is no equality. There is no place where equality exists. Yet you want the Arabs to start a Peace Camp of their own parallel to your Peace Camp. But they are not occupiers: they don't make you unequal; *you* create inequality. It is your problem that you have created, and you need to resolve it. The Palestinian public, as a result of its experience with the state of Israel, does not trust it. Who is responsible for the spread of the radical Islamic movement? The behavior of the Israeli government."

Issues of inequality created and fostered by the state are linked to the government's responsibility for Islamic fundamentalism by what is seen as tacit approval of it in the past when the PLO was seen as the enemy and religious Muslim institutions appeared (quite wrongly) to the Likud as politically irrelevant. In the last few years, as the signing of the 1993 agreement indicates, the construction of the "enemy" has shifted from the PLO to fundamentalist groups such as Hamas, whose leaders were expelled to Lebanon in December of 1992. Hannan voices her concerns regarding the spread and growing popularity of Islamic fundamentalism within the Israeli-Palestinian population: "Yes, I do have my own fears, unique to my community. There is, for example, the fact that some Muslims want to oppress me as a woman, as a nonbeliever, as a communist, and many other sides of my life. They do threaten my basic democratic principles, my belief in pluralism. There are as many shades and colors within the Palestinian society as there are in the Israeli-Jewish one."

A moment of unity is established at Haifa, as Daliah reminds the Israeli-Jewish women: "It is not just the Muslim Brotherhood and the Islamic fundamentalism; it is also ours, the Kahanes on our side. There are extremes on both sides." But this moment of agreement is short-lived, as several people in the Haifa audience ask the Israeli-Palestinian women what they are going to do about the fundamentalists in their community. Suheir responds to them: "You are asking here: 'Why is there Islamic Jihad? Why is there Hamas?' I don't ask you why there is Kach, why there is Moledet. It is not my task to explain why there is Hamas, if it is influential, and so on. I don't have to go talk to the Islamic Jihad, as I don't have to talk to the Communist Party or ask the people of my village why there are so many different views in the Palestinian community. In every society there are many different views. My job is not to bring about social cohesion. My job today is my struggle as a Palestinian woman. I am afraid as I walk on the street. If I look Arab I will be attacked by Jews, and if I look Jewish I will be attacked by Arabs. You are not the only ones who suffer; I, too, am going through hard times. . . . Why are we blaming the Jews? Because we are at the bottom; we are the oppressed; we are the ones whose heads are being stepped on all the time, not you. I have never hit Jews; I have never denied them a job on the basis of who they are; I have never refused to let them an apartment because they are Jews. I wanted to rent an apartment in Haifa, and I was told point blank: 'We don't rent apartments to Arabs.' You do not feel what we feel."

On the One Hand: Competing Anxieties Rock Solidarity

Occupying the position of a minority is a difficult topic to negotiate between women from two nations, each claiming for itself the experience of marginality, one in the past and one in the present. The occupier, who still has in its national discourse the horrors of a minority group and the fear for its survival, faces accusations of oppression and the other's fears and anxieties. It is not easy to negotiate this paradox, as Ann acknowledges; she expresses the hardships of minorities but at the same time voices fears about the survival of the state: "I know what Suheir is talking about. I have experienced it as a Jew when I lived abroad. But I also don't know where the borders are going to be if we do have two states. And you, Samira, do you want to stay in Haifa as a Palestinian, or do you want Haifa to be part of Palestine? This for me is the problem. We as Jews think that we want two states, but we are afraid that if we divide the country in the middle that this will be the end, and we will disappear. Today we hear Arabs who say: 'Let's throw them into the sea.' We think that we want two states, but we are afraid that, if there will be a Palestine, a large number of Palestinians will say that they do not want two states; they want one state. The new state would be able to open the door to Jordan and the Saudis, and, who knows, maybe all the Arab countries are waiting for the Palestinian state to do it."

Ann expresses the view of a number of Israeli Jews who are afraid that a Palestinian state will provide a launching place for an all-Arab war against the state of Israel. Fatina rejects this view of the future state: "I think that this is nothing but propaganda that the Arab countries want to destroy the state of Israel or throw its citizens into the sea, and they are only waiting for a Palestinian state to do so. The situation for Palestinians throughout the Arab world is pretty bad. They are being kicked out of every country; they are refugees going from one Arab state to another. If the Arabs want to destroy Israel, why would they wait to do it from a new and weak Palestinian state?

All the Arab states, more than 120 million people, are waiting for this tiny state of 2.5 million to throw Israel into the sea?"

On the Other Hand: A Palestinian Voice for Coexistence

Women peace activists struggle with the complex reality that in both communities there is a wide range of political views, from extreme fundamentalists who would fight to the last Jew and to the last Arab, at one end of the spectrum, to people who want to live side by side in peaceful coexistence, at the other end. While the Haifa conference reveals that a time of crisis brings to the surface fears kindled by extreme groups, like Jewish and Muslim fundamentalists, the conference in Kufir Yasif made space for Palestinian voices for coexistence that were drastically different from the image of an eternal enemy just waiting to kill all the Jews, which was heard in Haifa in October. A Palestinian voice for coexistence was presented in the Kufir Yasif conference by Tirzah, an Israeli-Jewish woman and a member of a vigil of the Women in Black. Tirzah asked to read in public a letter written by a Palestinian man who lives in the Occupied Territories to one of the vigils of Women in Black (at the Nahshon intersection); his peace position matched theirs, and the Kufir Yasif conference in July 1990 provided a context for a "peace-for-peace" exchange.

Tirzah told the women at the Kufir Yasif conference: "I stand in the vigil of Women in Black at the Nahshon intersection. One Friday afternoon, as we were standing in our usual place, we saw a truck from Hebron [a city in the West Bank] stop at some distance from the vigil. Two young boys, holding a case full of cucumbers, approached us. They put the case down and left. Under one of the cucumbers we found a note in Arabic that had a boy's name and a Hebron telephone number on it. A man from our kibbutz who comes to our vigil speaks Arabic, and that same evening he called and thanked the people. We thought that this was the end of it. The following week the truck came again, but this time it stopped closer to the vigil, and once again we were given a case full of cucumbers. We now have many pickles at home. This time there was a letter as well, and I have brought the letter to share it with you. The letter will be read in Arabic first, and then I will read a Hebrew translation of it."

Here is my translation into English of the letter that Tirzah read: "To the people that I love but do not know, in the name of God, Allah, the beneficent and the merciful. Dear brothers and sisters, I offer you my blessings and my deepest respect. Despite all the humiliation, the oppression, and the deprivation that I experience as a Palestinian, despite everything that our people face here and abroad for many years, and despite the tragic events that I witness daily as I travel from Hebron to Gaza and Ramallah, seeing your vigil for the first time at the intersection I felt in my heart that there are brothers and sisters among the people of Israel who fight for human principles that are acceptable to all of us in the modern era. There is no doubt that one day, together, we will win with the help of God, blessed be He.

"I don't know which of the suffering that I daily witness to tell you about. Let me say it briefly that our lives have become a flaming hell, and no one can put the fire out. I am convinced that your vigil makes a big contribution to keep us from despairing and from feeling that all is lost. I cannot even describe our situation as far as our safety is concerned. I therefore will simply tell you our material condition. Compared to many people of my homeland, I am relatively well-off. I have a truck and a store, and I work day and night, traveling about five hundred kilometers a day. That is, when I do get to work. I am an Arab driver who always suffers under the hand of the police, and the less said the better. The government demands a thousand dinar every month, and I have to take care of a family of ten children and pay my employees. The situation does not allow me to work more than twelve days a month. Add to it all the oppressive measures that are inflicted on us, such as confiscation of our merchandise under all kinds of pretexts. Or arbitrary rules such as the government's decision, two days ago, that we cannot bring in tomatoes and potatoes from Gaza. I don't know how to tell you what this rule means for farmers in the Gaza Strip.

"Dear brothers and sisters, I want to say to you that I strongly believe that we can face this hardship for many years, with patience and hope. But, if this is our fate, if the fate of the Palestinian nation is to live on this land, it is our duty, Arabs and Jews, to dedicate all our efforts to peaceful coexistence that will unite us in love, in cooperation, and in providing a future for our children. I have given you a gift to express my appreciation and respect on the one hand. On the other hand I send it with my little son so that this ten-year-old will know that not all Israelis are the border police, the army, the income tax, and all kinds of other hardships. The Israelis have suffered in the past as we are suffering today. They have experienced losses as we do now. They too have the right to live in peace and security and to enjoy freedom and respect rather than face fear and terror. A Chinese proverb says:

'Every journey of a thousand miles begins with one step.' I deeply appreci-
ate your courageous step that with God's help will lead us to the shores of
love and peace."

Tirzah's act in reading the letter at the conference in Kufir Yasif made
public space for one voice of a Palestinian under occupation and a glimpse
of the experiences of emotional suffering, economic discrimination, and
personal humiliation. It included parenthood as well—in this case a father
who wants his son not to stereotype Jews and who is deeply concerned
about the future of children. The letter draws attention to the political effectiveness of the vigil, to the fact that not only Israelis but Palestinians as well
are aware of women's peace activism. In Kufir Yasif the letter served as a
reminder not to stereotype Muslims as Hamas or fundamentalists, as it gave
a voice (in this case male) to those within the Palestinian community who
are willing to live in peace; these may include Muslims who are not necessarily seeking to destroy the state of Israel but who are willing to accept a
solution of two states living side by side in peace and security. For Israeli-
Jewish women peace activists the letter, like the conferences and the visit to
Ramallah, is an encounter with the problematic issue of occupation. The
reading of the letter was an act of creating a transnational space, however
fragile and transitory, with the writer and symbolically with Palestinians
like him and an indication of women's determination to confront the brutality of the occupation. The reading of the letter in public is to display the
paradox of women's peace activism: that the other side of solidarity is occupation; that, despite the Israeli women's objection to the occupation, they
are members of the community of occupiers and that they speak from within
that community, though in a dissenting voice.

The Relentless Construction of Sororal Transnational Solidarity

The reading of the letter implies what the confrontations in the Haifa conference make explicit, and both conferences reveal the problematics that
press on solidarity. The violent October events brought forth specific
national concerns and exposed the differential power relations between the
women of the two nations. But within, around, and beyond the problematic
differences women daringly construct unity. The three public events that I
have discussed in this chapter—the women's visit to Ramallah, the conference in Kufir Yasif, and the October conference in Haifa—are all public
events in which an ideology of coexistence was constantly reaffirmed.

The Haifa conference shows that, far from being an easy outcome of simply being female, solidarity is borne not out of a natural, gendered affinity but, rather, out of women's relentless efforts to create and sustain it. In the midst of the difficult and painful issues of inequalities within Israel and the unavoidable fact of occupation, the sororal transnational solidarity is founded in women's resolute determination to stand on a specific political ground, albeit a limited one, that is both national and transnational. In the women's solidarity visit to Ramallah, as well as in the two conferences, the political territory on which women stood united was the idea of two states for two nations living side by side in peace and security. The women's sororal territory is transnational in the sense that each group reaches across its own nation to establish an alliance with women from the other nation.

While scholars such as Anderson claim that the concept of the nation is a cultural invention, it has become for many people, including women peace activists, a natural emotion. Alberstein's epigraphic poem quoted at the beginning of this chapter proposes that love for a homeland is a natural feeling. In her poem Alberstein evokes the concept of family, so that love for the homeland, *moledet,* is equated with the kind of self-evident and selfless love that is attributed to families in Western culture. For Alberstein, though, as for women peace activists, feelings for one's homeland nation, while "natural," should not stop at the border. Alberstein's claim that "we are all responsible for the other" parallels many statements made by women in Kufir Yasif and Haifa. Within and beyond the anger, the pain, and the frustration is a sense of camaraderie that social justice does not stop at national borders. Female solidarity was carefully crafted by women like Hannan, even as they unmasked the inequalities and revealed the pain of oppression. At the Haifa conference Hannan reminded women of their gendered space: "We—women in particular—can say that there is coexistence, that there is coexistence in our struggle for equality, for peace, a struggle that we can testify promises an alternative. Our struggle should be a joint struggle on the basis of equality, of true solidarity, of mutual respect and trust, rather than suspicion and fears. We can act on coexistence here today, but we have to reject the relationship of occupier. Let us together show an alternative way. Let us women show what we really want."

In public events women of each nation construct the alliance simultaneously from within and across their respective nation. The alliance is meant not to challenge the concept of the nation but, instead, to recognize and affirm it. Because the women's alliance draws on the construction of the concept of a homeland as a natural entity and because they see it as the other nation's inalienable political right to nation-ness, the call for two states for two nations was prominent throughout the discussions. The fact that, despite the tragic events, the October conference was not canceled affirmed a commitment to women's solidarity. Ruth, the moderator, said: "I think that the tension in this room was very healthy, one of the healthiest things that I have experienced lately. It was honest and confused; it was candid and groping; it was not dogmatic, and this is beautiful. How to capture it and translate it into political concepts is a question for us."

The emotional responses of the women who spoke in Haifa unveiled not only differences but also the resilience of women's solidarity and the skillfulness with which it was reaffirmed time and again. Daliah, for example, was pragmatic in constructing a sororal territory. In acknowledging women's absence from organized politics in 1990, she offered political action that women could take: "Since we are women and we don't have political power and we cannot decide where the borders will be drawn, let us do what we can and what needs to be said and let us say loud and clear: 'We do not want the killings of men, women, or children. We are sick and tired of wars.' Let each woman get up in the morning and ask herself: 'What am I going to do for peace today?' What difference does it make where the border between the two states will be drawn? I say this because, when the borders are drawn, we will not be consulted. On that day when they start drawing maps and fixing borders we will go out on the street, and we will say that we want this or that. Until 1977 there was fear of Egypt, the most dangerous of Israel's enemies at the time. The Palestinians were not even considered as an enemy. We were told that there are no Palestinians. We did not even know then that a few feet away there were Arabs. In 1977 we were terrified of Egypt, and it turns out that it is possible to live with Egypt and not be afraid. So let us do something. So if it is Women in Black—and not all of them are ashkenazi women, but it does not matter whether we are ashkenazi or not—or if it is in Reshet or in any other women's group, every one of us will find her own place. The most important thing is to live and do something for peace. Let us say: 'Let us stop killing each other.' If you are a woman who cannot leave the house, write a letter to the newspaper. Every day that you don't send a letter another letter gets published. Write, all of you. Did all of you write something to the newspapers lately? Don't be silent. Do one thing for peace every day. When you do that you can ask yourselves what you have done for peace and not where the borders will be drawn." Women like Daliah realized in 1990 that, despite their ceaseless efforts to insert the peace position in the public sphere, to transform ideas into political facts, political leaders and not peace activists will draw the maps of peace as well. Many activists, though not all, were content to be the rank and file who would bring about peaceful coexistence and the end to occupation.

From the Israeli-Palestinian side came a forceful call to sustain transnational unity despite differences. Hannan declares: "Our struggle must be a joint one. We have much in common. I have in this room many Jewish friends, and we have been engaged in the same struggles. They feel my pain, and I feel their pain. We may feel upset and confused, but we must find that which unites us. As I came in I met Hannah, and we hugged, and we gave each other strength. We felt that we were in it together. Not that she is Jewish and I am Palestinian, but in our hug there was a moment of truth and an ability to go on." Dafna constructs a solidarity that must include justice for women of both nations as she argues that there is no viable "separate" justice for the majority only: "If there is no equality in the state of Israel to all its citizens, I too feel threatened. We are all threatened. If Israeli Palestinians have no equal rights in Israel, I as an Israeli Jew am equally endangered. I have no guarantee that tomorrow they will not do the same thing to me."

Some women, like Gabrielle, said that the Haifa conference empowered them in the midst of the divisive events. She recreated a transnational alliance: "I belong to the emotional section of the population. I felt very much the same way that Hannan did. I wanted to stay home, turn the TV off, and let me be detached. But I said to myself that maybe I should make the effort and travel to Haifa tonight. Perhaps the effort will be worthwhile. Maybe something will happen. Something *did* happen. Despite the mutual accusations that we heard here tonight, despite the guilt feelings, the fact that we are sitting together is meaningful. Politically, I do not believe that the conflict will be solved without outside intervention. I do hope that it will happen and soon. But for us it is imperative to go on together, to meet, to work, with the accusations and beyond them, and to continue to sit together. This in my view is most important."

While the conference in Kufir Yasif took place before the October events, it was already marked by a paradox of transnational female unity on the one hand and the differences between women of two nations on the other. Not only Israeli-Palestinian inequality was revealed, but women from the Occupied Territories talked about the inequality between occupiers and occupied. For Palestinian women from the Occupied Territories the alliance is both about what connects them with Israeli women for peace and what separates them. The photograph in *Hadashot* that is described at the beginning of this chapter unveils the connection as it masks the separation. Both elements are uncovered in the following remarks, which Suheir offered in Kufir Yasif: "Many of us came to this group as good friends because we were able to see so much and work together. Yet, I also say that in this group we are not equals. Some of us belong to the group that oppresses, and some of us are still among the oppressed. So at no point have we achieved parity. While we would have liked to, we could not overcome these psychological barriers, and they could not disappear. I say that, as long as I have a sense that as a Palestinian I go back from these meetings to the reality of my life, there is no security, and the anxiety is high on a daily basis. What I witness and go through leaves little hope that we can actually minimize the psychological dangers. I think that peace will really come when we work together politically to end the occupation and to bring equality and parity to both our people."

Israeli-Jewish women peace activists are well aware of the differential relations. This is revealed in the following observations offered by Sarit, one of the founders of the Women in Black: "At the beginning of the Intifada those of us who had been active in various groups against the war in Lebanon or in Beir Zeit solidarity or whatever were in fact shocked at the scale of what was happening but not at *what* was happening. All this had been happening before, and no one was paying any attention, and then suddenly it was on a massive scale—the abuses of human rights and so on. But there had been deportees, house demolitions, arrests, killings, for twenty-two years before that. The escalation brought it to public attention. People were in a state of emotional shock and horror, sadness and dismay. I think that women found themselves able to react, and of course women are allowed to have emotional reactions; nobody says to you this is inappropriate. So, if the initial reaction is of wanting to cry or feeling emotionally in a state of upheaval, it is easier to give expression to that if you are a woman. And, in fact, we had women who were either friends or acquaintances coming up to us saying: 'You are an activist, you know what is going on—what can I do?'"[9]

On the Borders of their Nations: A Women's
Transnational Territory

Women peace activists were cognizant of their marginal position in organized politics and realized, as Daliah notes, that when the peace agreement
is drawn the women are not going to be sitting at the negotiating table. What
emerged in the signing of the 1993 agreement would not have surprised
them because they knew all along that to be part of the final negotiations
they would have to be in the inner circle of organized politics or, in the
Israeli case, to be powerful male politicians. For many of them the goal was
and still is to end the occupation, to have two states for two nations, and neither of these has happened with the signing of the agreement. Yet, at the
same time, women wanted to establish themselves not only as utopian peace
dreamers but also as persons who understand the pragmatic politics of the
Middle East and who are fully engaged in thinking and planning for economic and other kinds of projects.

In Kufir Yasif, beyond and around these facts of painful differences of
occupation, the Women and Peace Coalition continued to forge a pragmatic
transnational solidarity: "We are planning two conferences, in close cooperation with Palestinian women from the Occupied Territories. Last year we
had a large number of European women, but this year it will be our conference, we and the Palestinian women. Since we think that the conference
must make a clear declaration of talking peace to the PLO, we wanted to
divide the event into two parts. One part will take place in Europe to include
talking to the PLO, which we cannot do here in Israel or in the Occupied Territories. The second event will take place in Jerusalem at the end of December 1990. The idea is to do something symbolic in Europe on negotiating
peace with the PLO and to plan for an international peace conference. The
event in Israel is designed to think about specific plans that are related to
peace, such as the issue of water distribution, the question of the settlements, the status of Jerusalem, and the issue of refusing to serve in the Occupied Territories. Women need to show what we think peace will actually
look like—to say how we can live in this area and not take each other's water
resources; how we can live in this part of the world with Jerusalem as the
capital of two states, Israel and Palestine. Between now and December
women will be asked to take on many tasks, to organize and to bring many
women to Jerusalem. If last year we had six thousand, this year we should
have sixty thousand, and this means a lot of work for us."

Women understand that to make their peace position successful the region has to be economically prosperous and that different claims on natural resources have to be negotiated. Yet they understand that some of the inequalities have to be confronted; in 1990 as well as 1993, for women in the West Bank, the occupation remained a reality, and the emancipatory status of Gaza and Jericho has yet to unfold. Any alliance with the Israeli women's peace camp contained the problems of occupation and inequality, as described by Nabiha: "From the time that we established the political platform of our organization, the Union of Women's Work Committees, it has been that the Union believes in a two-states solution and has been calling since 1967 for an independent Palestinian state in the Occupied Territories side by side with the state of Israel. Palestinian and Israeli women have engaged in meetings at various homes, and we have participated in each other's activities. In the early 1980s, long before there were so many groups working for peace, we strongly believed in the two nations coming together and learning more about each other and joining efforts for something that we both believed was destroying both nations, and that was occupation."

Though the signing of the peace agreement took place between male leaders, rank-and-file women have been, and remain, concerned with the nation. Anderson's nation as "an imagined community" is one from which women are mostly absent. This absence raises gender problematics, but it "is difficult to say in advance whether or how different feminisms must negotiate through or around national political discourses" (Parker, Russo, Sommer, and Yaeger 1992, 6). But, if women, like these Israeli and Palestinian peace activists, do see themselves as part of a nation, they need to negotiate through and around two nationalisms and through and around the inequality of occupation. One temptation could certainly be to replace Anderson's "deep horizontal comradeship" with a deep horizontal sororal comradeship. A horizontal comradeship is impossible in the case of women's public events, as national inequalities are obvious. Yet the three public events discussed in this chapter reveal that women choose to display action and power by carefully selecting what to unveil in public events: when to present sororal comradeship but to veil the inequality of the occupation. In some public events Israeli and Palestinian women choose, as Hannan Ashrawi did in her response in the interview in *Yediot Ahronot,* to construct a sororal comradeship, even if not a horizontal one. The conferences in Kufir Yasif and Haifa unveiled simmerings of differences and inequalities between women of two nations who, at the same time, draw on gender to construct coexistence.

Women's peace activism relentlessly exposes different kinds of simmerings. In the following public event sharp divisions surface within the Israeli-Jewish community. More specifically, fundamental disagreements emerge among religious Zionists and between religious and secular Israelis. A debate on peace with Palestinians draws on sacred texts so that Scripture becomes inseparable from contemporary Middle East politics.

CHAPTER 3 · A Socialist God of Justice: Between Fundamentalism and the Secular Left

You shall not oppress a stranger, for you know the feelings of the stranger, having yourselves been strangers in the land of Egypt. Six years you shall sow your land and gather its yield; but in the seventh you shall let it rest and lie fallow. Let the needy among your people eat of it.

—Exodus 23:9–19

God, who knows no favors and takes no bribe, but upholds the cause of the fatherless and the widow, and befriends the stranger, providing him with food and clothing. You must befriend the stranger, for you were strangers in the land of Egypt.

—Deuteronomy 10:18–19

Religious Women's Peace Conference in Jerusalem: Between the Secular Left and the Religious Right

On an evening in June 1990, in a hotel in Jerusalem that is frequented by religious Jews, four women panelists were sitting at a long table facing an audience of about a hundred people, mostly women. The panelists were addressing a conference entitled "Religious Women for Peace" *(nashim datiyot lemaan shalom).* This conference of religious women for peace, hosted by Oz Veshalom/Netivot Shalom, the religious Zionist peace organization, faced a Likud government that strongly supported settlements and stood solidly behind Gush Emunim (Block of the Faithful), the religious Right settlers. This particular conference aimed to create a public space in which a collective of religious women for peace could not only confront the state but also situate itself between the secular Peace Camp, on the one side, and the religious Right, on the other. The panelists and participants were concerned with the fact that Israeli society was (and despite the signing of the agreement still is) divided on the issue of a Palestinian state and on the return of land for peace. In addition, the conference reflected acute political ruptures between a secular majority and a religious minority (constituting about 15 percent of Israeli Jews) and fierce disputes between the Left and Right within the religious Zionist community.[1]

The conference participants considered two key questions: How should they position themselves as religious women peace activists within a secular Left? How should they challenge the Right politics of the Greater Israel settlement movement headed and inspired by the religious Gush Emunim? Religious women peace activists wanted to forge a distinct political ideology of an authentic Jewish peace anchored in the Torah[2] and fashioned in the image of a God of justice. Miriam, the moderator, expressed their dilemma in a pragmatic question: "Where do we, religious women for peace, place ourselves on the broad range of Israeli politics that spreads from the secular Left, with Shulamit Aloni at one end of the spectrum, to the religious Right [Gush Emunim] with Daniela Weiss or *rabbanit* [a rabbi's wife] Levinger at the other end? We have something in common with both, but we do not belong to either side."

Miriam's questioning statement began the process of transforming a Jewish peace ideology from mere talk into political fact—a fact embodied in the formation of a distinct collective. The collective was defined as Miriam differentiated "religious women for peace" both from the secular Left (Shulamit Aloni) and from the religious Right (Daniela Weiss). The Israeli Left, or the Peace Camp, reflects the broader division between a majority of secular and a minority of religious Israeli Jews. In 1990, religious women for peace saw themselves as part of the religious Left, and many of them were closely linked—if not structurally, at least ideologically—to Oz Veshalom/Netivot Shalom. The ideological position of Oz Veshalom/Netivot Shalom provided the ground on which the women stood as they performed an act that not only distanced them from women in the religious Right but created their own collective, "we religious women for peace," within and between the Peace Camp and the religious Zionist community.

It is useful to locate Oz Veshalom/Netivot Shalom in Israel's political map as an ideological space in which the women forge a collective of "we religious women for peace." Oz Veshalom/Netivot Shalom was formed through a merger of two previously distinct but related peace groups. Oz Veshalom came into being in 1975, and Netivot Shalom emerged after the 1982 Lebanon War. The names that each group chose for itself are rooted in sacred texts and signify God and Torah. *Oz Veshalom,* which means "Strength and Peace," is taken from Psalm 29:11: "The Lord will grant His people strength, the Lord will bless His people with peace." *Netivot Shalom* comes from the saying about the Torah: "Her ways are ways of justice and all her paths are peace." Oz Veshalom/Netivot Shalom is distinguished from the secular Left in that its peace activism is firmly rooted in Jewish biblical and rabbinic tradition. The women's political position says to the secular Left that peace in terms of justice is a traditional *Jewish* value, indigenous and authentic, and not a secular Western humanist claim or a product of European Enlightenment. Thus, as religious Jews, they separate themselves from the religious Right. To Gush Emunim the women signal an equal claim on Jewish tradition but a drastically different interpretation of God, Torah, and precepts, *mitzvot* (divinely commanded acts).

The conference of religious women for peace in Jerusalem revealed deep divisions within the religious Zionist community between Oz Veshalom/Netivot Shalom and Gush Emunim. Each religious group is aligned with a broader secular political position regarding the Israeli-Palestinian conflict. Oz Veshalom/Netivot Shalom is closely associated with the ideology of peaceful coexistence and territorial compromise represented by Labor and some smaller left-wing parties. Gush Emunim is closely associated with the Likud and the smaller ultra-Right parties that espouse the Greater Israel and an "only-by-force" ideology; Gush Emunim has spearheaded the settlement movement in the Occupied Territories, which Oz Veshalom/Netivot Shalom strongly opposes.

Cast in terms of religion, politics, and land, the dispute between Gush Emunim and Oz Veshalom/Netivot Shalom, between the women in the Jerusalem conference and women such as Daniela Weiss and *rabbanit* Levinger, is about what is "divisible" and what is "indivisible." Because for Gush Emunim land (the West Bank, the Gaza Strip, the Golan Heights) and religion are indivisible, women for peace distance themselves from it and stand together with men in the religious Left, who claim that a God of justice and Israeli politics are indivisible.

Fundamentalism: A Global Phenomenon in Local Versions

At first glance the women's conference in Jerusalem seems to be a local debate within the religious Zionist community, a question of where religious women for peace position themselves vis-à-vis the Gush Emunim. Yet the women's debate is also about the way in which local and global issues merge as the Gush Emunim version of religious politics raises an Israeli debate on Jewish fundamentalism. A number of Israeli scholars, such as Friedman and Lazarus-Yafeh, identify Gush Emunim as a Jewish fundamentalist group; they note the place of local fundamentalism in a growing global phenomenon,[3] but they identify the specific nature of the Jewish and Muslim versions.[4] The Jerusalem conference illuminates ways in which political disagreements about the Israeli-Palestinian conflict are framed by political activists who raise the question of Jewish fundamentalism in religious terms. The conference brings a rank-and-file dimension to the question of the meaning of a global phenomenon of fundamentalism in a local script of the Israeli-Palestinian conflict in which local resistance to fundamentalism has been generated within the religious community itself. Though Gush Emunim has been identified by Israeli scholars as fundamentalist, the question remains: What does "Jewish fundamentalism" look like from within the religious Zionist community? When women in the conference bring up names like Daniela Weiss and *rabbanit* Levinger, what meanings are attached to "fundamentalism," Gush Emunim style, that these women represent? According to Oz Veshalom, "Gush Emunim maintains that the messianic redemption of the Jewish people, and the unfolding of God's plan in history generally, are integrally linked to the 'wholeness' of the entire Land of Israel; any return, therefore, of these territories, or parts of them, to Arab sovereignty under a peace treaty would be against the will of God. To forestall such an eventuality, and to realize the *mitzvot* [divinely commanded acts] of 'conquering' and 'settling' the land, Gush Emunim has put its messianic principles into practice by spearheading the establishment of Jewish settlements in the West Bank, or 'Judea' and 'Samaria' if one uses the biblical name for that territory" (Oz Veshalom Publications no.1: 1).

Sacred Land: Jewish and Palestinian "Fundamentalists"

In the Middle East, Jewish and Islamic religious political groups that are identified by locals and outsiders as fundamentalists have placed the concept of "land" in the sacred realm. The faithful are called upon to guard whatever is defined as the "entire land" as a God-given precept. Ziad Abu-Amr, a Palestinian political scientist at Birzeit University, argues that "all Islamic groups, not only in Palestine but throughout the Muslim world, consider Palestine in its entirety as Muslim land, no part of which can be ceded under any circumstances" (1993, 9). In the summer of 1993, shortly before the signing of the agreement between Israel and the PLO, Abu-Amr sounded a warning signal for such an act: "The establishment of a Palestinian state in the West Bank and Gaza is . . . seen as sinful if it entails conceding the rest of Palestine to Israel, an illegitimate entity." Hava Lazarus-Yafeh notes the politically ominous aspect of fundamentalism in the region, observing that "in the Middle East, where tensions and strife between different religious communities are, unfortunately, rather common, fundamentalists—on every side—often inflame latent feelings of hatred and air them openly and violently" (1993, 52). But there is also the striking fact that, despite their enmity, the two groups also resemble each other in their identical construction of land as sacred and indivisible, as a thing to be defended unto death by the faithful. Coexistence, as envisioned by the Israeli and Palestinian leaders in September 1993, will be affected by these groups, whose similarity more than their differences locks them—or so it seems at the moment—in uncompromising positions.

The religious politics that glorifies land as sacred and God-given also permeates and is deployed by secular politicians, as the alliance between the Likud Party and Gush Emunim indicates. Five months before the signing of the agreement in Washington, D.C., a secular political leader of the Likud, the former prime minister Yitzhak Shamir, constructed land and nation as indivisible and sanctified by sentiments of attachment and a historical claim of ownership. He commented on the Labor government's declared intentions to negotiate land for peace: "Many people, men and women, walk around in the country these days and in their heart is a sharp, open wound. They cannot comprehend how people, led by the Israeli government, can part forever from large and precious territories, *shtachim gdolim veyekarim,* to which we have become so attached and feel so good about, and to hand over parts of our land to our enemies, who, we all know, have always dreamed of and desired to rob us of our land and our lives" (*Yediot Ahronot,* May 7, 1993).

On the other side of the conflict Palestinian scholars such as Abu-Amr note the position about land held by Hamas, the Islamic group in the Occupied Territories, which strongly opposes any peace negotiations. Abu-Amr says that the Hamas charter states: "What are called 'peaceful solutions' and 'international conferences' to solve the Palestine question all conflict with the doctrine of the Islamic Resistance Movement, for giving up any part of the land is like giving up part of the religious faith itself" (1993, 13). In both of these respective positions land has come to define the community of patriots and of the faithful. For Israeli secular Jews on the Right land has come to define patriotic parameters. Patriots fight for every inch of land; traitors give it away for peace. Groups such as Gush Emunim and Hamas, which regard each other as bitter enemies, in fact agree on this issue more than they would wish to acknowledge. For religious Jews on the Right as well as for

Muslim groups like Hamas, land has come to define the boundaries of faith. Both groups speak in similar religious idioms: it is a sin to give up land; the faithful should be prepared to fight for land unto death.

Religious women in the 1990 Jerusalem conference separated land from religion. They did not see land and religion as indivisible, and they objected to the sanctity attached to it, which supersedes all other considerations. Nurit said at the conference: "Gush Emunim says that there is precept, *mitzva*, for settling Eretz Yisrael, but there is no such *mitzva*, especially not when human life is at stake." According to people like Nurit, when land and human life are juxtaposed, human life supersedes land. Human life and *halakha* (Jewish law), rather than land and *halakha*, are seen as indivisible. To Nurit the saving of life is the greatest religious deed: "*Kol hamtzil nefesh keilu hitzil olam umloo* [To save one life is to save the whole world]." It says, she emphasized, "a life, *any* life. It does not say Jewish life."[5]

Distancing from Messianic Redemption, Fundamentalists, and Zealots

The discourse on Gush Emunim draws different terms. Religious peace activists mostly talk about this group in terms of its insistence on messianic redemption; others refer to it as a community of fundamentalists or zealots. But, beyond the different terms, religious peace activists insist on publicly distancing themselves from Gush Emunim. At the 1990 Jerusalem conference Miriam's question about how religious women for peace should position themselves constructs a women's collective that views Gush Emunim as a messianic redemptive group that seeks legitimation for settlements by claiming that it is acting according to God's will. This position is symbolically expressed in the names Daniela Weiss and *rabbanit* Levinger. Miriam's mention of them is more than simply pulling out at random two names of women in the religious Right. Daniela Weiss is a recognized leader of the Gush Emunim settlers in the Occupied Territories. She is a woman of considerable oratorical skills who has held the position of secretary-general of Gush Emunim. *Rabbanit* Levinger is the wife of Rabbi Moshe Levinger, who, according to Ian Lustick, is "the most prominent ideological guide of the fundamentalist movement" (1993, 109) and a settler in Kiryat Arba, at the outskirts of the Palestinian city of Hebron. In this version what scholars such as Lustick describe as Jewish fundamentalism was presented by the women as local and indigenous Jewish messianism and an insistence on a *mitzva* to settle the land at all costs.

Both the religious Left and scholars are engaged in a debate on what the latter call Jewish fundamentalism. The former, however, are concerned with the implications of what they call messianic redemption for the religious Zionist community; the latter focus on defining Gush Emunim as Jewish fundamentalism and placing it in a larger global context. Menachem Friedman (1993) identifies two local Jewish versions: Gush Emunim, which he refers to as "innovative fundamentalists," and non-Zionist as well as anti-Zionist ultraorthodox fundamentalists, whom he views as "conservative fundamentalists." Friedman describes all Jewish fundamentalists by using a historical Hebrew term, *"kanaim"* (zealots), used by ultraorthodox anti-Zionist Neturei Karta people to describe themselves.

It is perhaps not surprising that the name of the Palestinian Islamic fundamentalist group Hamas means "zeal" in Arabic and that fundamentalists on both sides not only fight over the same land but themselves make use of similar religious terms. In Jewish history the term *zealots* is fraught with memories of failed struggles and political powerlessness. The use of the term by Neturei Karta as well as by Friedman evokes the local Jewish revolt in ancient Israel against Rome, the first-century superpower. The revolt ended with the loss of Jewish political sovereignty and marked the beginning of two thousand years of exile. The use of *zealots* by Israelis can be seen as either heroic or as catastrophic, depending on one's view of the ancient revolt or, for that matter, on one's views on the Israeli-Palestinian conflict.

Religious peace activists in Israel often note similarities between the past (the revolt against Rome) and the present Middle East conflict. Then, as now, there were serious disagreements within the Jewish community; then, as now, there were rifts among those, like the zealots, who wanted to fight to the last Jew, and others, like Rabbi Jochanan Ben Zakkai, who called for a compromise with Rome in order to save lives. Ancient disputes about the hierarchical ordering of Jewish values—which value takes precedence over all others—also permeate contemporary debates within the religious Zionist community. Commenting on the need in this community for compromise to take precedence as a halakhic issue, Rabbi Lichtenstein, the head of Har Etzion Yeshiva in Israel, rejected Gush Emunim's position on the indivisibility of land and Torah: "No one who knows what the sanctity of Israel means can sign away part of the Land of Israel without feeling that a painful operation is involved. Nevertheless, people undergo surgery" (Yudelson 1986, 22). He denounced the failure of rabbis who favor a land compromise for the sake of peace, justice, and human life to say so publicly, calling their silence "a desecration of the Holy Name, *Chillul HaShem.*" Given the significance of public events as contexts to transform talks into political action, Rabbi Lichtenstein's dismay at the rabbis' silence is quite clear. The absence of a rabbinical voice for peace was of great concern to women in the Jerusalem conference as well, because the public acts of Gush Emunim, whose concept of land as taking precedence over the value of life have come to "represent the entire Torah world" (23).

"Fundamentalists" Are People We Grew Up With

This drastic division within the religious Zionist community, however, does not necessarily produce an image of fundamentalists, or Jewish messianism, as (demonized) others opposed to the modern (Western) world. Lazarus-Yafeh argues that fundamentalism "seems to be a global wave of negative reaction to modernity and Western values, brought about by a variety of factors of varying importance in the different context of each one of these religions" (1993, 43). Yet, in the local Israeli context, this broad definition is called into question in the case of Gush Emunim because the group clearly fosters the concept of nation-ness and the indivisibility of nation-states. This idea of the indivisible nation-state, as Anderson (1983) notes, was conceived in the European womb of modernity and nurtured in its embrace of Western values. More important, despite the differences over the Israeli-Palestinian conflict and the nature of God and Torah, the debate within the religious Zionist community between the Left and Gush Emunim is not for and against modernity as much as it is two opposing religious understandings of modernity. Both groups accept the concept of nation-state, and both, unlike ultraorthodox Jews, do not retreat from the modern world. Members of the two opposing groups often come from the same social and cultural world, and both resent what they see as a complete secularization of Israeli culture. "Both opposing trends accept *Halakha,* meaning Rabbinic law in its historical unfolding, as a binding, normative authority. The two trends do not emerge from different socio-economic backgrounds; they both come from the Labor movement, the kibbutz, and the urban middle class; both trends grew out of the same educational and cultural milieu. Nor is there clear-cut correlation between political extremism and religious, ritual observance" (Tal 1986, 7).

In fact, some women peace activists have actually moved from the religious Right to the religious Left, having been first drawn by what they call Gush Emunim's dedication and idealism and then repulsed by its treatment of Palestinians. Gush Emunim has taken some elements from religious Jewish socialism—its early emphasis on kibbutzim and on communal villages, *moshavim*—to weave into its particular genre of nationalism. Tova, one of the panelists in Jerusalem, described the common cultural world shared by religious Zionists, in which socialist elements were incorporated into that community from the Yishuv (prestate) to 1967. During that period religious Zionism (represented by the political party Hapoel Hamizrahi) was ideologically close to Labor, and its socialism was expressed in the number of kibbutzim that it established. Beyond living in communal settings, socialism for religious Zionists was easily incorporated into a religious way of life and broadly interpreted as doing productive work (in a Marxist sense), such as agriculture, working for social justice, and leading a halakhic way of life.

Some religious Zionists used, and still use, the word *bourgeois* as a derogatory term. Tova noted that for some religious Zionists there was a mixture of socialist/Zionist ideas and bourgeois aspirations, which she rejects: "I grew up in a very Zionist home. It is somewhat amusing to say so because I grew up in Israel, and the myth is that native Israelis are not Zionists. But this is not necessarily the case. I grew up in a home that was ideological, active, and Zionist. I grew up on stories of my parents' struggles to go to Palestine, to become pioneers, to work hard to build the country. Responsibility for the task of building the country was the strongest sentiment at home. On the other hand, there was also a bourgeois message to me: not to make problems, to advance in life, to be financially secure, to be a good girl, to marry a religious guy, and so on. When I grew up I searched to fulfill the Zionist dream. I was brought up to implement, to do, not just to theorize. Well, Gush Emunim were doers; they were religious Zionists who went to settle in the territories. I must confess that for a brief period I was absolutely charmed by their act. To this day I have appreciation for their self-sacrifice and their idealism, their antibourgeois lifestyle. But at the same time I have had some major doubts. Temperamentally, I feel closer to Gush Emunim settlers than to the bourgeois of Tel Aviv, who turn me off, even though we may be together in the Peace Camp and in feminism.

"But beyond the temperamental affinity to Gush Emunim I have some fundamental issues with their enterprise. One of these issues was of the people of Israel, *am Yisrael.* They have forgotten the people; their priorities are all wrong. There is so much to do in terms of social justice, in development towns. I also could not understand how they can totally ignore the Arabs. All the messianic vision can be very convincing from a Jewish perspective, but you can only sustain it as a closed system. I could not accept it. I could not understand how people can close themselves off and not see all the Arabs who live there. The territories are not exactly empty space. And to this day I cannot comprehend it, this ability not to see human beings, not to see people who have their own national aspirations. It is important to follow Buber's idea, and we have to see these people as us and not as them. I may not like them, and I may be very critical of them, and sometimes I may think that they do hideous things. But I realize that they are autonomous human beings. This is how I ended up joining Oz Veshalom / Netivot Shalom, religious Jews for peace. For me peace was not isolated from issues of social justice. This was very important as I grew up in my parents' home, and it is still important to me."

Women like Tova grew up in communities that during the early years of the state noted differences between socialists and bourgeois people and were exposed to socialist ideas such as the value of work, *avoda,* which were firmly woven into an understanding of God and Torah. In some of these communities, in urban settings and in religious kibbutzim, there were members who saw Judaism and socialism as totally compatible. Some of the daughters of these communities, such as Tova and Nurit, were in the Jerusalem conference. Nurit recalled that her father told her that God was the first socialist and quoted from the Bible every possible line that showed the many ways that God cared about all people. In 1967, however, the religious Zionist community split into two major groups, as Gush Emunim took a turn to the Right. It replaced the socialist concept of "Torah and Work," the emblem of the religious Zionist youth movement, Bnei Akiva, with a nationalist Torah and the settlements in an attempt to claim direct continuation of the original religious Zionist project.

For women in the Jerusalem conference, religion, peace, and social justice are intimately linked, and it is on these issues that they saw themselves as different from Gush Emunim. Is the land empty or populated? Are Palestinians a nation or "mere" Arabs who could go anywhere? These are the questions that separate the conference women from the people with whom they grew up, those who, like Daniela Weiss, became settlers. Religious women peace activists thus align themselves with Israelis (seculars, scholars, and others) who object to Gush Emunim's blindness to other people's national aspirations and its members' willingness to settle as though the land were empty of people. Israeli scholars such as Ehud Sprinzak offer a similar view on Gush Emunim's denial of nation-ness and demonizing of Palestinians into enemies, which leaves no room for coexistence: "Gush Emunim's position on 'the Palestinian question' is sharp and unequivocal: the problem does not exist and is no more than a vicious ploy by the Arabs, who want to destroy the State of Israel, furthered by Leftist Jews who refuse to see the Arabs' true intentions. Eretz Yisrael in its entirety belongs to the Jews by divine command. The Arabs, whoever they are, have no collective right over the land, and the issue, if there is one, is of individuals who must find a way to live under Jewish rule. The universal principle of self-determination—even if it might have some relevance in other places—does not hold in Eretz Yisrael" (1993, 125). But the 1990 women's conference in Jerusalem reveals that there is more to their struggle with Gush Emunim than a disagreement about Israel's occupation of the West Bank and the Gaza Strip, about Jewish settlements in these territories, and about Palestinian nation-ness.

At the conference the struggle over political positions in the Israeli-Palestinian conflict were intertwined with religious philosophical questions: What is the nature of Judaism? What is the nature of God? What is the foundation for an ethical way of life for Jews in Israel? These questions were addressed both directly and indirectly when religious women talked about their peace position and quoted the epigraphic verses from the Bible emphasizing God's words: "You shall not oppress a stranger, for you know the feelings of the stranger, having yourselves been strangers in the land of Egypt" (Exodus 23:9–19). Nurit, an active member of Oz Veshalom / Netivot Shalom, said: "We in the religious Left frame our thinking in Torah that has been distorted by the religious Right, who disregard some basic rules in their approach to Palestinians. They ignore the whole Jewish concept of a "stranger-resident," ger-toshav; they disregard the issue of social justice, rooted in Judaism, which is sensitive to the stranger, ger, and in rules such as the prohibition on slavery, and a Jewish way of life that is anchored in the Jewish memory of slavery. They forget that it is incumbent on us to remember that we were slaves in Egypt and that this should inform our identity and our acts. The laws are not only concerning slaves but all those who are powerless—the widow, the orphan; the prohibition of taking a poor person's last possession to pay a debt, these are all designed to defend the weak. For it is said, 'God who knows no favors and takes no bribe, but upholds the cause of the fatherless and the widow, and befriends the stranger, providing him with food and clothing' (Deuteronomy 10:18–19)."

For religious Zionists on both sides of the political divide of the Israeli-Palestinian conflict, the nature of Torah, in the broad sense of Jewish tradition, and the conflict are inseparable. While both frame their political positions in religious terms, Gush Emunim sees it as a religious (messianic) precept, *mitzva,* to settle the West Bank and the Gaza Strip, while the religious Left maintains that "the social and spiritual cost of holding on to the disputed territories is too high for the Jewish state to tolerate, if it wishes to remain faithful to Jewish values and *mitzvot* that pertain to interpersonal and intercommunal relations, not just the people-to-land relationship" (Landau 1986, 1). The religious Right talks about a *mitzva* to settle the land and not to relinquish an inch, and the religious Left talks about a *mitzva* of saving human life—not just Jewish life—as superseding all other precepts.

Who Owns God and Torah?

Religious women peace activists were uneasy that religious Zionism has become identified locally and internationally with Jewish fundamentalism and called on the religious Left to bring forth the fact that Judaism is concerned with peace, ethics, and justice. They stressed the need to reclaim Jewish rules for ethical conduct that Gush Emunim has eroded and expunged from religious Zionism. Janet Aviad, one of the leaders of the Peace Now Movement, raises the question of how messianic ideas that have been on the margins of religious Zionism have come to dominate it. She asks in an article published by Oz Veshalom why the religious Right rather than the Left has gained political popularity: "The fascinating and difficult question for anyone concerned with the development of religious trends in Israel is why a group like Gush Emunim, which had been peripheral and whose politics run counter to the original principles of religious Zionism, has leaped into a position of dominance, while a group like Oz Veshalom, more genuinely linked to the traditions and ideals of religious Zionism, appears the peripheral phenomenon today" (Aviad 1986, 31).

In facing the religious Right, panelists and participants in the Jerusalem conference were concerned with what they saw as Gush Emunim's appropriation of the right to represent God and Torah.[6] Rachel, one of the panelists, proposed to reclaim this sole ownership of the interpretation of Judaism and argued against what she considered the reluctance of the religious Left to do so: "When the religious Right attacks us I think that we underestimate what is happening. The interpretations that the religious Right gives to texts have to be heard; we need to recognize that some of the things they claim are, unfortunately, in the texts somewhere. What we must do is what Judaism has always done: we need to deal with a constantly changing reality. We offer innovation and novel exegeses, and probably they give a more fundamentalist and more simplified interpretation of texts."

It is clear that the issue has become a struggle not only over who will define God and Torah but also who will define the identity of religious Zionist Jews in Israel. In my own conversations with religious women and men on the Left, the men often expressed annoyance at being automatically identified as fundamentalists merely because they wore a skullcap. Yotam, a young religious man, said, "I am sick and tired of people looking at me and saying 'settler,' *mitnahel,* just because I wear a skullcap." His comment captures his annoyance with Gush Emunim for robbing him of his identity as well as his resentment that secular Israelis so easily stereotype a religious person as a settler.

A close association between religious Zionism and Gush Emunim has become a concern for religious women and men peace activists: "The religious Jew has acquired a new image in the eyes of the public, an image antithetical to the values of Judaism. Judaism is the source of humanism. The *Halakha* commands us to love human beings, *all* human beings, for they are created in God's image. Our being a chosen people does not give us the right to act like arrogant overlords or oppressors—just the opposite is true. Our chosenness requires us to spread the light of eternal Jewish values: justice, peace, mercy, loving kindness, and fraternity to all creatures. The new model of the young Jew with the knitted skullcap, armed with an Uzi, acting on the basis of 'might makes right' instead of 'right makes might'—this image distorts the true character of the Torah. In so doing, it leads to the gravest sin possible according to *Halakha,* namely, the desecration of the Divine Name *(Chillul HaShem).* There is no repentance or atonement for such a sin, the meaning of which is that if a religiously observant Jew acts in an unbecoming or unsuitable manner, he creates in the eyes of others a negative image of the Torah and even, as it were, of the Creator" (Glass 1986, 38). A key question emerges about what constitutes appropriate religious Zionist behavior.

The act of settling the territories and behaving as occupiers is defined by people in the religious Left as a religious transgression—the desecration of the Divine Name, *Chillul HaShem*—but is defined as religious precept, *mitzva,* by the religious Right.[7]

The dispute within the religious Zionist community is in some ways inseparable from a struggle within the Peace Camp with secular Israelis about the meaning of peace and of "Western" values. The women raised the question: What kind of peace is the Israeli one? Is peace a Western product *adopted* for the local dispute, or is peace a local product *rooted* in local Jewish history and most suitable to resolve a contemporary local dispute? Many religious peace activists have said, when they talked about why they organize separately from the larger peace group, that peace and justice are authentic and historical Jewish values ignored by secular Israeli Jews presenting these issues as a Western product of the Enlightenment. Humanism and justice, according to the religious peace activists, are a local, indigenous Jewish product, forged in ancient Israel and guiding ethical political behavior in the contemporary Israeli-Palestinian conflict. For religious peace activists God is an inclusive humanist God, and Halakha commands Israeli Jews to behave in an ethical way, to love all human beings because all are created in God's image. Jewish Halakha, then, is an indigenous product; it has a crucial place in defining what is ethical political behavior. This emphasis on ethical Jewish politics is a statement to both seculars on the Left and religious Jews on the Right.

Sacred Words in a Sociopolitical World

Framed in Appadurai's (1991) concept of "word and world," the struggle within the religious Zionist community is not just about the politics of the Israeli-Palestinian conflict; it is also not a struggle between sacred words and a secular world. The contestation is within the word—that is, within shared texts—about the meaning of *word,* in this case sacred word. Both sides, the religious Right and the religious Left, are engaged in a process of locating the "right" word in the text, the right meaning of God—the undistorted meaning—in order to legitimate action in the sociopolitical world. If human beings are created in the image of God, that image is crucial: if God is a nationalist warrior, human beings are justified in such behavior; if God is a God of peace and justice, human beings should reflect or aspire to reflect such a God. Religious women for peace talked about an inclusive Ruler of the universe, as opposed to an exclusionary nationalist God of Israel alone. At the Jerusalem conference Rachel stated what she considers Gush Emunim's construction of God, texts, and society: "I think that the religious Right uses the word *peace* in a very narrow sense, that is, a peace for Jews only, security for the Jewish people safeguarded by God, in a homogeneous society that 'transfers,' or oppresses, or kills the 'other.' When they give this kind of meaning to the word *peace,* I am afraid that they support it by quoting very literal texts."

There is a clear understanding for women like Rachel that the Hebrew Bible includes numerous, sometimes contradictory ideas. She, like other Israeli Jews (both secular and religious), turns to words of the sages to argue for action in the world as it is experienced: "When we want to emphasize what our notion of peace is we must remember, and remind others, that Jewish tradition highly values change and addresses the realities of specific historic times. One of my favorite stories in Jewish culture is the one regarding Rashi [a famous eleventh-century Jewish scholar who wrote an extensive commentary to the Bible and the Talmud]. It is said that in Rashi's old age he told his grandson that had he been young he would have written a new commentary to the Torah, because things change, and there is an ongoing dialogue between a person and his tradition, between a person and former generations, between a person and a reality that is always changing before his eyes."

The concepts of "change" and "dialogue" emerge as important themes in all women's peace conferences—changes from belligerence to peace, from settlements to giving up land for peace, from banning a dialogue with Palestinians to negotiation. For religious women such as Rachel social change and cultural continuity are proposed in the same breath, not as binary oppositions but as a unitary concept. Change does not indicate modernity and a break from tradition; rather, it reaffirms Jewish tradition that is by nature in a process of change as it responds to time and events, as Rachel's story of Rashi illustrates. To promote peace is to propose political change that is cast not only in contemporary ethical issues but calls on a long line of Jewish religious leaders to legitimate a peace position against Gush Emunim, which justifies its position by claiming that it is God's wish. Knowing God's wish is seen as a messianic idea and is distinguished from the nature of God and the nature of Torah. Religious peace activists, like Landau, resist any knowledge of God's wish: "The Jewish people have suffered greatly in the past from messianic movements that claimed to know God's plan for humanity in any particular generation. For the time being, until we receive further instructions from the only reliable Source, we Jews have a revealed and revered tradition that teaches us that all human beings are created in God's image and are worthy of being treated with dignity, respect and compassion." (1986, 1–2).

When religious women for peace struggle with Gush Emunim over an understanding of God and Torah, there is an aspect of what Richard Handler calls disputes "over ownership of the past and of cultural property" (1991, 67). Rachel urged the conference participants to engage in a dialogue with Gush Emunim by paying close attention to the texts. She sees the collective cultural property as a repository of earlier struggles over meaning in the ancient Jewish community, as reflected in contradictory passages in sacred texts: "I emphasize the need to be vocal about it because when the religious Right attacks us we seem to underestimate its power. They use texts that, I am sorry to say, do include discriminatory exclusionary comments. Yes, it is true that Psalms 122:6–7 says: 'Pray for the well-being of Jerusalem; may those who love you be at peace. May there be well-being within your ramparts, peace in your citadels.' But what kind of peace is this? A citadel, ramparts, living in a fortified city with a Jewish society inside? It is hard to say that a narrow, exclusionary, siegelike peace that the religious Right talks about is not written anywhere in our sacred texts. But what we must emphasize is that Judaism has always engaged in particular historic events and dealt with changing realities, and so must we engage in new commentaries. When we talk about peace we must say that we are followers of Aaron, who was a seeker of peace, and we must ask ourselves what we need to do so that there will be peace with Palestinians here and now and not in some utopian place." Biblical figures are employed to legitimate and guide religious Jews' quest for peace; Aaron is recognized by women and men as a symbol of peace: "Of all the figures in the Bible, Aaron, the high priest, is said to most exemplify the ideals of peace and peacemaking—along with priesthood in general—and is depicted as one whose entire personality is directed toward alleviating conflict . . . a lover of peace, a pursuer of peace, and an instrument of peace between people" (Gopin 1986, 38).

Thinking within the Nation of God beyond the Nation

In this women's mirror is a reflection not only of global/local struggles regarding the negotiating of religious traditions, politics, and modernity but also a discourse on what Appadurai (1993, 411) refers to as "thinking beyond the nation." Appadurai's call to the intellectual community to recognize the social forms that are engaged in thinking beyond the nation parallels the call of these women to think beyond the Israeli-Jewish nation but without surrendering nation-ness. This is not a case of postnational aspirations but, rather, of arguing for the need within the Israeli religious Zionist community to think beyond the nation; it is a call to recover God from the fundamentalists' messianic grip, to recenter in religious Zionism a transnational, socialist God of justice, one who cares about all human beings. Against this God, according to the women, is a formation by Gush Emunim of a nationalist, particularistic, and aggressive Jewish God.

How do people determine whether God is beyond nations? For religious women sacred texts are one source of determining the nature of God, as exemplified by biblical figures whose actions are seen in line with God's will. Rachel said in the Jerusalem conference: "To talk of real peace in this complicated country of ours we must expand the concept of peace and say it loud and clear, using Jewish sources that speak of tolerance and say that our Father Abraham was very creative when he said to Lot: 'Let us separate: if you go north, I will go south and if you go south, I will go north'" (Genesis 13:9). When biblical persons think beyond selfish needs, if they make choices of compromise, and when they do not sanctify land, they provide guidelines for contemporary decisions. To the participants of the Jerusalem conference Rachel had this to say: "We have not only the right but the responsibility, the duty, to turn to Jewish sources to give us the strength to think of a changing reality. We should turn to Genesis and take example from Abraham, who had the courage to change, to give up land when it was necessary. By suggesting to Lot to divide the land between them rather than fight Abraham was creative. God told Abraham that the land was his, but, despite God's promise, Abraham decided that the wisest thing would be to divide the land, and what he did was something creative. He took tremendous responsibility when he chose to give up land. I think that we need to be as creative as Abraham was."

To extend politically beyond the nation and work toward a peaceful coexistence, Rachel said, is a long process that will require a great deal of empathy: "Where is it possible to draw strength from our heritage for a dialogue that is empathetic? Empathy always reminds me of the famous Hasidic story about the rabbi who spent a long time with every Hasid who came to see him. The rabbi was asked, 'Why does it take you so long?' and he said:

'What do you mean? When a person comes to consult with me I need to take off my clothes, and he has to take off his clothes because I need to wear his clothes when he tells me his problems. Next, I have to give him advice, so I take off his clothes because now I need to put on my clothes so that I can advise him. It takes a long time because you need to be both yourself and the other."

Jewish texts provide legitimacy for stretching beyond the nation to consider a "land for peace," as a compromise, which Gush Emunim emphatically opposes. While women such as Rachel turned to texts at the conference, they also noted an absence of rabbis willing to support publicly a peace position; others, however, insist that there are rabbis who do take this position. Shimon Glick, who speaks from a religious peace position, says that "it would be inappropriate to 'count' rabbis, but if we were indeed to take a poll, it seems that the majority, both quantitatively and qualitatively, does not, a priori, oppose return of territories if in the opinion of responsible political and military leaders such a step is indicated in order to ensure the safety of the community" (1986, 38). Whether Glick is right in his estimate of support for peace among rabbis, in Israeli politics this does not matter so much. What really matters is what the rabbis say in public, and their public silence does not translate their private support for peace into a political fact.

In positioning themselves against Gush Emunim, religious women for peace publicly construct their image of God who cares for all humans. At the heart of the debate between the religious Left and Right is not only a struggle on the meaning of peace, land, and *mitzvot,* but also a struggle regarding the nature of God: What kind of God is the Jewish God? The question of the nature of God is linked to humans, who are created in God's image. Adin Steinsaltz, a renowned Israeli Judaic scholar, writes that "one of the definitions of the name 'Man' or 'Adam' is likeness, *domeh,* to the Supreme. For, like God, man creates the world in the image of himself," and notes that "man may therefore be viewed as a symbol or a model of the divine essence" (1980, 117, 118).

While Steinsaltz may use the word *man* as an inclusive term for humanity, the masculine word is embedded in a religious culture and has serious implications for women, who struggle not only for an equal place in Israeli society but in the synagogue as well. Yet in the struggle with Gush Emunim religious women and men peace activists aim to recover God from the religious settlers. God's image is not just a spiritual concern but also takes on political dimensions: If God is a God of justice or if, by contrast, God is an exclusionary nationalist, it follows that humans who have likeness, *domim,* to the Supreme will choose a different course of political action. Defining the nature of God profoundly determines the actions of human beings.

Women and men in the religious Left undertake to denationalize God, to "redeem" the Redeemer from Jewish fundamentalists by restoring social justice to *HaShem,* the Name, as Rachel, one of the panelists in the conference, suggested: "We say that every human being was born in God's image, and we believe that we have a mission to bring justice and peace to the world in the name of God, *beshem hashem.*" Religious women peace activists are worried that nationalist messianism will sweep the religious Zionist community's understanding of religion, of God and of Torah—an understanding from which political issues are inseparable. Within the larger context of Israeli society a socialist God who cares about all human beings also means a different kind of a Jewish state from the one that would be shaped by a nationalist, exclusionary God.

Shifting the *Mechitza* in the Synagogue

For religious women and men, God and Torah are not a private matter between individuals and their religious practices but, rather, a way of life that permeates all spheres of social activity. Difference, however, impinges on this common ground that religious women and men share. Women's exclusion from full participation in the crucial spheres of Israel's social life and from most positions of power in organized politics extends to the synagogue as well. In synagogues in Israel and orthodox synagogues outside of Israel, women are not equal members, they do not count as part of the *minyan* (prayer quorum of ten), nor can they lead the congregation as rabbis, cantors, or Torah readers. The divide, *mechitzah,* between women and men in the synagogue has structural and symbolic aspects; it is more than a concrete "thing," more than the mere allocation of a separate physical space, because it creates the reality of a divided ritual for women and men within the synagogue. Men perform the rituals; women are the audience.

If God cares about all human beings and all are created in the image of God, women must be included in this image. How and what implications does this inclusion have for religious women peace activists who sit in the synagogue behind the divide? Because women's space marks their unequal membership, the *mechitzah* is more than a material part of the building: it symbolizes unequal allocation of space to women. In addition, because men are the agents and performers of the rituals, only they have access to all sacred objects such as the Holy Ark and the Torah scrolls. The *mechitzah* constitutes the separation not only between women and men but between women and sacred objects.

Yona, one of the panelists at the Jerusalem conference, recounted an event in which she made a public gesture of equality—she touched a sacred object as she took the Torah in her hands: "Once on Simchat Torah, when we were carrying the Torah in a circle dancing in the street outside the synagogue, I asked a young man to give us women a Torah scroll. He gave it to us, and I started dancing with the Torah. The band continued to play, though they were in shock that a woman would dance with a Torah. The women froze for a second and then began to dance around me, but not a single one of them would take the Torah from me. A few minutes later I returned the Torah, and I will never, never do it again." A sacred object may be both coveted and feared, as the women were adamant in their refusal to touch it; the fear may lie not only in the religious but also in the social realm, and religious women may want to avoid condemnation and therefore avoid touching or taking sacred objects. While Yona made a gesture of equality she found herself isolated and alone; despite the fact that the women danced, no one wanted to cross the line and take in her arms a sacred object that only men are allowed to hold and dance with.

As my conversations with religious women peace activists reveal, the attempt literally to shift the *mechitzah* spatially is to shift ritual and spiritual boundaries. Batya and Yona told me about their unsuccessful attempt to change the location of women's space in their synagogue. "We have a struggle in our synagogue about women's place," said Batya. "Our town is basically a small traditional community. We have more than a dozen synagogues, and several more are in the process of establishing themselves. Our synagogue can be defined as modern orthodox and is ashkenazi in its services; however, we incorporate mizrahi elements, such as some customs, cantors, and liturgy. It is unique in our town that we allow women to be members in their own right, to pay membership dues, to have a right to vote in all the meetings, and to sit on all committees. We just renovated our synagogue, and when the renovations started we, a small group, a few families, wanted to expand the place of women in our community because we are struggling with forging a way of life that is Jewish, Zionist, and *halutzi* (pioneering). We asked to relocate women's space, *ezrat nashim,* which is on the

balcony at the top of the stairs, to a space side by side with the men's section—separate and behind a divide, *mechitzah,* of course, but alongside the
men and facing East (the direction in which Jews pray), which the balcony
does not face; there is precedence for this kind of space in synagogues. What
seemed crucial to us was the sense of equality. We did not propose to abol-
ish the balcony; we simply argued that this is a young community with children, and strollers, and the stairs are hard for older women too.

"We wanted more space and something more egalitarian, but there were
practical reasons too, because expanding the synagogue alongside the men
would provide a large space for meetings and lectures, it would be easier for
mothers to take the children to the bathroom (which is on the first floor), easier to watch the children in the playground, and better for the children, who
could more easily go from mothers to fathers, and so on. Well, our proposal
created quite a storm; we endured some difficult weeks. What hurt most was
the silence of close friends in the community. People sat there and listened
to the horrible things that a small minority uttered and did not rise up, did
not voice objections. The attacks on us for our suggestion to build an additional women's space by a few people were vicious. We lost."

The fragility of solidarity of what constitutes a "we" collective of like-
minded people is evident in Batya's dismay at the absence of support from
friends and more obviously within the synagogue community, which sees
itself as different from other synagogues in town, more progressive regarding
women and more "Left" in the political orientation of its members, many of
whom support the position of Oz Veshalom/Netivot Shalom. Change and
tradition are linked as Batya calls for greater equality for women and at the
same time insists that the very change (women's space alongside the main
synagogue) is not halakhically revolutionary and has precedence in both
ashkenazi and mizrahi synagogues; therefore, the request is legitimate.

Domestic concerns invade public space as motherhood, child care, and
respect for the elderly are invoked to construct the requested space as a practical consideration. The other side of what Susan Sered Starr (1992) calls
religious women's "domestication of religion" is the deployment of domestic concerns to forge public changes for women in the synagogue. The category "we religious women" is marked by differences as women's relationship to their religious communities varies from acceptance of their place to
various forms of overt and covert resistance and includes a wide range of
both accommodation and rebellion. Women may actively reproduce their
position in their religious community by strongly monitoring one another's

behavior, as Tamar El Or (1992) notes for a group of ultraorthodox *(haredi)* women in Israel. Women may forge a parallel religious sphere for themselves within exclusionary religious systems, as Sered Starr observes in a community of elderly mizrahi women in Jerusalem, and they do so by creating a wide range of personal rituals. Others, like Batya, bring women's struggle to the public domain and attempt to widen their space within the *edah* (holy community). For women peace activists there is a parallel between their peace acts and their actions in the synagogue. In vigils and conferences as well as in the synagogue women make a space for their position and attempt to transform ideologies into facts and acts.

The Significance of Facing East

Beyond the material space in the synagogue, the women's request to face East was an attempt to enlarge women's spiritual and ritual sphere. Women's "privilege," the fact that in Judaism they are exempt from prayer, is also the sign of their exclusion, so that when women present themselves not as casual worshipers but as persons who take prayers seriously, who want to face East, it threatens the traditional divide between them and men, who in the synagogue hold a privileged position. In the particular case of Batya's synagogue, acknowledging that women have a right to face East when they pray in the synagogue alters the relationship between prayer on the one hand and membership in the community on the other; it means that, if women face the same direction as men, it will minimize difference and will add a spiritual dimension to their existing bureaucratic privileges, unusual for most synagogues, such as membership in their own right and the right to join all committees. To move the divide from the balcony to side by side with men must have been beyond the boundary *(gvul)* that the community was ready to advance; the few families who wanted to shift the gender boundary further found that they could not do it. Rejecting the women's request was not a question of change against tradition but, rather, a matter of transgressing gender boundaries within the synagogue community.

For religious women for peace, activism for equality in the synagogue meant yet another transgression—this one across the boundaries of a religious community. Yona, who was one of the women who put forth the proposal, alluded to this issue: "Clearly women do not want to disturb men's prayers. But women are asking similar considerations for their needs. Some people saw it as a feminist struggle, but the absurdity is that in the balcony the women are extremely exposed; those who object to the change say: 'What is the problem? The women can see much better from the balcony.' I find it upsetting that, yes, I see everything, but I am a passive spectator, while the man is at the center. I don't even mind sitting in the back of the synagogue and not side by side, because then I feel that we are on one level, and while I barely can see the men I know that they and we are praying to the same Creator of the Universe [boreh olam]. Since I am an orthodox Jew, I accept the fact that men run the service and not women, but we all pray to the Creator of the Universe. When we sit upstairs, however, I feel that it is as though it is a bullfight, and they are bullfighters, and I am watching and clapping. It is intolerable for me, simply intolerable, that man and not God is at the center of the service. It is a relationship between actors and spectators: they are onstage, and we watch. We accept the strictures of the separation of the sexes in the synagogue in order to pray to God. But the balcony turns the prayer experience into something false and inauthentic."

Yona's dramatic analogy between the synagogue services and bullfights is not necessarily intended to claim that there is something aggressive about them as much as it is intended to mark a deep separation between those who are seen in all the splendor of their performance and the act itself is almost forgotten. For Yona services mean a spiritual communication with God that the present synagogue structure denies to women. Gender equality is not confronted directly by women like Yona, who seek social justice but who also say, "I am an orthodox woman," and do not question the customary Jewish belief that women "disturb men's prayers" by their mere presence. Working their way around these gender problematics makes women peace activists such as Yona find that at times a quest for prayer as an authentic experience is a way to claim space alongside the main synagogue, so that it will be a public fact on the ground of an enlarged and more equal women's space, without actually having to spell out any ideas about equality.

Feminism in the Synagogue: Who Owns Torah?

In the Jerusalem conference Miriam, the moderator, talked about gender equality and what she saw as a reluctance on the part of religious women to identify themselves as feminists: "The word feminism was missing tonight from our discussion, and for me feminism, or Jewish feminism, is not a dirty word. I am not saying that all the women here tonight define themselves as feminists, but I myself do, and I do think that the incorporation of feminist values and a commitment to Jewish tradition is linked to what Rachel noted as a relationship between change and tradition. If we as peace activists struggle with discriminatory Jewish texts that exclude non-Jews from the category of human, we also must face the fact that Jewish tradition includes stereotypes and otherizes women and that it excludes them from the study of Torah. We do not have religious leaders in our generation that can serve as models. We must be the pioneers and be our own models. If we can have dialogues between Israelis and Palestinians and among Israelis, we surely can have a dialogue between women and men and, God willing [beezrat hashem], we will prevail."

In conferences and in the synagogue religious women for peace engage in transforming ideas about gender equality into a political fact by increasing their rights in the religious sphere. Religious women who struggle for equality attempt to redefine their place as persons within a religious context and aim to turn an ideology of equality into a political fact. Yet to do so does not mean that women will use the word *feminism*. In conversations with religious women for peace it was clear that using the word *feminism*, or avoiding it, is politically motivated. When women choose to do so they want to emphasize female solidarity and are silent about it when they think that to do so would be politically foolish. Yona noted: "To the question of feminism and whether our struggle in the synagogue is a feminist one, I have two responses, a tactical and a fundamental one. My tactical response is that we [women] think that it is very bad to wave the feminist flag in our synagogue and generally in Israel in all kinds of contexts. It is a bad idea because it sounds provocative and would be perceived as such if we came and said to the members in our synagogue that we want the women's space alongside the men's section because we want equality. Because to them it would not seem an equality issue but as a provocation. But when we come and say that the change will be good for families, it is good for older women, who don't want to climb stairs, it is good for this or for that, our request seems fine. To speak of women's equality is not productive and entails frustration." The lost fight over women's space in the synagogue illustrates that, while women like Yona may assess the situation correctly, their avoidance of the word *feminism* does not guarantee political success. Members of the community may still read feminism behind and within the domestic arguments of "older women and children" and resist attempts to create a new, more egalitarian women's spiritual space in the synagogue.

Whether religious women reject the concept of feminism or publicly embrace it, some of them fight for greater equality within their religious communities because they feel empowered as religious women. Thus, women take on roles allocated to Jewish men, as Miriam's opening statement in the Jerusalem conference indicates: "It is customary in our organization [Oz Veshalom/Netivot Shalom] to open conferences with a homily [dvar Torah], and with your permission I will start with a reference to Torah. All four of us on this panel are religious women who struggle for peace, and all of us are involved in education. During my research on education for women in Jewish history my attention was drawn to an interesting phenomenon. It is common knowledge that in Jewish tradition men only are commended to study Torah. Baruch Epstein, the author of Torah Temimah, describes in his memoir, Mekor Baruch, a debate that he had with his aunt Rayna Batya, a scholar in her own right. Epstein says that Rayna Batya was worried and sad that women's honor and value was minimized because they were forbidden to study Torah. Epstein explained to his aunt that women are exempt from it because they do not serve in the army and are also exempt from serving in God's army. His rationale draws on a long-honored tradition in Judaism.

"One of the metaphors that we have for learning Torah is a metaphor of combat, and up until now it has generally been men who have learned Torah. Many sayings of the sages and other historical sources describe an atmosphere of the study of Torah that is aggressive, masculine, competitive—even violent. Some of my friends commented on the title for this evening, "Religious Women's Struggle for Peace," and said that struggle (maavak) is a masculine term. Their comments are similar to Gilligan's notion of 'a different voice,' which argues that women have a different approach to ethics and moral issues than men. I want to be fair and note that the Jewish sages displayed different forms of relations; among them some were less competitive and more supportive. But these were not the dominant voices. I wonder whether women can bring a different approach to the study of Torah and also to political negotiations. Could women bring a less competitive, more congenial, and supportive spirit? I hope that this evening will provide a model for this spirit. I hope that with the entrance of women to the world of Torah study and to the political negotiations that they will be able to contribute to the peace process, that they will be able to influence those negotiations in a more peaceful direction, less competitive, less aggressive, and more supportive way; that they will bring peace among people and between nations."

However careful women may be to avoid the word feminism, to offer a homily *(dvar Torah)* is to bring an act of gender equality to the religious sphere. Such a public act is a shift of a divide in the religious community, which has traditionally allocated this role to Jewish men. Miriam transforms an ideology of an "equal yet different" women's voice into a political act as she draws on a debate between a male Jewish scholar and his female relative, a scholar in her own right, to legitimate women's right to Jewish scholarship. She used a feminist viewpoint by focusing on gender differences to suggest that much of traditional Torah study displays an aggressive male approach that resembles a battlefield, and quoted a Western scholar, Gilligan, to argue for a local women's voice of peace, a voice that could be brought to both the study of Torah and to political life in Israel.

Miriam could offer a homily in a public space outside the synagogue, an act she could not perform in the synagogue. Tova noted that even in her synagogue, which she considered to be progressive, women are excluded from offering homilies: "Our community does allow for women to teach mixed classes in the synagogue. Yet we have not yet arrived at a time that a woman can give a homily in the synagogue." Religious women like Miriam may not offer a homily in the synagogue but may perform this role in public events, such as peace conferences, so that secular space becomes sanctified by bringing in sacred texts and Jewish customs. Thus, while women such as Miriam aim to bring a religious perspective of a God of Justice to a secular Peace Camp, there is also a message to the synagogue community. The secular but public event can turn into religious space by means of a homily and so widen women's rights within the religious sphere.

The women's peace conference in Jerusalem is not only about the politics of the Israeli-Palestinian conflict; it is also about women's right to say a *dvar Torah* and to sit in a synagogue side by side with men, facing East. As religious persons, these women peace activists engaged in dialogues with other religious persons who would like to keep the women's space in the synagogue unchanged. The space that they share with secular women like Aloni, at a peace conference, can be used to restructure the religious space they share with men in religious Zionism.

Protesting the Occupation with Shulamit Aloni and Observing the Sabbath without Her

Religious women peace activists face divisions not only within the synagogue and the religious Zionist community but among women's peace activists as well. While gender and peace provide elements for solidarity with secular women like Shulamit Aloni, differences emerged in the Jerusalem conference in 1990 around the significance of Judaism to public culture and of a halakhic way of life as a pragmatic concern. Both religious practices and Jewish values become issues in peace activities and threaten to unglue the unity of "we women for peace." At the Jerusalem conference Hagit spoke of the difference that observing Shabbat, the Sabbath, creates in peace activism: "I stand in the Women in Black Friday vigils, and I feel an outsider [she used the Hebrew word *chariga,* "deviant"]. In a few weeks there will be a peace conference in Kfar [Hebrew for the Arabic Kufir] Yasif on Shabbat. I feel that there is no room for religious women who follow a halakhic life *(shomrot mitzvot)* and for their self-expression. I am told that I am in the minority, and I don't know how to make a difference. Perhaps if there were at least five or more of us, we could make a difference." In response to Hagit, Ruth suggested that more religious women get involved in other peace activities: "Every Sunday morning there is a vigil organized by Reshet [a women's peace organization] in front of the prime minister's office. It is important to have a delegation of religious women there as well."

Religious Zionist women, like Hagit, not only feel threatened by Gush Emunim but also see themselves as outnumbered and marginalized among secular women who share their politics of peace. Such women have a sense of urgency to make their presence known, a need rooted in the knowledge that they are a minority in a mostly secular society and want to make their presence felt in the women's peace camp. Miriam addressed the issue of religious women's sense of being a minority, saying that it may be more a perception than a reality and that there are probably more peace activists than people realize: "I would like to note that there are a number of women in this room who wear black on Friday [stand in the vigils] and observe Shabbat. It will be a good idea to meet one another at the end of the evening and to exchange telephone numbers and to know that there are other religious women peace activists."

To be represented is more than a refusal to be ignored or silenced; it is also to make public space for the fact that there is a religious Left. As Yael noted: "There is resistance in the Left to hear that there is a religious Left. The fact is that the Left organizes demonstrations on Shabbat, and it is hurtful." There is a sense among religious peace activists of marginalization within the larger Peace Camp that parallels the sense that religious Jews have within Israel's secular society of having to fight hard for a Jewish way of life in a secular society that seems to them more intent on Western culture than on Jewish culture. It is not that religious peace activists reject Western culture but, rather, that they see secular Jews as rejecting Jewish culture.

The issues regarding culture that came forth in the conference mirror a wider struggle over public culture in Israel and raise some key questions: Is Israeli culture both a local product and a global import? Is Israeli culture authentic (in the case of religious peace activists, it means a Jewish core; does this core include mizrahi tradition?), or is it a generic, "imported" Western culture? Is it an indigenous secular blend of both?

Sarah, a religious woman peace activist, uncovers some of the women's concerns about the Peace Camp: "The religious ashkenazi world has experienced in the last two hundred years a process of secularization from the tradition that does not characterize the Sephardi mizrahi communities. Israeli mizrahi Jews see the Left as having no identification with Jewish tradition; let me give an example. Peace Now has published a pamphlet, 'Everything you wanted to know about the West Bank and you did not dare ask.' The publication included mostly newspaper items; the only nonjournalist source was *The Little Prince*—undoubtedly a lovely book, but there was not a single Jewish source, not a single biblical or Talmudic quote, not one midrash, not even a quote from Jewish folklore. When I asked a Peace Now leader, why this absence, he shrugged his shoulders and said: 'Because I am not familiar with it.' "

As religious women peace activists see it, they are familiar with both cultures and can distinguish between these two cultures, but secular Jews are blind to Jewish culture. Religious women in the Left often mentioned that, when the secular leadership of the Peace Camp speak publicly, they often quote from Western literature but make no references to Jewish texts; religious women see this omission as not so much a matter of ignorance as a deliberate move away from Judaism, which they find insulting. They view the Left as insensitive to their Jewish way of life, because many of the peace activities and conferences are organized around leisure time. In Israel this is Friday afternoon and Saturday; Sunday is a workday. A halakhic way of life and the nature of Shabbat emerge as a difference between women peace activists, since Shabbat for religious women means a curtailing of most mundane activities. Yet beyond restrictions that Halakhah requires, Shabbat is a holy day of ritual activities that are family centered and are of utmost importance to religious women.

Miriam acknowledges that there is an issue for religious women who have to make choices about which peace activities they will join on Shabbat: "In addition to the Shabbat that I spent in Brussels at the women's peace conference with Palestinian women, I also spent a Shabbat in Ktziot [the site of an Israeli prison for Palestinians], and we had quite a large group of women and men. The organizers reacted very favorably to everything we did from prayers, the blessing of wine, and songs, until the afternoon, when they wanted to dismantle the camp and were shocked to hear that we could not move and could not even sit in the buses until the end of Shabbat. They very much liked the positive side of Shabbat, but the prohibitions it entailed made things more difficult. I really think that it boils down to a personal decision whether one joins peace activities on Shabbat, because on that occasion I felt a duty to be there on Shabbat in Ktziot, but I will not be in the coming conference in Shfayim or in Kfar Yasif, and I don't remember the many other events that are planned. I do think that there is a clash of values here. At times the value of the demonstration or event determines my choice; at other times the value of celebrating Shabbat in our community, in our home overrides and is favored over feeling isolated and lonely. It is not that I choose to be a Leftist or to be religious. I am both all the time. It is simply that when an event is planned for Shabbat one side has a preference over the other, and we must all choose."

Miriam's account reveals both a practical and a cultural divide between secular and religious; for many secular peace activists Shabbat rituals may seem exotic, strange, or a backward diaspora culture, depending on their views on religious rituals. But many of them may be ignorant of what a halakhic life means and, as Miriam noted, would not realize that their religious coactivists could not leave Ktziot before the formal end of Shabbat, which is in the evening and is marked by a specific time or the visibility of three stars in the sky. Scholars such as Myron Aronoff argue that the "segregation between ultra-orthodox, orthodox, and non-orthodox Jews is almost absolute in terms of residence, education, and service in the army (even among the national religious who serve in the army, most do so in homogeneously religious units), and marriage" (1989, xix). In the Jerusalem conference Judy addressed the social and cultural separation between secular and religious Jews in Israel that, in her view, has deepened in recent years and is topographically symbolized in segregated neighborhoods: "In the early years of the state there was a stronger sense of national unity and differences between a secular public, and an observant person was much less pronounced. We lived together, we resided in the same buildings, in the same neighborhoods, and shared neighborhoods have now become rare." Whether this view of the past is nostalgia or reality is less important than the fact that, even for religious Zionists and secular Israelis who do live side by side in the same towns or villages, and often in the same apartment buildings in cities, the divide exists. Residing in the same buildings does not mean that secular Israelis are familiar with the synagogue or a religious Shabbat beyond some general knowledge; often friendships do not cross these lines and almost come to a halt on Shabbat.

In some sense, then, there is a kind of an invisible *mechitzah* between religious and secular Jews that appears at Shabbat; the lighting of candles and communal prayer on Friday night signals the onset of a social and cultural separation that keeps apart religious and secular Israelis, even those who have close ties of friendship. Secular and religious women peace activists who stand in the vigil of the Women in Black go home to a different Shabbat; the black dress and gender provide solidarity among women, but a halakhic way of life means differences between them. In some respects, while they stand in the vigil religious women share space with women like Shulamit Aloni, but when they go home on Friday afternoon they have more in common with Daniela Weiss and *rabbanit* Levinger.

Shabbat, more than the rest of the week, brings about this divide as religious Jews focus on the synagogue and rituals, and it is a day that for them precludes watching television, listening to the radio, traveling, or any form of working that secular Jews may engage in. It is also a day of intracommunity relations for religious people, a day of socializing and sharing Shabbat meals. To engage in peace activities on Shabbat means that religious people perform rituals in the company of secular people, who are spectators, as Miriam noted. However politely or rudely secular activists may react to Shabbat rituals, the point is that these rituals are not part of their cultural practices; religious women engaged in peace activism on Shabbat, while keeping halakhic rules, see themselves as a minority within a secular Peace Camp.

Because religious women peace activists see themselves as an excluded minority within the category "we women for peace," they share a peace space only partially. Some, like Hagit and Yael, see themselves as silenced or ignored. They and women like Miriam, who ask, "Where do we, religious women for peace, place ourselves on this broad range in Israel's political spectrum?" reveal a constant collective dread of a threat to the group's existence and to its religious way of life, even when there are no specific events to trigger it. When something actually happens, such as a peace conference on Shabbat, it becomes incorporated in this sense of dread felt by religious people and supports the collective anxieties experienced by them and other groups that see themselves as numerically or socially marginalized in Israel.

Collective anxieties are nurtured by a sense that a group's most elemental concerns are disregarded or ignored by those in power. Rachel, one of the panelists in the Jerusalem conference, told the women about her experience at a conference that took place in the United States, which she contrasted with what she saw as the disregard for religious activists in Israel: "Last year, we were in a conference in New York that included representatives of the PLO. The conference was organized under the auspices of Columbia University. The person in charge was an orthodox rabbi, and there were no planned activities on Shabbat. The plenary meeting was on Friday afternoon, and the organizers did not allow for non-Jews as well to have any activities on Shabbat. We resumed at the end of Shabbat. The food at the reception was all kosher, as was the wine. I felt as if a miracle had happened; Messiah has come [yemot hamashiech]. I asked myself: 'When will I be so fortunate to experience it in Israel? I don't think that it was easy, but since the activities took place in the public eye of American Jews the organizers knew that they would be in trouble if they gave a public forum to a conference that included the PLO but was insensitive to Jewish concerns. They knew that they had to be careful not to give this kind of a message. They made every effort to work it out so that both groups would be included."

A Religious Minority, a Secular Majority: Who Owns Public Culture?

In the larger existential anxiety—the survival of the state, shared by many Israelis on the Left and on the Right—are micro-anxieties concerning the survival of groups within the larger national collective. The sense of marginalization in the secular Peace Camp noted by religious peace activists is lodged in this wider Israeli context. Yet, despite the fact that the numbers favor secular Jews, they too are worried about their way of life; from their perspective it is the broad category "religious people" (datiim), which they see as competing for the nature of public life in Israel. They perceive the datiim as having political power that is disproportionate to its numbers. Both secular and religious Israeli Jews, in fact, are threatened by what they see as the other group's wish to impose its beliefs on them, to silence them culturally and restrict their actions in the public and domestic spheres.

Secular Israeli Jews fear the encroachment of Jewish halakhic rules into public life, from restrictions on public activities on Shabbat to the food that can be served in restaurants; they already face an invasion into the domestic realm in marriage and divorce laws and mundane issues such as the kind of food they can buy in stores to cook at home, which precludes nonkosher food.

In January 1993 a group of secular peace activists met in Tel Aviv on Shabbat for a social lunch without the religious comembers of the group. This was not an act of exclusion but, rather, a reflection of separate Shabbat activities. Because the religious activists were absent, however, the conversation turned to the conflicts between the two communities. Yohai, one of the leaders of the peace group and a social science scholar, said to me that I should plan to come back and study the next important struggle that would take place in Israel: "The real struggle in this country is not between Israelis and Palestinians and not between ashkenazim and mizrahim but between secular and religious Jews. When the peace issue is settled, the real fight, which is obscured now by other problems, will surface. This will be a vicious fight because it will be a fight for the character and identity of Israel."

On Friday, May 7, 1993, *Yediot Ahronot* published an interview with two secular authors, Ephraim Sidon and Yosi Aboulaphia, that reveals some of the existential anxieties of secular Jews in Israel. The authors had recently published a book of fiction for children that deals with relations between secular and religious Israeli Jews, and the interviewer, Amalia Argaman Barnea, asked them: "You wanted very badly to hurt the feelings of religious people *[datiim]*?" Sidon responded: "I don't want to hurt religious people but I don't want them to hurt me. This is not an antireligious book. This book, I emphasize, is against the passivity of secular people. I have nothing against religious people. It is their right to achieve whatever they want through political means. But if someone pulls my ear and I don't say anything—this is my problem. As a secular person I constantly become more cowardly, but basically I am against all coercion. My parents raised me in an ideological Laborite home, and I belonged to the [Left] Hashomer Hatzair youth movement. I love the Bible, and my favorite subject in high school was Talmud—that is, until a teacher said to me that to study Talmud I need to put a skullcap on my head. That makes me angry because it means religious coercion. Secular and religious will never compromise because the secular will never say: 'OK. I will eat a little bit kosher and you will eat a bit nonkosher, *traifa*. The red lines are marked by the religious, the compromise has to come from us, and the erosion [of rights] is always in my direction. An ultra-orthodox, *haredi,* person can live among seculars and aside from the fact that a miniskirt might upset him, no one will harm him. A friend of mine, B. Michael, is a religious man who lives near Mea Shearim [an ultra-orthodox neighborhood]. How often do you think the air was let out from his wheels? And why can a Lubavitch Hassid come and talk to my son's class, but I cannot come to a religious school?"

In this account it is a secular Jew who sees himself excluded, marginalized, and even physically threatened, if not directly at least vicariously through his friend. The religious person, according to Sidon, has the right to go to secular school to proselytize, while he, Sidon, cannot go to religious school and express his views. Like religious women peace activists, Sidon feels excluded and imposed upon; for him, as for women peace activists, home is where ideas are formed. A secular home as well is held as the source of ethical values, and Sidon sees his childhood as formative in his defense of a secular public life. While religious women peace activists talk about the absence of Jewish tradition from the lives of secular Israelis, this is not necessarily the way secular people see it.

Clearly, Israelis are aware of the fact that beyond the ratio between secular and religious, there are political deals made by every Israeli government with religious parties, even with the non-Zionist ultraorthodox parties, in which support for the large secular party, whether it is Likud or Labor, is exchanged for a number of concessions, including religious legislation. According to scholars such as Charles Liebman, this political exchange system needs to be monitored and balanced, because "excessive demands in the area of religious legislation threaten them [religious politicians] with public backlash whose shadow, even now, looms on the horizon. The religious parties are aware of their minority position in Israeli society and are anxious to avoid confrontations with the nonreligious majority at both the political and the social level—a confrontation they can only lose" (1993, 284). Secular Israelis (including peace activists) fear that they will be coerced to lead a halakhic life because the public sphere will be determined by deals driven by political ambitions of individuals and parties.[8]

Each community, the secular and the religious, feels that it is on the margins of Israeli society, expressing anxieties of powerlessness in a public culture defined by the other. It was not surprising that the fragility of peace solidarity was revealed in Tel Aviv in 1993 as it was revealed in the Jerusalem conference. In Jerusalem the religious women voiced their anxieties and fears: in Tel Aviv it came from the other side. With the religious members absent, the support and affirmation for the seculars' views were resounding. Stories were told of attempts to impose a religious, halakhic way of life on secular Israeli Jews, and the group of secular peace activists who gathered for a Shabbat lunch, all of whom live in Tel Aviv, agreed that it was still relatively free from the kinds of strictures that characterized Jerusalem, what some people called its ultraorthodox stifling atmosphere. The consensus was that many secular Jews were leaving Jerusalem because it had become an oppressive city for secular Israelis.

A Partial Solidarity: Whom Do We Demonstrate With?
Whom Do We Pray With?

Women's comments in the Jerusalem conference in 1990 about their sense of exclusion in the Peace Camp mirrors profound conflicts that rock from within a society already shaken up from without. Rachel, one of the panelists, said: "As religious women and men in the Left, it is quite tough for us. But I think that from a practical perspective the Left's disrespect for Shabbat and the sanctity of Judaism cuts the very branch on which the Peace Camp sits. Because the reality is that there are many, many people, including some who do not identify themselves as religious, who do not drive on Shabbat and who don't light a fire on Shabbat. They may watch television or go to a soccer game; they may do many things. But Shabbat is Shabbat somewhere in their hearts. It therefore frightens me that the argument in the Left is that it is convenient to have activities on Shabbat because it is the only free day and it is important that the activity will get publicity in the 9 P.M. news on television. And therefore it is imperative to break the sanctity of Shabbat to desecrate Shabbat. In this shortsighted act there is an absence of long-term thinking of the future of the Jewish people, and the Left comes out the loser. The practical aspect of connecting to a larger Jewish public comes at the price of making our lives a bit more complicated by avoiding Left activities so that we do not desecrate Shabbat."

Religious women peace activists reveal that in addition to the Middle East conflict and the question of occupation, Israeli society struggles with internal fractions and discords. The cloak of existential anxieties that hangs over Israel's relations with its Arab neighbors and with Palestinians also spreads over relations between various groups within the state. Anxiety meets (real) fears in ways that often sharpen internal friction, such as those between secular and religious, so that each comes to view the conflict as a matter of the survival of its way of life. To Israelis and to outsiders who are familiar with Israel's divided political life, the women's dilemma expresses tensions between two collectives: "we secular" and "we religious." Each becomes a meaningful collective when the two engage in a dialogue over public culture in Israel, which at times takes on adversarial dimensions that overshadow other solidarities such as "we peace activists."

The 1990 women's conference in Jerusalem expressed, in debates about the nature of God and Torah, the fierce struggles between the Left and Right within religious Zionism about Palestinian rights and the future of the West Bank and the Gaza Strip. As a women's conference, however, it also brought forth issues of gender and of the paradox of female unity ceaselessly constructed and differences that constantly intrude on women's solidarity. Categories such as gender, religion, and political positions are pliable and shifting rather than fixed, so that whenever any of these are employed to provide unity and solidarity they can do so only partially. Religious women employ gender to emphasize a unique female contribution to the peace process; at the same time, they also establish the limits of the category "we women," as Miriam phrased it, to describe the position religious women take between the secular Left and the religious Right, by standing between women like Aloni and those like Weiss. Religious women for peace reject the secularism of the Peace Camp and strongly object to the settlement movement of religious Zionists on the Right, making it difficult to forge women's solidarity that does not become fragile on each side. The Jerusalem conference displayed a paradox of women's shared space and a divide, a *mechitzah,* that separates them. There is a divide between religious women for peace and secular women with whom they share a peace position but with whom they cannot pray. But the synagogue also does not provide grounds for solidarity among women. There is a divide between religious women for peace and religious women in Gush Emunim who hold a Greater Israel position but with whom women like Judy and Miriam may pray together metaphorically or literally. But there is yet another divide: while they can stand side by side with Daniela Weiss in the synagogue, they cannot share space with men in the religious Left with whom they do share a political position of coexistence with Palestinians.

A shared peace position thus exposes a range of conflicts and at times profound disagreements among women peace activists. Gender, which often provides the glue of unity, is occasionally seen by some women as irrelevant in light of other, more meaningful political alliances. The category "we women for peace" in the Israeli-Jewish community is, as I note in the next chapter, shaken by mizrahi women as they challenge what they perceive as ashkenazi blindness to mizrahi life experience in Israel.

CHAPTER 4 · East Confronts West: What the Left Eye of Israel Does Not See

*As long as Israel defines itself culturally as a Western
country it rejects its Eastern side. As a people we were born
here in the East. For generations Jews in the diaspora have
repeated Judah Halevy's words, "My heart is the East and I
live at the edge of the West," but today many Israelis think:
"My heart is in the West but I live in the East."*

　　　　　　　　　　　　　　　—Katya Gibel-Azoulay

*Most Ashkenazi women are against the oppression of
Orientals, only they do not really believe that Orientals are,
in fact, oppressed.*

　　　　　　　　　　　　　　　—Vicki Shiran

Mizrahi Women for Peace Raise a Question of Solidarity

In July 1990 about 130 women for peace and 5 men from the Peace Camp gathered in Tel Aviv to participate in a conference entitled "Peace and Identities in Israeli Society: The Place of Mizrahi Women in Political Activities." This conference, jointly sponsored by Reshet Nashim Leshalom and a women's studies program at Tel Aviv University, invited a panel of mizrahi (Oriental) women to explore why there was such a small number of them in peace groups.[1] Instead, both panelists and mizrahi participants changed the focus and talked about a history of ashkenazi injustices to mizrahim. While affirming a peace position, the women rejected a solidarity based on gender and peace that informed groups such as Reshet Nashim Leshalom, claiming that the groups' leadership and structure is ashkenazi and exclusionary. Mizrahi women's rejection of solidarity in gendered peace activism revealed an Israeli social and cultural divide: Westernness was closely associated by panelists with ashkenazi wealth, affluence, and social and cultural privilege; Easternness was seen as a rich but disparaged culture and as associated with mizrahi poverty. Mizrahi women in the Tel Aviv conference linked their refusal to join women's peace groups to a divide between mizrahi and ashkenazi communities; they forged a different kind of solidarity, a collective of "we mizrahim" as they raised issues of discrimination—that is, economic, political, and cultural inequalities within the Israeli-Jewish community.[2]

In broader terms the Tel Aviv mizrahi women for peace insisted that a discourse on justice for Palestinians raises questions of the meaning of justice for women's peace groups. Panelists and participants argued that justice is indivisible and universal (it applies equally to all groups) within and beyond nations; justice to Palestinians is linked to justice within the Israeli-Jewish community. Panelists noted, however, that for the Israeli Left and for women's peace groups, justice is divisible and partial: it has different meanings for their concern with Palestinians and their concern with mizrahim.[3] Similarly, panelists said, feminism is concerned with gender equality but uninterested in justice for mizrahim. For mizrahi women who support both gender equality and coexistence with Palestinians, therefore, neither peace nor gender can be taken for granted as a ground for collective action with ashkenazi women.

At the conference panelists insisted that the very question of why there is no adequate representation of mizrahi women in peace groups needed first to confront the fact that Jewish society is divided into two communities, mizrahi and ashkenazi, marked by inequality; in addition, they called attention to not just discrimination against mizrahim but what they considered a denial of discrimination by ashkenazi women. Gila, one of the panelists, said: "It is sheer nonsense to claim that ashkenazi and mizrahi women are natural allies in the feminist struggle. As a mizrahi woman with consciousness and as a feminist, I have a problem. As a woman and a human being, I need today a more encompassing social awareness; I realized that the women's movement deals only with one dimension, with women's oppression by men. The women's movement in Israel was established by ashkenazi women, who shaped it, and I think that they never had a serious discussion of their relation to mizrahim. Ashkenazi women are 100 percent against the oppression of mizrahim—if it exists. But, they say, where is there discrimination? I am always shocked that they don't see any; they simply do not see it."

Mizrahi women identified themselves at the conference as holding both feminist and peace and coexistence positions. But these political positions did not transcend the ashkenazi discrimination to forge a ground for collective action among women. Panelists and participants questioned whether there was equal sororal space for them within the Peace Camp or within women's groups. A historiography of mizrahi experiences permeated the discussion, and accounts of the past gave further substance and meaning to the panelists' challenge that women's peace groups are inhospitable to mizrahi women for peace. Remembering the past, women brought to light the gap between Israel's ideology of *mizug galuyot* (ingathering of exiles) and the immigrants' experience of discrimination.

The women at the conference talked about a mizrahi experience of exclusion that began when they arrived in the 1950s as immigrants to the newly established state of Israel. Though at that time ashkenazim were dominant in Israel both numerically and politically, the large numbers of mizrahi immigrants changed the numerical distribution. But the panelists argued that the large mizrahi immigration did not alter the initial political imbalance, which was manifested by a persistent exclusion of Eastern culture. Women in the Tel Aviv conference talked about discrimination *(aflaya)* far beyond mere economics, as they raised issues of Israeli identity and the absence of mizrahi culture from this identity. Vered, one of the panelists, said: "Israeli society is Israeli in name only. The fact is that there are Israelis, and there are mizrahim. I—and I can speak for many of my women friends— do not feel that we belong. We feel alienated, *menukarot*. We can have, theoretically at least, common goals with ashkenazi women, and I include peace and even what you call feminism in it. But cooperation never happens. The first encounters bring a sense of alienation in these groups—and I speak of the Left in general, including women's groups."

Women panelists in the Tel Aviv conference established a collective of "we mizrahim" to talk to a collective of the Left and to women's peace groups. The panelists' collective was forged in a shared experience of persistent inequality that stretched beyond the Peace Camp; their comments on ashkenazi women's blindness to an endemic discrimination parallel similar comments by mizrahim in ways that transcend gender and class differences and allowed the panelists and the participants to forge a mizrahi collective. Israeli scholars such as Sammy Smooha note that, despite gains made by mizrahim, "inequality is an unrelenting source of deprivation for Oriental Jews in Israel. Its political potency stems precisely from the national consensus against ethnic inequality and yet the failure to eliminate it. . . . Orientals feel relative deprivation and witness the inability of the system to satisfy their needs and to bring them up to par with their Ashkenazi brothers" (1993, 325).

Like the women at the Tel Aviv conference, Smooha identifies both the inequality and the denial of it. While he argues that the denial itself perpetuates the condition, some mizrahim speak of their emotions of anger against ashkenazi refusal to see what mizrahim consider injustices inflicted upon them in Israel. There is also a strong resonance of these themes in conversations that Amos Oz had with mizrahi men in Beit Shemesh, a town populated mostly by mizrahim, and the women who spoke at the Tel Aviv conference. The men who spoke to Oz live in a development town, not in one of the center cities, and many of them were working-class mizrahim. The panelists in Tel Aviv were middle-class and upper-middle-class professional mizrahi women who lived in the three major cities of Israel. One of the things these mizrahi women and men share is a view that, despite the economic gains of some mizrahim, Israel has failed to eliminate inequality. A man in Beit Shemesh said: "See what shame is: they gave us houses, they gave us menial work, they gave us education and took away our self-respect" (Oz 1983, 32). Another man said to Oz: "I would forgive you [ashkenazim] everything except my dignity, my parents' dignity and the dignity of my ethnic group, *eda*" (35). The women's account in the Tel Aviv conference and the comments offered by men in Beit Shemesh highlight a shared view of a pervasive ashkenazi blindness to the divide that constitutes both economic discrimination and an exclusion of mizrahi culture, because it is seen as not a (Western) culture and because it is perceived as a wrong (Middle Eastern) culture.

In mizrahi discourse on the Israeli concept of "one nation," the idea of solidarity with ashkenazim is rejected. The panelists' refusal to forge a sororal solidarity with ashkenazi women parallels a similar refusal by a mizrahi man in Beit Shemesh, who said to Oz: "You want to put an end to hatred? First you [ashkenazim] must come and say nicely: 'Sorry. We have sinned, we are guilty, we have betrayed'" (ibid., 41). While Smooha uses the term *ashkenazi brothers,* the panelists in Tel Aviv argue that, despite the common goal of peace and coexistence with Palestinians, for the time being there is no sisterhood or brotherhood with ashkenazim; the refusal is lined with what these mizrahi women and men see as ashkenazi denial of social inequalities and cultural erasure.

The women in the Tel Aviv conference also confronted the state as they talked about a denigration of Eastern culture that began with the first encounter of mizrahi immigrants with their homeland. Panelists described the state's demand that mizrahim shed their cultural identity: They talked about a persistent exclusion of Eastern culture from the construction of Israeli identity; they spoke of an exclusion of mizrahi culture that is more difficult to confront than economic discrimination because it is less immediately obvious; unlike income, it is harder to quantify and identify.

One of the difficulties in locating the exclusion of mizrahi culture from Israeli identity is because it has never really been clear in public discourse what an Israeli identity was—or is. It does not, for example, include its Israeli-Palestinian citizens, and it is not strictly Jewish, because it severed itself from adherence to Jewish laws, Halakha. In a deliberate rebellion the pioneers and founders of the state rejected the Eastern European Jewish identity of the shtetl, a symbol of ashkenazi diaspora, oppression, and Jewish parochialism; instead, they constructed an invented blend of Jewish secular/socialist life of a new liberated and liberating, autonomous, mostly secular, mostly ashkenazi "Israeli," in which even the term *sabra* (native-born Israeli) took on these attributes. Within the Israeli-Jewish community there was never an explicit position on how ashkenazi (or for that matter how secular) this identity was, or should be, and how mizrahim (or religious Jews) were expected to assume such an identity. Yet women's peace conferences reveal that for various groups the ashkenazi/secular center defines Israeli identity, leaving them on the margins; groups such as religious Jews, discussed earlier, or mizrahim, as the Tel Aviv conference indicates, are anxious about their collective existence in a public culture that seems to exclude them. Moreover, the question of cultural authenticity came up in the Tel Aviv conference as well. Religious women for peace distinguish themselves from secular women, whom they see as expressing Western/humanist rather than Jewish/humanist values. In the same way, mizrahi women at the Tel Aviv conference distance themselves from ashkenazi women, whom they view as holding an ashkenazi/Western (foreign) culture and ignoring a more indigenous mizrahi/Eastern culture.

Mizrahi women described a sense of alienation that is lodged in a wide range of social, economic, political, and cultural inequalities. While mizrahi poverty was one of the key issues raised in the Tel Aviv conference, the sense of alienation was often constructed in terms of the exclusion of mizrahi culture from Israel's public life. Panelists stated that both social discrimination and cultural exclusion are not a thing of the past, an early phase in an immigrant experience, but, rather, a present-day fact of life for mizrahim who were born in Israel (sabras) who should feel at home but instead experience alienation.[4]

The question of what is divisible or indivisible underlined the discourse in Tel Aviv. Against the claim of unity among women for peace (gender, peace, and solidarity should be indivisible), panelists and participants constructed solidarity and social justice as indivisible. On this ground they forged a mizrahi collective. On this ground of the indivisibility of solidarity and social justice, mizrahi women saw the attempt to recruit them to women's peace groups as mere talk of solidarity, what Gila described as "a claim that ashkenazi and mizrahi women are natural allies," but with an absence of acts that would transform this talk into political facts; panelists noted the absence of acts of solidarity with mizrahi people, such as working in, and for, poor neighborhoods and development towns.

At the Tel Aviv conference—a public event—women established the political fact of discrimination and revealed equality in Israeli society to be mere talk. Solidarity, according to mizrahi women, means not only ideologies of equality but certain acts (of social justice), such as the elimination of economic, cultural, and social exclusions; above all, it requires a collective acknowledgment of discrimination, a refusal to deny it exists. In Gila's words, it would mean leaving behind ashkenazi women's question: "Where is there discrimination?" and acting to confront it.

What Lies beyond Discrimination?

The issues that women confronted in the Tel Aviv conference were much more serious than discrimination. Panelists talked not only of the denigration of mizrahi culture but of hidden racism (casting pejorative features on people for no other reason than their being members of a particular group—in this case, mizrahim).[5] Panelists and participants argued that the very language used to describe mizrahim, such as "primitive" (without culture) and "violent" (an Eastern inferior/wrong culture), cast pejorative images on people based on their membership in a particular group. The phrase "hidden racism" *(gizanut smuya)* was used by mizrahi women when they refused solidarity with ashkenazi women. Smadar, one of the panelists, said: "As far as I am concerned, the issue addressed in this conference, 'the place of mizrahi women in political activities,' is a false one. Reshet, the group that sponsored this conference, and other women's groups, are like all the Left groups; they are ashkenazi groups. Me, I am a mizrahi woman. I don't want to explain or define the meaning of mizrahi. I am a mizrahi woman. My response to you and to your question—why mizrahi women don't join you—is that you need to talk among yourselves, you need to examine your stereotypes, you need to explore the alienation between the two communities and to be honest about the hidden opportunities available to one group but denied to the other. I cannot tell you why mizrahi women don't come to political activities. What I can tell you is that you need to talk among yourselves about your hidden racism toward us. The exploring is yours to do." The fine line between denigration of mizrahi culture and hidden racism that was expressed in the Tel Aviv conference reflects a broader mizrahi experience. In Beit Shemesh a man gave a local voice to this generalized pejoration of mizrahim when he said that, no matter how badly ashkenazi people in the kibbutz behave, they always end up being "the beautiful Israel and we are the criminals. Hoodlums. Mob. The ugly Israel" (Oz 1983, 40). The women's construction of a "we mizrahim" collective encompasses mizrahi men (like the men in Beit Shemesh) and women who were not physically in the Tel Aviv conference yet were part of it, because they all face this hidden racism.

Different Centers (Women's Groups) but the Same (Mizrahi) Margins

At the Tel Aviv conference mizrahi poverty was defined within a power relationship of privilege that spilled over to peace groups. Dalia, the moderator, said: "One of the mistakes of the Peace Camp—and I define the Peace Camp as those who aspire for a political solution based on mutual recognition between the two nations and two states for two nations side by side in peace and security—was a great reluctance to link the two topics of peace and social injustice." Women questioned the meaning of justice and equality in the Peace Camp and noted that the Left emphasizes justice for Palestinians but lacks an interest in justice for mizrahim within Israeli society. They noted the absence of mizrahim in positions of decision making and leadership within the Peace Camp and in women's groups. In their discussions they showed how groups on the margins that espouse ideologies of equality can at the same time produce within themselves centers of power that create internal inequalities and privileges. In the case of the Israeli Left panelists saw a political fact that mizrahi women and men for peace are absent (and in their view excluded) from the leadership of the Peace Camp. Ashkenazi women occupy the center of the margins (women's peace groups), while mizrahi were relegated to the margins of these margins.

At the Tel Aviv conference mizrahi women insisted that a fundamental change has to take place in women's peace groups to make it possible for mizrahi women for peace to engage in a dialogue with ashkenazi women from a position other than the margin. Gila said: "I think that solidarity with ashkenazi women can happen but on condition that they become more open. Mizrahi women and men in Israel are, through no fault of their own, at the bottom of the class system and are the weaker group. To have a dialogue, I demand a stretching of the hand, that ashkenazi women must reach out so I can see that a women's group organizes conferences to learn about the problem of mizrahim in Israel. This is what I did when I wanted to learn about the Palestinian issue—I went to them. I went to them to understand, to learn, to listen to their folklore, their way of talking about Jews, because as a Jew I have caused them suffering that was not their fault. I suggest that the ashkenazi women in Reshet—and I am convinced without researching it that most of them are ashkenazi, as they are in most of the peace groups—will sit down and with honesty, deep honesty, reflect and examine the issues. Then we will be able to be a multitude of women powerful and strong, mizrahim, ashkenazim, and Palestinians."

The Western Birthplace of Reshet

Brussels, the birthplace of the idea for Reshet, was seen by women panelists as a metaphor for the sense of marginalization of mizrahim in women's peace groups because it symbolizes ashkenazi preference for the West and a rejection of the East. The Brussels conference was initiated by a Belgian-Jewish ashkenazi couple, Simone and David Souskind, who have been active in bringing together Israelis and Palestinians for peace talks. An Israeli reporter described the gathering as a transnational event: "The participants, who came from Israel and the territories, as well as from Arab and European countries and the U.S., a handful of local and Arab journalists, and half a dozen PLO officials, listened for two and a half days to lengthy reports on conditions in the territories" (Sela 1989). But when word of the Israeli delegation to Brussels got around it turned out that not a single mizrahi woman was included. According to Katya Gibel-Azoulay, a political activist and an advocate for social justice for mizrahim in Israel, events then took an international turn: "The leader of a small but vociferous group, East for Peace, contacted the sponsor in Brussels and demanded the inclusion of mizrahi women. He charged that it was scandalous that a conference of this nature be held without any mizrahi presence and threatened to contact several prominent and influential Jewish families in France of North African background. After several international telephone conversations, one mizrahi woman, a professor at Haifa University, was added to the list" (1993, 4).

For the panelists who came to the Tel Aviv conference at the invitation of Reshet the story of Brussels is particularly linked to what mizrahi women described as a historic preference in Israel for the West (meeting in Europe) over the East ("Why not Spain?" some women asked), of ashkenazi dominance of the center, and of mizrahi placed at the margins. From the perspective of women peace activists who went to the conference in Brussels, however, the event looked a little different. They saw it, instead, as a successful breakthrough in a dialogue with Palestinian women, in which Israeli and Palestinian women forged a ground of sororal solidarity across national boundaries. Shulamit Aloni, now a minister in the government, highlighted gender solidarity as a transnational ground, when she said in her address to the Brussels conference: "We are no smarter than men. There are, however, things men don't know. They are fascinated by glory, they are ready to go to war because this is part of manhood. Those who stay behind and suffer are the women. They are left with the ashes [and] the graves of heroes" (Sela 1989).

For mizrahi women, however, Brussels was a conference from which they were excluded. What they saw was the omission of mizrahi women (partial justice) and a conference that failed to bridge the divide among Israeli-Jewish women concerned with peace (partial solidarity). For them the very trip to the West was punctuated by the absence of the East. The ground on which the conference in Brussels stood—the exclusion of mizrahi women, despite the last-minute addition of one mizrahi woman—provided another political fact of inequality for the Tel Aviv conference. Moreover, the choice to have a peace conference in Brussels (and not Madrid) was seen as a political act of ashkenazi peace activists who prefer the West to the East.

The East: No Culture, Wrong Culture

Renato Rosaldo's (1989) discussion of the ways in which groups get labeled as "people without culture" or people with a "lesser culture" reflects what panelists saw in the mizrahi immigrants in Israel. Panelists argued that, because mizrahim come from the Middle East, they were and are still seen in Israel as both people without culture (because they do not possess Western culture) and as people with a "lesser, inferior culture"—an Eastern, Arab, and undesirable culture. Vered said at the conference: "People prefer to see us not as having a rich cultural world but, rather, want us to go through hell to become so-called human, because the concept of mizrahi is linked to negative images."

The panelists' accounts of immigrants who were seen to have no culture and the wrong culture highlight a broader, ongoing debate on mizrahim in Israel in which the media, scholars, politicians, and various other commentators participate. Shlomo Swirski, an Israeli scholar, presents a position that parallels those expressed by the panelists. He notes the crucial part that the country's leaders played in the cultural struggle between the state and mizrahi immigrants; he speaks specifically on the role of Israel's first prime minister in the no culture/wrong culture approach to mizrahim: "Ben Gurion, speaking to the top command of the Israeli army in 1950, stated: 'Many of these immigrants come to us without the most elementary knowledge, without a trace of Jewish or human (!) education. There are two reasons for this. First, they are the product of a period of destruction, a period of world wars, a period of material and spiritual deterioration caused by a shake-up in all human institutions. Second, they come from dark, oppressed, and exploited countries'" (Swirski 1989, 27).[6]

Political leaders such as Ben-Gurion presented mizrahim with the double bind of not having a "culture" (Western) and having the "wrong culture" (Eastern). Smooha speaks of an Israeli construction of mizrahi culture as flawed and dangerous: "At least until the mid-1960s, Oriental [mizrahi] Jews were viewed as culturally inferior and threatening, and were also strongly pressured to assimilate. Later, in reaction to the cultural change Orientals have undergone, their protest, and the revival of ethnic pluralism in the United States, Ashkenazic attitudes have partially been mitigated. The Ministry of Education and Culture introduced the program of Oriental and Sephardic Heritage aimed to enrich the curriculum and Oriental history, literature, and folklore. The national television and radio channels were also opened to Oriental folk culture, which used to be considered low and kept underground" (1993, 321).

Virginia Dominguez joins the debate on mizrahi culture in Israeli society; she notes that the more recent acknowledgment of mizrahi history, culture, and folklore has been designated as mizrahi "heritage," while the word *culture* has been reserved for Euro/ashkenazi expression. She argues that this distinction manages in one stroke to both keep the hierarchy and appear to change it. These kinds of changes create, says Dominguez, "the illusion of cultural equality promoted, on the surface, by the relatively new official policy of legitimating cultural differences" (1989, 124). Mizrahi women at the Tel Aviv conference would probably not consider new approaches, such as that of the Ministry of Education and Culture's making space for mizrahi heritage, as more than mere talk. Such moves by the state were seen by the women as producing benign "ethnic" folklore without the "negatives." The no culture and wrong culture of mizrahim were now turned by the state into popularized, exotic, but assimilable ethnicity.

The Question of Ethnicity and Social Class

Ethnicity in Israel, in popular and scholarly productions, means only Eastern (mizrahi) but not Western (ashkenazi) Jewish roots. Accordingly, Israeli scholars who engage in the debate on the place of mizrahim in Israeli society speak of a link between "ethnicity" (Eastern roots) and social class (income) but have different interpretations regarding the nature of these links. Dan Horowitz and Moshe Lissak, Israeli sociologists, argue that one of the reasons for the absence of a strong class sense (e.g., working class) in Israel has to do with the fact that mizrahi immigrants tended to perceive economic differences not as class issues but as ethnic concerns. The sociologists note that, "when ethnic origins and socioeconomic status overlapped, people who came from Muslim countries responded to it in ethnic and not in class terms" (Horowitz and Lissak 1990, 131).

While Horowitz and Lissak indicate that the discrimination was essentially economic but that mizrahim perceived differences not as a class issue but as an ethnic concern, Swirski takes a different view, one that parallels the arguments made in the Tel Aviv conference. He proposes that it is the fact that mizrahim were seen to have no (Western) culture and the wrong (Eastern) culture that perpetuates economic inequality: "The ethnic division of labor is being reproduced by an ideological apparatus that presents the low social, political, and economic standing of the Orientals as a result not of the class nature of Israeli society but of the fact that they came from non-modern and culturally backward societies. In other words, it puts the blame for the low position of the Orientals on the Orientals themselves. This ideology stems both from the general European feeling of superiority over people of the Third World, which Ashkenazim share, and from the sense of superiority acquired by veteran Ashkenazim as the creators of the Zionist movement for Jewish political revival. This ideology has been elaborated by the Ashkenazi elite in Israel—from politicians and social scientists to educators and journalists" (Swirski 1989, 27).

An economic argument for the mizrahi secondary position in Israel holds the promise of social mobility; once mizrahim enter the middle or upper middle class, or the elite, the problem will go away. But the Tel Aviv panelists insisted that, beyond economics, discrimination has to do with mizrahi culture and is not so neatly remedied. It can also not be fixed, the women argued, because mizrahim do not want assimilation; what they want is equality as a cultural collective in Israeli society and a partnership in defining Israeli identity to include Easternness. Mizrahi women in Tel Aviv said that people who come from Muslim countries have an Eastern culture that they want to maintain, but, as they see it, this right has been systematically denied to them. Vered, a conference participant, said: "The steamroller of the melting pot has left its bruises not only on the first generation but on the second generation as well. As a result of the lack of familiarity with the mizrahi world in Israeli society, people associate mizrahi with backwardness, poverty, and environmental ugliness." For women panelists in Tel Aviv both social class (a large proportion of mizrahim in the working class and in poverty) and a deep sense of cultural alienation (of Eastern culture) combine in intricate ways to marginalize mizrahim, to turn them into "ethnics."

Easternness Excluded from Israeli Identity

Panelists in Tel Aviv argued that, in the case of mizrahim, Israeli identity defined itself by discrediting Eastern Jewish traditions as backward, inferior, and undesirable qualities, as opposed to an "Israeli" Western (by implication progressive, superior, and desirable) identity. Women talked about the impact of the melting pot position regarding mizrahim and the state's efforts, more openly in the early years, and more subtly ever since, to expunge Eastern identity from the immigrants in the hope that they take on an Israeli identity.

Some Israeli scholars express a similar view that the Israeli establishment actually engaged in such cultural distinctions and extinctions. They debate the East-West cultural identity of Israel and offer different understandings on these distinctions according to the value that they themselves place on Western culture. In 1969 Joseph Ben David, an Israeli sociologist, expressed the superiority of Western culture as a position that was embraced voluntarily not only by mizrahim but by the region as a whole: "I don't think that mizrahim want to give up the achievement of Israeli society. The fact that they identify with ashkenazim and do not want to be like the rest of the Middle East indicates that they want to become Westernized and do not want the rest of Israeli society to become Easterners. By the way, this Eastern and Arab region no longer identifies with the so-called Eastern values that I hear about. The region wants to advance European style economically and in education and is rebelling against the Eastern tradition" (90).

The panelists in Tel Aviv would not agree with scholars like Ben David. The women viewed such an identification with the West as imposed upon them and argued that mizrahim had to pay a price for it. Such identification, according to the panelists, required a painful mizrahi complicity in the silencing of Eastern culture and in becoming "ashkenazi." Women talked about the price paid for trying to comply with the pressure to agree, that "they no longer identify with so-called mizrahi values" and instead "identify with ashkenazim." Penina said: "For me as a Sephardi woman something happened to me in the feminist movement. I did go through a process of becoming ashkenazi. Part of it goes back to my childhood and my youth, when I was ashamed of my family name, which was very Sephardi. And much later I still only whispered to women: 'You know, I am really Sephardi.' 'What? You don't look like one.'" The pressure to deny mizrahi culture and the price that had to be paid for it was expressed by other participants in the Tel Aviv conference. Yet the women's position should not be taken as a gendered perception only of middle-class professional mizrahi women. It is shared by other mizrahim across gender and class lines who see the pressure to shed their mizrahi culture as an act that distances parents and offspring. This position was echoed in conversations Amos Oz had with mizrahi men in Beit Shemesh. A mizrahi man said to Oz: "You should ask, who taught the children early on to mock their parents, to mock their elders, to mock religion and [our] customs?" (1983, 30). In Tel Aviv panelists and participants talked about what it meant for mizrahim to fit into an Israeli identity in the early years of statehood and into a construction of the "ingathering of exiles." The state aimed to give all immigrant communities not only a home in a Jewish state but to endow them with a new identity as well.

Old (Diaspora) Identity and New (Israeli) Identity

The construction of a new identity for Jewish immigrants (in this case for mizrahim) has antecedents in the early years of the Yishuv. For the Jewish immigrants of the prestate period a new identity was linked to existential anxieties and the desire to ensure the collective Jewish survival; survival required not only a homeland but also a refashioning of identities. For the pioneers *(halutzim)* who came to build a homeland during the Yishuv days, identity was not fixed but replaceable. Accordingly, they rejected Jewish Eastern European cultural traits.

There was, as I noted earlier, an ideology that claimed to endow Jews with a new "positive" identity under the belief that an undesirable Eastern European, parochial, "shtetl" identity could be discarded, like an old coat, upon arrival on the shores of the homeland. This faith of the early pioneers that they could actually give birth to new collective and individual "selves" also permeated their position that the new mizrahi immigrant could, and should, do the same. While this obviously is not the only ground for the exclusion of mizrahi culture from Israeli identity, ashkenazi pioneers did consider identities as "things" that people could step out of and leave behind, as they left their homes and communities in Eastern Europe or the Middle East.

While the pioneers refashioned themselves from what they considered, in socialist terminology, as an unproductive and oppressed people into "productive," free, and mostly secular Jews, it was less clear how the new identities would be acquired by mizrahi communities, or what exactly was entailed in "becoming" Israelis. For mizrahi immigrants, becoming Israeli meant denying Eastern culture and embracing a new identification with the West.

With statehood, however, an identity of a "new Jew" of the pioneer Zionist ideology was no longer sufficient. What became important as Israel faced massive immigration was an Israeli identity that all immigrants, including Holocaust survivors, were expected to embrace. While the state recognized the Holocaust and commemorated it by making various public spaces for it in the Yad Vashem museum in a national remembrance day, Yom Hashoa, it ignored the actual experience of survivors. Holocaust survivors' experience symbolized, in an extreme form, everything that the pioneers believed must be discarded (powerlessness in the form of diaspora). Survivors evoked collective existential anxieties and were a reminder of what the founders of Israel sought to distance themselves from—collective Jewish powerlessness; the powerlessness associated with Jewish diaspora in the collective memory threatened the still budding Israeli identity.

The wish for a new collective Jewish identity that marked the Herzlian concept of a safe homeland and that had taken on a socialist formation by the pioneers was strong in the newly emerging state and played a part in silencing the trauma of Holocaust survivors. Zipporah, the daughter of such survivors, who was born and grew up in Tel Aviv, said: "Most of our friends and neighbors were also Holocaust survivors. I did not think that there was anything peculiar about them. Everyone we knew had nightmares, woke up screaming, and cried for no apparent reason. But it was an iron law in Israel not to hark back to the past, to think only of the future. Of course there were public commemorations, an endless stream of commemorations. In school we soon learned everything about the Holocaust. What we were remembering and mourning were the dead. Nobody gave a thought to the damage being inflicted on the living" (qtd. in Sichrovsky 1991, 51–52). Batya, also a daughter of Holocaust survivors, said: "What I hated and dreaded most when I was a child was summertime. It was a time when the numbers on my mother's arm would be there for all to see and people would know that she was a survivor and was one of the despised people. People like my parents were despised in Israel, and I was ashamed of them." She noted, however, that mizrahim see their own collective exclusion from Israeli culture but do not see the similar exclusion in the experience of Holocaust survivors.

An alliance of immigrants against the state's exclusion of mizrahi culture and the suppression of the Holocaust experience from public culture did not emerge. Instead, rivalry and animosity between the two immigrant communities were occasionally expressed in conversations with women like Batya, who are angry that mizrahim see only their exclusion and ignore the experience of ashkenazi refugees. From a mizrahi point of view the rivalry takes on the opposite direction, as some mizrahim see Holocaust survivors as a privileged group in Israeli culture. In Beit Shemesh a mizrahi man expressed this animosity when he said: "If an old Polish man will write in Yiddish his Holocaust memories, his mistakes will be taken care of, it will be nicely arranged and put in a book. But if I would come and bring from my memory stories straight from life, how we were exploited, how we were mocked, I will be told: go home. This is not Hebrew, this is dirty, this is bitter, you use offensive language" (qtd. in Oz 1983, 40–41).

The absence of solidarity among immigrants may derive from the fact that, while a survivor identity was no more encouraged than a mizrahi one, it was possible for survivors to become part of the ashkenazi community and therefore "melt" into the desired, if elusive, Israeli identity. The refusal to agree to women's solidarity in the Tel Aviv conference is grounded in a mizrahi exclusion from this identity; the panelists noted that a cultural price was exacted not only from adults, who were stripped of their culture and their past experiences, but from their children as well. Mizrahi offspring (and children of survivors) were ashamed of their parents, of their kin, of their ancestors. Vicki Shiran, an Israeli scholar, recounts the price of shame that cultural exclusion exacted from her: "The most problematic aspect of this process at the time was the need to despise Orientals [mizrahi]—to despise my parents, my grandparents, many people whom I loved—and to view them as directly responsible for their inferior status in Israeli society. . . . It was obvious that I and others like me would have to go on being 'Orientals' for a long time." Shiran describes her desire to transform her mizrahi identity into an Israeli one: "Obviously, I hated my 'Oriental' identity. From the day I learned to tell the difference, I yearned to assume the identity of an 'Israeli'; naturally, I longed to resemble its true representative, the Ashkenazi male. In this context, my womanhood was a privilege that might relieve my inferior 'Oriental' status: by marrying an Ashkenazi, I could rise in class. Among many Oriental families, marriage to an Ashkenazi male was considered a formula for success, the breaking of a social barrier" (1991, 305).

A Genetic Solution to Cultural Unity: Intermarriage

Shiran's observation that a woman's marriage to an ashkenazi was one way to resolve social and cultural exclusion was also expressed by women at the Tel Aviv conference but from different perspectives. Some women took issue with intermarriage between ashkenazim and mizrahim as evidence of social and cultural equality and a sign that mizrahim are actually making it in Israeli society. Yael, one of the panelists in Tel Aviv, said: "We [Israeli Jews] have an ideology that we are all one people, *am echad,* and we really need the mizrahim because we are surrounded by enemies. But in this ideology of 'we are one people' there is a delegitimization of any mizrahi organization. They have all been perceived as opposition, as something wrong. We are being told a myth that the gap between mizrahim and ashkenazim has closed. But upon close examination of numbers we see that the educational and the economic gaps have not only not closed but widened. We are being told: 'But there are so many mixed marriages.' I think 24 percent. Even if it is between mizrahim [and not among different mizrahi communities] and ashkenazim, it is a very low percentage, and it takes place mostly in the middle class. In the upper class marriage is mostly between ashkenazim, and in the lower it is among mizrahim. Intermarriage takes place in a small segment of the population." Moreover, panelists argued that "mixed marriages," far from redressing the cultural exclusion, may further legitimate the negation and denigration of mizrahi culture.

In addressing the question of intermarriage, panelists' comments join a larger Israeli debate in which scholars and other commentators participate. Smooha, while taking a mostly critical view of the claim that intermarriage is a way to achieve equality, notes that "mixed marriages comprise nearly one-quarter of all marriages" (1993, 323). Yet panelists' accounts revealed that the very cultural concept of "mixed marriages" is both an acknowledgment of ethnic gaps and a perpetuation of difference highlighted by the notion of "mixed." Similarly, scholars such as Shiran argue that differences between people are affirmed, not denied, in the act of intermarriage. She notes that differences are underscored when "Ashkenazi families perceived Oriental women as warm and subservient creatures, whose assumed capacity for serving Ashkenazi males compensated, to some degree, for their inferior status. A common Yiddish proverb illustrates this point: 'A Frenk is a chaye; a Frenkina, a mechaye' [an Oriental is a beast; an Oriental woman is a bliss]" (Shiran 1991, 305). Shiran notes that such views and the promise of a mixed marriage as a road to Israeli identity makes mizrahi women complicitous in the erasure of their culture.

Mizrahi women in the conference did not view intermarriage as a panacea. Yael saw intermarriage as one way of silencing mizrahi culture. Mizrahim, according to her, are not allowed to have a distinct identity in Israeli society: "For the Palestinians within Israel there is hope because they are cognizant of their situation, and they organize, and they struggle. But the moment mizrahim organize, people say: 'Shame on you. That is not nice, that is unseemly behavior.' Until mizrahi women and men take on the struggle there will be no social change. The last wave of [Ethiopian and Russian] immigration is staring in the face of all those who kept insisting that 'the gap has closed, everything is fine, we intermarry, we are one people.' All of a sudden it transpires that Ethiopians are not getting what the Russians are getting."

Panelists saw claims that intermarriage is a sign of equality dissolve into mere talk when claims of equality were placed side by side with actual state policies that displayed differential treatment of Ethiopians and Russians. Intermarriage thus had no substance as a fact of equality for mizrahim. Swirski takes a similar position when he notes that "Israeli politicians and social scientists alike tend to stress the importance of intermarriage as a means of 'erasing the barriers between the ethnic groups' and of creating 'a one and unified people.' The rise in the proportion of interethnic marriages, from 9 percent to 20 percent at the present, has been hailed as a clear sign that the 'ethnic problem is disappearing.' . . . What lies behind the celebration of intermarriage is, rather, a belief that it can lead to the 'uplifting' of the oriental partner, either through the transfer of the genes of the Ashkenazi partner to the couple's children, or through the influence of the 'cultured environment' that the Ashkenazi partner imposes in the home" (1989, 22).

Swirski's observation of marriage as a cultural elevation of the mizrahi spouse highlights yet another aspect of the debate—that marriage is seen by some Israelis as a genetic/cultural way to make the "ethnic problem disappear." Israeli political leaders such as Moshe Sharet participated in the debate regarding mizrahi identity and intermarriage. Sharet, like other politicians, was concerned that Israeli society be united and struggled with concepts such as the melting pot that would create one nation. As one of the founders of the state, Sharet talked about an Israeli identity that will evolve eventually as a result of a process of *mizug galuyot,* the ingathering of the exiles, that would address nature (genes) and culture (mizrahi), but he believed that it would be a long process. The simplest and easiest way, he said, would be through intermarriage, but that too would take too long. It was, according to Sharet, not enough to be born in Israel, a sabra. For Sharet an Israeli identity required more than birth in the homeland and went beyond being educated in Israeli schools—in other words beyond a birthright and culture. He predicted that even second- and third-generation mizrahim will exhibit ethnic features (Gabriel and Ziv 1973).

The melting pot ideology, however, was never directed toward the ultraorthodox community, which exhibits non-Western lifestyles and did not take on an Israeli identity. None of the leaders of the establishment in the early years of the state, or now, have ever suggested that intermarriage would reduce any gaps or used it as measure of the ultraorthodox assimilation in the state. In fact, their nonassimilability is accepted as a matter of fact that requires no cultural debate. The state did not display the same tolerance toward a mizrahi identity that it extended to the ultraorthodox identity. The panelists noted that an Israeli identity required an assimilation of people of Eastern culture but were not concerned with how to assimilate ashkenazi immigrants—including the recent Russian immigration. They noted that the state produced both an ethnic cultural and a social margin of mizrahi immigrants, who were sent by government agencies to development towns on the country's periphery.

Mizrahim on the Margins: Development Towns as the
"Second Israel"

Jerusalem, Tel Aviv, and Haifa, the three major cities in Israel, have come to symbolize different aspects of Israel's political life.[7] Jerusalem is seen as the more religious, or ultraorthodox, space; Haifa as the more mixed city of Israeli Jews and Palestinians; and Tel Aviv as the most Israeli city—the most urban, the most Westernized. All three cities are at the center of Israel culturally and politically, and development towns are at the margins of both. Women panelists established an East identity in a space (Tel Aviv) that represents Israel's "West" side. Smadar expressed a mizrahi perspective of the significance of spaces marking the divide: "The majority of the mizrahi population does not live in the small streets surrounding Shenkin Street in the old part of Tel Aviv. Most of them do not live in the north of Tel Aviv. The majority of mizrahim live far away from the center of the country, in Maalot, in Shderot, in Netivot, in Ofakim. They are uninterested in much of the society gossip news, in the latest fashions of so and so, the latest trendy pub, or how to cook an expensive piece of meat with herbs that can be purchased only in a particular store in the Latin quarter in Paris." Smadar expresses what Israelis actually know: that the northern part of the city is synonymous with ashkenazi privileged culture—the equivalent of New York's Upper East Side and an exclusive ashkenazi birthright. The south of the city (and of the country) is associated with what is called the "Second Israel," a euphemism for a mizrahi population and poverty.

At the Tel Aviv conference panelists join a broader discourse in Israel that identifies development towns as geographic spaces and metaphors of mizrahi powerlessness (and silencing of their culture). Yael emphasized that equality will not be a fact in Israeli society "until such a time comes when Ofakim will be a town not only of mizrahim, when Morasha will no longer be a poor neighborhood attached to a city with rich people." Swirski participates in the wider Israeli discourse on the meaning of space—development towns as margins—as an indication of the mizrahi economic, social, and cultural position: "The clearest pattern of differentiation is that between the central urban centers and the so-called 'development towns' located mainly in peripheral areas: most of the Ashkenazim reside in the former while the Orientals predominate in the latter. The development towns, established between 1952 and 1964, absorbed much of the immigration in those years, as part of the government's policy of population dispersion. These towns became overwhelmingly Oriental; by the mid-seventies, more than 90 percent of the foreign-born residents in Ofakim, Shlomi, Netivot, and Hatzor . . . were Orientals. All Oriental groups were—and still are—over-represented in the development towns, compared to central cities and suburbs" (1989, 22).

Women in the Tel Aviv conference talked about development towns as spaces in which mizrahim were relegated to social and economic margins of Israeli society. These were the sites at which immigrants were required by state representatives, housing, employment, health, and education to agree that essentially they had no culture—only some "primitive" customs, the sooner discarded the better. This kind of official position was expressed in the account given by Batya Goor, an Israeli ashkenazi author, of an ashkenazi old-timer who was in charge of administering the affairs of the first years of a development town. He said: "I felt a bit like a leader. I am more developed, *mefutah,* I came from Europe and I thought to myself: 'Here are Jews, brothers who came from undeveloped countries. I am a leader. I have something to give them" (Goor 1990, 118). A sense of cultural superiority and disregard for mizrahi culture accounts for the fact that in planning the development towns state officials ignored cultural needs or wishes of the people.[8] Oz writes after his visit to Beit Shemesh: "What did the planner [of the place] know and what did he want to know about the lives, customs, and wishes of the immigrants who were brought to this place? Did he know the inhabitants? And if he did know them, was he in agreement with the dominant view of the 1950s that these people must be changed, and at once—change them completely—and change at all costs?" (1983, 26). The accounts of the panelists in the Tel Aviv conference join this broader debate in Israel on how a valued Euro/ashkenazi culture and the exclusion of Eastern/mizrahi culture played a part in the creation of what Israelis call the Second Israel, development towns and poor urban neighborhoods.

Mythologized Mizrahim

The spaces identified in Israeli discourse as the Second Israel emerge in the Tel Aviv conference as places in which, as Vered said, "people associate mizrahi with backwardness, poverty, and environmental ugliness" and the places on which myths that disparage mizrahi culture were foisted. Goor tells how such myths regarding mizrahim are constructed: "The sense of superiority exhibited by the host society [toward mizrahi immigrants] was expressed in various areas, including prevalent myths [of their ignorance]. Take, for example, the myth of the toilet bowl and the watermelon. It was told that the new immigrants did not know what a toilet bowl was and put watermelons in it. While it is impossible to establish when this myth came into being . . . the host community had its own reasons to go on to view this [mizrahi] immigration as primitive" (1990, 126). The story of the watermelon is a metaphor of the double bind of being seen as both a people without culture (ignorance of Western technology: a bathroom) and having a lesser culture that stores food (watermelon, a typical Middle Eastern product) in the wrong space.

The watermelon myth, however, is an inversion of what often really happened. Documents and accounts disclose that for many mizrahi immigrants who came from urban spaces their first encounter with Israel was a culture shock because living conditions were "primitive" and they were far away from urban centers. Goor tells a story of an encounter between Uri, a young Israeli ashkenazi, who was a school principal in Maalot in the 1950s, and an immigrant mizrahi family: "He had a vision, this school principal. He imagined to himself how this family would embrace him, how the woman will touch the walls of the apartment with excitement and gratitude . . . no one said a word . . . he looked at the bowl of fruit that he had placed on the table and saw the woman turning on the switch. There was no light. . . . As he stood there waiting for voices of joy [at being in the homeland] the woman said: 'There is no electricity' and started to cry" (ibid., 73–74).[9]

The first encounter with the new homeland for mizrahim was often mythologized into inversions of reality. In Israel's public narrative stories were not told about immigrants, for whom the absence of electricity in the middle of nowhere in a strange land was the last straw, but of a bountiful state offering a modern haven (bathrooms) to people who come from so-called primitive societies (who put watermelons in toilet bowls). In this narrative development towns are contrasted with cities of "culture" like Tel Aviv, where the presumption is that bathrooms are properly used and watermelons properly stored. Geographic separation has emerged on the ground, creating two kinds of Israelis: "Orientals and Ashkenazim in Israel have tended to live further and further apart. Though it is difficult to present exact overall figures, it is clear that the majority of Orientals [mizrahim] now live in neighborhoods, towns and villages which are overwhelmingly Oriental" (Swirski 1989, 21). For women panelists Tel Aviv, the place of the conference, was also the space of social (economically affluent) and cultural (site of the production of high and popular culture) privilege; it signified ranked places of ashkenazim (center) and mizrahim (margins and the object of denigrating myths).

Living in the East and Pining for the West

The panelists at the Tel Aviv conference also raised the question of East-West identity, which they located in a wider Israeli national debate that has long roots in Jewish culture. The East-West duality goes back at least to Judah Halevy, a twelfth-century Jewish Spanish poet whose poems appear in school textbooks and various anthologies used in Israeli schools today. Gibel-Azoulay employs Halevy to remind Israelis that "as long as Israel defines itself culturally as a Western country it rejects its Eastern side." Her epigraphic quote given at the beginning of this chapter refers to Halevy's famous poem "My Heart Is in the East," in which he expressed his yearning for Zion and his wish to see the Holy Land. Halevy did in fact begin the journey East, but he got only as far as Alexandria and died there. To be in the West and yearn for the East has been reversed, according to Gibel-Azoulay. The problem, she says, is that Israelis have rejected their own Eastern identity and with it have also socially rejected mizrahi culture. Women panelists noted that the construction of Israeli identity has preferred an impossible and deceptive Western identity—deceptive and impossible because first and foremost the country is geographically in the Middle East, and more than half of its citizens, mizrahim and Israeli Palestinians, incorporate Eastern culture. Dafna said: "Anyone who goes to Europe for two weeks knows that we do not live in a European country. All of us, including the ashkenazim, are not part of European culture; we are all a product of Israeli-style Oriental culture."

It is within the broader Israeli debate on its East or West identity that women panelists in the Tel Aviv conference take a strong pro-East position, commenting on the fact that Jewish culture was forged in the Middle East. The debate on Israel's identity as East or West and the consequences that the debate has for mizrahi culture did not just emerge in the women's peace conference; it has been part of various discourses between academics and Israeli policy makers. In 1969, for example, the question of an East or West identity of Israel and the position of mizrahim in Israeli society were the focus of such a conference at the Hebrew University in Jerusalem, entitled in Hebrew *"Mizug Galuyot"* (The Ingathering of Exiles). While the English title, "The Integration of Immigrants from Different Countries of Origin in Israel," was longer, it was not any clearer about the locations of these "different countries." Both the Hebrew and the English title did not explicitly state that the immigrants discussed were mizrahim, described by a number of the participants as immigrants from Muslim countries.

Yohanan Peres, an Israeli sociologist, said that ashkenazim and mizrahim talked at the Jerusalem conference in 1969 about creating a single society in which all communities will be "at home" yet molded in a European fashion that, Peres said, means ashkenazi. Drawing on a study that he conducted among ashkenazim and mizrahim, Peres argued that ashkenazim tend to see this oneness in what he calls a "missionary" approach, of bringing mizrahim to "our cultural level, the more European," and that many mizrahim speak in similar terms of learning from ashkenazim. "The desire on the part of mizrahim to acquire European traits does not fall behind the ashkenazi desire to impart these traits," he says, noting that the desired unified "Israeli identity of immigrants is constructed on the perceived ashkenazi identity" (Peres 1969, 87). Whether mizrahim desired to acquire European traits or felt compelled to do so, panelists at the Tel Aviv conference argued that the price mizrahim paid for this act was extremely high.

Some sociologists at "The Ingathering of Exiles" noted the absence of mizrahi panelists in the conference and raised the issue of East-West, asking whether an acknowledgment of the Eastern heritage would be enough to reduce the divide or if it would necessitate that ashkenazim give up some Westernness: "The question that we [ashkenazim] always ask is 'What can we give you? To be more polite or more liberal? And what can we give you permission to do? To eat mizrahi food, to have mizrahi dances, to keep different tradition, fine.' But these are not serious issues because serious and central questions require a different kind of a question that I have not heard here yet: 'Are we willing to give up Westernization or part of it?' . . . in addition to what we will give you permission to do and what you are expected to do, we need to ask what are we willing to give up to create a new society" (Antonovski 1969, 89).

In 1990 the panelists in the Tel Aviv conference raised the same question, still unanswered some thirty years later: "Are we willing to give up

Westernization or part of it?" Dalia, the moderator, took a strong pro-East position not as mere talk but as a fact on the geopolitical ground: "In organizing this conference, we thought that the time has come to discuss with honesty the issue of the identity of our society and to ask the question: Where is it facing, East or West? We hope to be able to do it in an amicable atmosphere. Lately there has been some legitimation to talk about our society as being a Mediterranean society, as Amos Oz defines it, but let us face it: the truth is that we belong to the Middle East, and the emphasis is on the East, because, after all, Israel is not located in Western Europe."

Homelessness Looks Mizrahi

The debate on East-West identity in the Tel Aviv conference included the link between mizrahi identity and poverty. Panelists and participants made references to the organized protest of homeless families that took place in Israel in the summer of 1990. July 1990, a month that was a time of relative tranquillity in the relationship between Israelis and Palestinians, was also a month of intracommunity tension between ashkenazim and mizrahim. It took the shape of people who pitched tents and settled in public parks not far from the University of Tel Aviv and in various places around the country. Despite the location, the colorful tents, and the noise of children, these were not families on a camping vacation but, instead, families, couples, and single people who could not afford to buy or rent apartments and had been living in crowded conditions with their more fortunate relatives. They were called in English "homeless" and in Hebrew *chasrei diyur,* meaning literally "lacking housing." The women panelists at the Tel Aviv conference called the acts of the homeless *hitnachalut* (settlement) and protested the Likud government's disinterest in helping poor Israeli Jews to have adequate housing. Yael made the link between the topic of the conference and the homeless tent dwellers: "The reason for the absence of mizrahim in peace activism is not because of hatred of Arabs or because of political obtuseness. It is not difficult to find the mizrahi woman in social struggles and in the protest of the homeless; the struggle is carried out by mizrahi women."

In raising the issue of the homeless at the Tel Aviv conference, gender solidarity and justice to mizrahim were prominent. The ground for the women's refusal of solidarity included their view that poverty in Israel has an ethnic face and that ashkenazi women deny that face. Women panelists as well as the media noted that the homeless were mostly mizrahim, who saw their predicament as ethnic discrimination and expressed resentment of what they considered the government's favoring of ashkenazim, both the settlers in the Occupied Territories and the Russian immigrants. At the conference women uncovered the issue of justice (universal or partial). Yael said: "All of a sudden it transpires that Ethiopians are not getting what the Russians are getting; all of a sudden we see who the homeless are, who are the poor; it is all coming out into the streets." A sense of alienation was, according to a number of articles in various Hebrew papers, at the heart of the protest by the homeless. Smadar, one of the panelists in the conference, made a similar observation and noted that the journalists who wrote about the homeless were themselves mizrahim: "The majority of the homeless who are living in the tents now and are protesting are second- and third-generation mizrahim who suffer poverty and discrimination. Yet, while the facts are quite clear, there are many who are unwilling to talk about the total correspondence between the homeless and ethnic identity [motza adati]. However, obviously, the facts speak for themselves. Who were the journalists who first noted it? Those who have social consciousness, those who are themselves mizrahim."

The *Jerusalem Post* observed a strong sense of alienation among the tent city people and described almost all the camp dwellers as "children of immigrants from Arab countries, who believe the government has always discriminated against Sephardi Jews." The *Jerusalem Post* article also highlighted the sense of being literally without a home in the homeland: "Most families live in old army tents with dirt floors covered with mattresses and cots. In several instances two families share a tent and in some cases, large families with as many as nine children are packed together in the tiny confines. Sleeping outside is not an option on cold, dewy summer nights in Jerusalem. Mothers complained their children are suffering from flu and other illnesses" (July 20, 1990).

A Mizrahi Voice on Peace, Social Justice, and Solidarity

The link between justice, peace, and solidarity was given a mizrahi voice as the panelists in Tel Aviv reinscribed the political fact of tent cities, which turned up in many places in Israel, and confronted ashkenazi women about their actions on behalf of the homeless. Smadar, noting that mizrahim could, if they so desired, join peace groups (gendered solidarity), wanted to know how many ashkenazi women from the Left have joined the homeless cause (social justice). She said: "No one stops mizrahi women from joining these small peace groups of ashkenazi women. No one stops us from coming at one in the afternoon to the vigil, and no one prevents us from coming on Friday at two to the cultural Tzavta meetings. No ashkenazi woman impedes our coming, but we don't come. I hope that I will not sound provocative when I say that no one is stopping the ashkenazi women, not this month, not last year or the previous year, from coming to the parks where the homeless are protesting, to the development towns and to poor neighborhoods. Yet no one in this conference is investigating why they don't come and why they, who care about the peace process, are not conscious of social justice. No one has even put it on the agenda. It is a mistake and a question. It is beautiful that the ashkenazi women, the liberals, radicals, those who want change, wish to make peace with the Palestinians who kill us, yet where do they stand regarding mizrahi men and women? For them to come and tell us that we are politically passive is in my view problematic. There are politically active mizrahi women, but they are among the leaders of the homeless, in neighborhood associations, and so on."

Smadar's remarks resonate comments made by the homeless themselves, who are in a different economic situation from Smadar but share with her the experience of the mizrahim sense of endemic discrimination. Etti Levy, a homeless mizrahi woman, who demonstrated in 1990, raised the question of whether justice was for all: "Why do I have to return to a temporary camp when Soviet immigrants are being given new housing?" (*Jerusalem Post,* July 20, 1990).

For mizrahi women in Tel Aviv justice for the homeless shapes solidarity. The women are connected to the homeless mizrahim not by class ties but by ethnic solidarity; their alliance is not with those of similar economic means and ideological peace positions but with whom they share a mizrahi culture. It was clear for panelists that their collective includes indigent mizrahim and not ashkenazi peace activists. Solidarity rests on social justice. While mizrahi women refused gestures of gender solidarity in Tel Aviv, the homeless refused similar attempts by the state to forge a "one nation" alliance to convince the protesters to leave the parks and accept promises that the state will solve their problem.

Women at the Tel Aviv conference spoke of the response of ashkenazim to the homeless as the familiar blindness to such discrimination. Reiterating mizrahi refusal of gender unity, Tamar described how ashkenazi women see the homeless: "They say to me: Listen, I know mizrahim. Do you know how much money they earn? Do you know that in the tent city, it was on TV, there was a couple that earns three thousand shekel? Do you know how hard it was for me and my mother? Do you think that I don't have a mortgage to pay? Well, we start the discussion nice, nice; we both talk about the fate of these unfortunates; but soon it turns out that they [the homeless] are all black [shehorim]. Feminist ashkenazi women are feminists, but they belong to the oppressing group and to the blind public in Israel. If we will do an honest and probing analysis, someone will have to pay a price, and it is Jewish ashkenazi women who will have to pay it. Because they are more privileged than mizrahi women, more than Palestinian women, and more than mizrahi men."

An Israeli journalist, Hanna Kim, joined the public discourse about the homeless protest and noted the mixture of apathy and antipathy that greeted the phenomenon: "The indifference and hostility that the tent cities faced have revealed the denial of many citizens. The reaction has revealed the cooperation between the media, the ruling political party [Likud], and the parties that we call 'Left.' All of them united to create in the eyes of the public an image of freeloaders who disturb law and order" (Al Hamishmar, September 18, 1990).

Like the women panelists at the Tel Aviv conference, Kim raised the issue of the Left's partial justice, a justice that does not include mizrahim. Kim claims that the Left has not become the advocate of and for the homeless mizrahim. "Some of its leaders still exhibit a surprisingly primitive thinking: they blame the powerless sections of society for bringing this calamity on themselves by voting for the Right. . . . The tent movement of the homeless could have been a litmus test for the Left. For these [homeless] families have labeled themselves 'settlers' with good reason. They did it on their own. In my conversations with many of them I heard anger and resentment against the Gush Emunim settlers. The tent movement could have delivered a political message of a smaller but more just Israel, much better than Peace Now. But the Left has not taken up their cause and did not help them create facts on the ground because the Israeli 'Left' is a political Left [in the Israeli-Palestinian conflict] but is a Right in its position on social issues. The 'Left' is alienated from its true public and is mostly occupied with the Palestinian issue and did not assist the tent dwellers. . . . At the first sign of a large movement of thousands of people the Left, like the Right, yearns for law and order" (ibid.).

What Constitutes Grounds for Solidarity?

In the Tel Aviv conference mizrahi women refused gender solidarity within the Left. It was not a matter of mizrahi women's denial of peace with Palestinians but, rather, their refusal to make peace a ground for a "we" women's collective that was at issue. The failure of gender to provide unity in this women's conference reflects different constructions of solidarities (peace and gender or Easternness). In the Tel Aviv conference social justice for mizrahim challenged gender solidarity but displayed a transgender, trans-class mizrahi solidarity for women who hold both a peace and a feminist position. For women at the conference mizrahi solidarity meant establishing, in a women's public event, an act of exposing the absence of social justice from the Left's political agenda. The women in the Tel Aviv conference illuminated a wider public discussion on political solidarities. The solidarity that the Left thinks should be there with mizrahim is juxtaposed by the panelists rejection of such a solidarity because of the Left's silence on social justice. Instead, it constructed a mizrahi solidarity that transcended party politics.

The media participates in the discussion on solidarity between mizrahim and the Left and offers a wide range of views. Boshes, an Israeli journalist, writes in *Haaretz:* "The Second Israel and development towns were never included in the agenda of the Israeli Left and between them there has been alienation and political distance. Development towns are considered the bastions of the Right, including the extreme Right" (*Haaretz,* October 22, 1990). Not only mizrahi panelists in the Tel Aviv conference but several ashkenazi participants made similar observations regarding a gap between the Left and mizrahim. Miriam, an ashkenazi religious peace activist, forged an alliance with mizrahi women when she said in the Tel Aviv conference: "I confess that I am an ashkenazi woman from academia, but I too feel alienated and marginalized in the Left. I would like to mention something that has not been said tonight. In the last two hundred years the ashkenazi world has gone through a process of secularization and a move away from tradition. This process does not characterize the mizrahi communities. Israeli mizrahi people are much more attuned to Jewish tradition, in the family, the community, and cultural life. I think that they see the Left as devoid of national pride, devoid of identification with Jewish tradition."

Yet some people in the Left have another view. They bring forth the issue of solidarity and ask why it is that mizrahim do not join the Peace Camp. Several days before the Tel Aviv conference *Yediot Ahronot* published an article by Tzvi Kesseh, "Where Is East, Where Is Peace," in which he placed the blame for mizrahim's marginal position in the Left in the mizrahi lap: "The ashkenazim founded Zionism, the mizrahim made it come true. Without their immigration, it would have been possible to establish but not to sustain a state. And today the state's fate is in their hands. If they continue to support the Right, they will be responsible. In surveys, about 54 percent [of mizrahim] are willing under reasonable conditions to talk to the PLO, but there is no change in voting. It seems that the lack of sympathy toward the Labor party stands in the way of voting. Their response is that it is not ideological but that 'the Left is not responsive to us.' Stop the nonsense. Forty years have passed (since mizrahim's immigration to Israel). The fate of the country is in your hands. If you cannot vote for the Left establish a Left of your own. . . . The response of mizrahim's social issues is Left. But in the voting booth they choose Right. Explain it to me" (*Yediot Ahronot,* July 23, 1990).

Kesseh's view is that there are common political interests that should forge solidarity and rally mizrahim to vote for the Left. But views like his are the kinds that panelists in the Tel Aviv conference identified as a false ground for such solidarity. Beyond issues of alienation, Israelis like Kesseh introduce political issues such as the election and the significance of votes. If mizrahim are alienated in the Left, they are not likely to vote for political parties such as Labor and Meretz. Indeed, mizrahim have been identified by various surveys and political commentators as Likud voters. The panelists at Tel Aviv saw the mizrahi vote for the Right from a different perspective. They insisted that what is missing in the Left is broader justice and noted the various (political) associations between Arabs/Palestinians and mizrahi culture and identity. Tikva said: "It is true that mizrahim vote more for the right-wing parties. There are numerous reasons for it. One of them certainly is that we look more like Palestinians, that our color is black, so that mizrahim may feel that they need to put a deeper barrier between themselves and Palestinians. We have to see that immigrants who brought mizrahi culture with them brought it into a country where the Arab is the enemy, and Arab culture is something to be ashamed of. I need to erase Arabic, which is my language, and be ashamed of Eastern culture, which is my culture. We know that we belong to the lowest rung on the social status, and we want to assimilate. We know that Jews, not Arabs, constitute the center of power—so what can we do?"

In its refusal of sororal solidarity the conference illuminates the fact that it is mizrahim who compete with Palestinians in the workplace, but the Left is silent about it. Tamar, one of the panelists, said: "As you all know, the lives of mizrahim in development towns are dominated by issues of survival, of making a living, and they work side by side with Palestinian laborers and compete with them for jobs. Life in development towns is a constant struggle. That means that nice ideas on peace with Palestinians is not an abstract issue for them but a daily question: 'How will I make peace with the Palestinian worker with whom I compete daily?'"

Women noted that the struggle for economic survival is a potential space of friction between mizrahim and Palestinians, but they argued that it is also a potential space for identification (of suffering but also of a shared Eastern culture), which ashkenazim in peace groups refused to recognize. At the Tel Aviv conference Tamar, recalling an earlier peace conference in Spain, said: "Anyone who participated in the peace conference in Toledo was aware of the special atmosphere, the chemistry between mizrahim and Palestinians; there was a sense of a shared culture of people who have lived together."[10] The vote for the Right masks this kind of cultural identification.

Similarly, some Israeli scholars note that the vote for right-wing parties takes place not on ideological grounds of the Greater Israel but, rather, in the mizrahi position that the Left has discriminated against them and wants to erase their Eastern culture: "It was the Labor establishment, dominating all centers of power at the time, that engineered the policies that resulted in ethnic stratification. It propagated the ideology that the Oriental immigrants were a lost generation of the desert and posed a threat to democracy and Israeli culture. Their needs were said to be less, and they should be grateful for whatever they were accorded. While it was not clear whether they could be decultured or recaptured, their children were expected to completely assimilate into Israeli life. To the great injury inflicted by the discriminatory policies, a grave insult was added by this paternalistic ideology and humiliating stereotyping" (Smooha 1993, 319–20). Accordingly, mizrahim vote for the Likud Party "because they see in it, rightly or wrongly, a means for social mobility and status attainment. For them Labor is responsible for their predicament and represents Ashkenazim who enjoy status and privilege" (323).

A mizrahi man in Beit Shemesh said to Amos Oz: "Begin [the leader who brought the Likud to power in 1976] came, and believe me my parents straightened their backs in pride and dignity. . . . Begin respects their faith" (1986, 31). Men in Beit Shemesh who spoke to Oz resented the Left because they consider it blind to mizrahi justice. A mizrahi man said: "When you [Labor] were in the government you hid us in holes, in development towns so that tourists won't see us, so we won't give you a dirty image, so that the tourists will think that this is a white country. But now we are through with it. We have come out into the open. You still don't get it, because of your arrogance. It is as though you have inherited this state from your father. The state of Israel is from the father of Labor? Not from the Torah? Not from our sweat? Not from our manual work? Not from our blood?" (qtd. in Oz 1983, 36).

What the Left Eye of Israel Does Not See

The Left and women's peace groups were seen by the panelists and some of the participants in the Tel Aviv conference as holding the same partial justice, which ignores social justice within the state, of the ashkenazi center within the state and in the Peace Camp. Dalia said: "It brings me to the question of why mizrahi women avoid joining the peace movements. I want to emphasize this issue because there are a number of issues familiar to those who are active in the peace efforts, since in the women's peace conferences and meetings on the lists of speakers there are almost no mizrahi women. For many years the Eastern Jewish communities [edot hamizrach] were accused of enabling the Likud's success and their general tendency toward the Right; the consensus was that in the poor urban neighborhoods and development towns there is no one to talk to. But among mizrahim it is possible to find those who we can talk to. The aim of this evening is to strive toward cooperation and to begin to think of strategies that will promote the goal of social justice and peace."

Panelists recognized the gap between the Left and mizrahim and expressed the hope that the Left would focus on domestic social justice as well. The very term Left (smol) was challenged because it was seen by the panelists to be unconcerned with social injustices that have touched the lives of mizrahim in Israel. Women argued that intracommunity and intercommunity justice are made of a single political fabric. Justice is indivisible: it cannot have two different faces. Tamar said: "Without vision on social justice we will not be able to achieve our goal to change the policy of occupation and the status quo. Without a peace vision we will not be able to influence the distribution of economic and human resources that will close the social gaps within Israeli society in the Israeli-Jewish community and

Israeli-Palestinian community. And, above all, only through linking social justice and peace we will be able, after an agreement between us and the Palestinian nation, to aspire for cooperation between all the states in the Middle East."

Women noted that justice has to be encompassing—it must include all groups—but said that the Left is quick to emphasize common peace goals with mizrahim but unwilling to acknowledge the deep divide of discrimination. Vered said: "When I talk to [other] mizrahim a number of them say: 'When the Left talks about justice, it speaks of Palestinian justice but not of our justice.' I agree. The Left is concerned with justice for Palestinians, but when it comes to the working class, to the daily struggles of mizrahim for their existence, their life conditions, their well-being, to discrimination against mizrahim, the Left is insensitive. Moreover, the Left demands that I will apologize and even demonstrate proof of my intentions. This hypocrisy turns me off; I don't feel good in joining people with whom I don't feel partnership." Panelists see the Israeli Left treating justice as divisible: it is recognized where Palestinians are concerned and denied when it comes to mizrahim.

Feminism, Solidarity, and Justice

Feminism was also questioned as a ground for solidarity between mizrahi and ashkenazi women: Is feminist justice universal/indivisible or gender specific? Does it include concerns of class and ethnic justice? Panelists talked about ways in which mizrahi identity, class, feminism, and peace activism are both linked and separated. Tamar said: "I see myself as a mizrahi and a feminist woman. I am a member of the feminist community that most mizrahi women are very angry with and very critical of and are unwilling to join. I call it a feminist community because I think that there is such a community even if sometimes I am uncomfortable in it because I am a minority. It is a problem, because the women who started the feminist movement are ashkenazi women from academia. Economically and socially, they could afford to be feminists. I say that they could afford it because, as a feminist, you devote time, you need the kind of a job that will allow you to be active, and it also means that, if you commit to feminist activism, you move in feminist circles and create links with other feminists.

"There is a parallel with our situation regarding the ashkenazi society. We have to become part of it. Mizrahi women had to find a place in the feminist community because we did not come and say: 'Let us do something new, a joint effort.' When we joined we had to make a place for ourselves in an existing structure. For me, as a mizrahi woman, it was very difficult. I was lucky to have a job that enabled me to do it, even though I am not an academic, and I made connections, and that too is important, just as it is for a mizrahi in the ashkenazi establishment. It is much harder for a mizrahi woman, who does not have the connections that ashkenazi feminists have among themselves. So a mizrahi woman needs to invest much time and be involved in many activities to make a place for herself. I think that is tough for us. I have been to a number of meetings of peace groups. Where do they take place? In homes of [privileged] members. Because I am in the minority, I don't say much about it. I am not saying that it is deliberate, but we find ourselves in the same trap of the larger Israeli society of the Left, of peace activists talking among themselves. It is hard for mizrahi women to find a place even in the feminist community, and most mizrahi women are not being approached; there are a few of them, and they are not easily accepted. Until we make a massive effort to change the situation, it will remain difficult."

Panelists argued that feminist justice is divisible and equality is limited because feminist groups have a center and margins. Mizrahi women who are active in feminist and peace groups note boundaries that run along Eastern and class lines and see themselves as a minority. In the Tel Aviv conference mizrahi women also established a collective of "we mizrahi women," contesting what they see as a collective of ashkenazi "we women for peace." Women talked of an ashkenazi society in which mizrahim had to find a place and in which there was no question of restructuring the whole (Israeli identity, Israeli culture) together: "We have to become part of it." Those who joined the feminist community noted that, as mizrahi women, they had to fit in, to accommodate themselves to an ashkenazi leadership and structure.

Mizrahi women saw that the same serious barriers that exist in the wider society permeate women's groups and that the groups espouse an ideology of gender equality in Israeli society that does not include equality for mizrahim. Several panelists saw an analogy between a denial by some Israelis of the scope of the injustices caused by the occupation and a denial of the injustices to mizrahim in Israeli society. Yael said: "The atmosphere here this evening is very tense. It reminded me of my first meetings with Palestinians, because, as a Jewish woman, it was very hard for me to hear their recriminations. My early reactions were that it is impossible that I am wrong or that I wrong other people. But it was a beginning for me, and I hope that this will be a beginning for many women who are angry right now. This is an invitation to reflect. The aim is not to turn the word *ashkenazi* into a curse; it is not to turn the tables around. But it is an attempt to rethink the issue of mizrahim and to do it in a good way and even as shock therapy in order to understand the other side. There is still great discomfort in talking about ashkenazi women, but it is important to understand that thirty or forty years of walking around with this stigma of being mizrahi for those who came as immigrants and for those who were born here is a burden. It does not mean that [Israel] is exactly like South Africa and its relationship between whites and blacks, but it is in the nuances, in the small things that accompany a person from childhood throughout life. When I came back to the Jewish side to talk about injustices to Palestinians people said: 'Why don't they [Palestinians] rebel? Why don't they start a movement of their own? Why don't they have a "Peace Now" movement?' We need to be more attentive, to listen more, and to try to understand what is going on. We need to understand the conflict not in terms of who is guilty but to understand that mizrahim feel that they do not belong in peace organizations. Why don't mizrahim start their own movements? Because they are the powerless. It is the same issue as for Palestinians who are citizens of Israel, not to mention those in the Occupied Territories."

For women like Yael, feminism is not seen as ground for solidarity; it lacks the substance of a social fact of indivisible justice or of indivisible equality. The panelists in the Tel Aviv conference speak of the limits of equality and a sense of power differentials that cannot be transcended by the gender unity that marked other conferences, including the stormy Haifa conference. Smadar insists on the indivisibility of justice: "Women's groups suggest that I become politically active in their groups. But I feel alienated. I don't feel closeness to these women. What do they offer me? Usually it is 'Let us solve that [the Palestinian] problem, and then your problem will be taken care of as well.' But I object to it because, while the Palestinian problem does bother me, I see other daily, burning concerns for mizrahim as well."

The Tel Aviv conference constructed the position of mizrahi women on justice: that it cannot be parceled out, divided, given to some and deferred to others. The call for solidarity that they hear sounds to them as an attempt to assimilate them into what they see as an ashkenazi project of peace politics. They rejected an ashkenazi view that justice is divisible and that groups will just have to wait their turn before it can apply to them. Nurit said: "I have a feeling that we are hearing a claim: 'Let us first solve the feminist question, and then we will turn to the second one of ethnicity.' I hear it from the Left all the time. They come to us and ask us to support them, and eventually they will find time for our problems as well." What mizrahi women rejected at Tel Aviv was not the concept of feminism or of peace but, rather, what they considered their limits, their boundaries (gvulut), in their respective constructions of justice. The women said that, in the various political groups that call for justice for Palestinians or for women's equality, no space was made for justice and equality for mizrahim.

Unmasking Social Denials

The conference in Tel Aviv on mizrahi women in peace activism revealed and unmasked the broader issues of partial justice versus justice for all within the Israeli-Jewish community between mizrahim and ashkenazim. The conference told an Israeli story of what is already out there in the social world: partial justice, cultural exclusions, and the limits of solidarities. Mizrahi women in Tel Aviv identified denials of discrimination and limitations of justice and equality. The women called on ashkenazi women to acknowledge certain unpleasant social facts, from discrimination to hidden racism. To bring up these issues in the public events in Israel establishes facts on the ground of partial justice and the limits of solidarities (peace, gender) as well as their scope (stretching across gender and class). Panelists and participants talked about a belief that social facts not acknowledged publicly don't exist and that these facts can be denied as long as they are not brought up in public events. A faculty member at Tel Aviv University, Shifra, told of her efforts to find a room on campus for the conference: "When I approached the university to give us a room for this evening's symposium on mizrahi women and peace, the response was familiar, from previous requests concerning various feminist activities: 'Why differences?' 'Why say women?' As though I have no right to call it a conference regarding mizrahi women. It is as though, in having this conference, we actually create a problem that was not there, and, if we only will not name the problem, 'it' will not exist. It is as if what we hear tonight and what we know that is taking place can be wished away."

Partial justice (not for all) and a contested Israeli identity (East or West) were unveiled by women at the Tel Aviv conference. They spoke of "difficult problems" that some or many Israeli ashkenazim, people in the Left, and feminists would have liked to take off the national agenda. The conference displayed the limits of justice and equality in a country that sees itself as one people *(am echad)*, a home for all Jews, and a place where equality is a highly valued ideology, where the Peace Camp and feminist groups take a justice position. It also revealed the links between local and global; between cultural identity, the Middle East conflict, and the lure of the West. The Tel Aviv conference thus established a fact of a contestation rather than a consensus on a (fixed) Israel identity. Women asked, "Is it East (local), or is it West (global)?" and made a strong case for an inclusion of Easternness on cultural and political grounds.

Mizrahi women spoke publicly of what it means to be "displaced" culturally in one's own country; to be "out of place" with people on the Left, with whom one could theoretically share ideological positions on justice; and, finally, to be in a "marginal place," even in women's peace groups or among feminists. Women made this clear when they publicly exposed the divide between the ashkenazi and the mizrahi communities. Smadar argued that ashkenazim know little about Eastern culture and are unfamiliar with lived experience of mizrahim: "Most mizrahim are interested in the basics and the daily issues of their lives. But most of the [ashkenazi] journalists live in Tel Aviv. One woman journalist went to work in a factory in one of the development towns and the whole country cheered. Why? After all, this is the stuff of journalism at its most elementary—to go and write about the lives of others. When the writer Batya Goor went to Ofakim and wrote a long and interesting article on mizrahim in *Politika* the whole country talked about it. Why? Because journalists come to these places like anthropologists going to an unknown land. But these journalists have no idea about the cultural and spiritual world of the people they are writing about. They do not have a clue about what truly concerns these people and what they would really like to talk about."

Panelists questioned ashkenazi women's genuine concern with social justice and stated that, when the choice is between standing together with mizrahi men (whatever their position on peace or women's rights) or ashkenazi women (peace activists and feminists), they choose solidarity with mizrahim. Tamar said: "The ashkenazi women could tell their friends and acquaintances that the problem of discrimination is large and deep. Instead, they tell them: 'Listen, there is a lovely conference tonight on mizrahi women. It should be quite interesting.' My question is: 'Do we come here together to learn what has turned Israeli society into this nonsolidarity society?' I feel not solidarity but anger with feminist women. They don't think that they need to invite me and other women who know a different version to give an altered view of Israeli reality, a version that is simply at odds with historical accounts that we heard before. Do these discussions focus on immigrants; is there talk about discrimination; is there talk about a long differential treatment of not just Ethiopian Jews versus the Russian immigrants but about how, all along, the mizrahi immigrants were being treated in contrast to ashkenazi immigrants? It is important that you have conferences to investigate these issues. Because when I have to choose between my male mizrahi friends, who are chauvinists, and feminist ashkenazi women, who belong to the oppressing class and who wish to remain blind, I choose chauvinist mizrahim. I choose them because my ethnic identity is stronger."

While mizrahim, like ashkenazim, come from different communities and mizrahim recognize their own internal differences, these have become insignificant. At the national level the category of mizrahi, rather than any specific identity—for example, Yemenite, Moroccan, or Algerian—has been embraced as the ethnic identity. The shared experience by all of these communities in Israel accounts for the forging of a mizrahi collective when facing ashkenazim. Women's refusal to allow a ground for unity with ashkenazi women thus opens up questions for feminists who would like to employ gender as a ground for solidarity but must face the limits of female unity.

A New Order in the Region

Three years after the Tel Aviv conference and several months after the signing of the agreement between Israel and the Palestinians, Shimon Peres, the minister of foreign affairs, envisioned a new era, "the shaping of a new Middle East," and spoke of bringing hope to the region, "which has been laden with much distress and despair." He stated that "Israel will make every effort to ensure the agreement becomes not just a political document but a successful reality—politically, economically, and socially. Economic growth, political identity, and social justice are interfused" (Peres 1993, 57). How much of it will be translated from mere talk into political facts of justice in the Middle East is yet to unfold. The Tel Aviv conference raises the question of Israel's contested identity and how the vision of the new Middle East era will alter the East-West contestation. The conference reveals that justice positions as elements in the promise of a new era are not sufficient and that some justice positions can in fact be divisible, partial. Israel faces issues of social justice not only between Israelis and Palestinians in the West Bank and Gaza, not only between Israeli citizens, Jewish and Palestinian, but within the Israeli-Jewish community as well. Women's refusal of gender unity in the Tel Aviv conference and their insistence on an indivisible justice (for all) indicates that for these women solidarity can only be claimed where there is (indivisible) justice and reconsideration of an East-West cultural identity.

For Vicki Shiran the masking of social justice is seen when ashkenazi women (and men) "do not really believe that Orientals are oppressed." Hedda Boshes, an Israeli journalist, describes the mask in functional terms, which means that, given Israel's many political issues (e.g., the Palestinian conflict), this is not the right (social) moment to deal with inequalities of mizrahim. Injustice to mizrahim, according to Boshes, is "a difficult problem that we would have liked to take off our overcrowded agenda" (*Haaretz*, October 22, 1990). The Tel Aviv conference therefore indicates that envisioning, as Peres does, a new Middle East with Israel as an active state in the region will entail a process of reforging Israeli identity between its geography in the Middle East and its deep yearning to belong to the West. The conference showed how the intracommunity conflict between mizrahim and ashkenazim is rooted in a tension in Israel itself between concepts of East and West as both geographic and social-cultural facts. Gibel-Azoulay identifies this tension in the chapter epigraph: "My heart is in the West but I live in the East."

In a practical, political sense Israel could not, until the recent signings of the agreements, truly belong to the East. During the years of the Middle East conflict the region was closed to Israel and the question of where it belonged culturally could easily tilt toward the West, partly because Israel was not accepted as part of the East. But, beyond the fact that it was rejected by the other states in the Middle East, within Israeli society this pining for the West meant a rejection of the East, a rejection that in the local context brought about cultural erasure and social injustice to mizrahi people. For Israel change in the politics of the region begins, as I note in the following chapter, with the 1992 elections and a shift toward peace and coexistence. This drastic political turnabout could also bring a change in the position of mizrahim, from an inferior one to a culturally authentic group of the region. Yael said at the Tel Aviv conference: "Ashkenazi culture has rejected the mizrahi culture because it resembles Arab culture. In doing so, Ashkenazi culture is cutting off the arms that it could have used to embrace this region. I ask myself how accurate is it to claim that these arms have been amputated. Demographically and numerically, the Eastern culture has a majority in this country."

CHAPTER 5 · A Political Upheaval: Meanings of Peace and Coexistence

Suddenly everyone understands
that the world must survive
that it is imperative to change direction
because it is impossible to stand
on the verge of calamity
forever
because it is urgent to repair, and right away
before we will all, God forbid, be destroyed.
                              —Bracha Serri

There is talk about co-existence
but I don't follow co-existence
there is only existence
or non-existence.
                              —Bracha Serri

We knew that the public wanted to punish the Likud. I
expected that we will get a majority, but I did not believe
that punishing the Likud would be so severe and our victory
so great. The people knew how to punish the government
that has made so many mistakes.
                              —David Libai

A Turnabout: From Greater Israel to Peace and Coexistence

In June 1992 a public event of profound significance took place in Israel: after fifteen years in power, the Likud Party lost the elections, and the Labor Party, together with Meretz, formed an essentially Left government, including its position on the Israeli-Palestinian conflict. State politics had been altered overnight. Israelis on both sides of the divide of the Israeli-Palestinian conflict knew that a crucial shift would take place; an ideology of "peace and coexistence" would replace the Likud's ideology of a Greater Israel. The ideology of peace and coexistence was transformed into a political fact in a public event, as the new prime minister, Yitzhak Rabin, addressed the Knesset on July 13, 1992. Rabin turned this ideology into a political act as he out-

171

lined peace and coexistence as the bedrock of Israel's new domestic, regional, and global relations.

For the Left (Labor and Meretz) the magnitude of the ideological shift from mere talk of peace to political facts was instantaneously apparent when a number of peace activists took on positions of power in the new government and in the Knesset's various committees. Women peace activists, who had feared that the Likud would win again, faced a new political reality as some of their own comrades on the Left, including women, were elected officials. It appeared that much of their peace politics would now become state policies.

The 1992 government also included the mizrahi Orthodox Shas Party (considered, correctly or mistakenly, among the religious parties to be the closest to the peace position). The new government was also assured support in the Knesset by five Israeli-Palestinian members of Knesset. While the Israeli-Palestinian political parties were not invited to participate as partners, the government's open alliance with them signaled a major domestic political shift in Israel's relationship to its own Palestinian citizens. A policy of exclusion of Israeli Palestinians during the Likud government was swiftly replaced by a promise of inclusion Rabin made in his inaugural address in July 1992: "There are substantial gaps between the Jewish and Arab communities in a number of spheres. On behalf of the new government, I see it fitting to promise the Arabs, Druse, and Bedouin population that we shall do everything possible to close those gaps. We shall try to make the great leap that will enhance the welfare of the minorities that have linked their fate with our own" (Rabin 1992, 4).

Israelis have described the elections not as a change, but as an upheaval, a turnabout (mahapach), to signify their realization that not only domestic policies would take a sharp turn but that foreign policies as well would be drastically altered. The measure of the political turnabout/upheaval was marked by Rabin's call on Israel to abandon an official isolationist position and instead to "join the international movement toward peace, reconciliation and cooperation." Rabin made it publicly clear that regional policies would take a new direction and that the new government "made it a prime goal to promote the making of peace and take vigorous steps that will lead to the conclusion of the Israeli-Arab conflict" (ibid).

Israelis on both the Right and on the Left could tell that the elections marked the dawn of a monumental political turnabout. According to their political views, Israelis either hoped for or feared a future in which events such as the signing of the agreement between Israel and the PLO in Washington would take place. After the 1992 elections various leaders within the Left have used the word *mahapach* to express their exhilaration at the electoral victory. When the election results became known, Yitzhak Navon, Israel's fifth president, said: "Today is a great day. This is an upheaval, *mahapach*, that should have taken place several years ago but was delayed, and now we won it" (*Haaretz*, June 24, 1992). Member of Knesset and peace activist Yossi Sarid of the Meretz Party said: "For 15 years I have waited for the word *mahapach*. I still have a trauma concerning this word from 1977 [when the Likud came to power]. The word has come and I am a happy person" (ibid).

The same upheaval that the Left celebrated was the one that the Right has dreaded. Yitzhak Shamir, who would eventually be very critical of the handshake between Rabin and Yassir Arafat, the PLO chairman, described his reaction to the 1992 election: "When the anchorman announced a turnabout, *mahapach*, in favor of the Labor Party, it seemed impossible to me. . . . I felt as though a storm had hit me." In a recent article Shamir revealed that his shock was beyond a personal loss and an end to his political career: "I felt something entirely different. A deep anxiety for the fate of Eretz Yisrael filled my heart. I knew that this new government will give up vital positions that the Likud and I protected and that it will put an end to Jewish settlements in Judea, Samaria, Gaza and the Golan Heights. Rabin would become prime minister [and defense minister] and Shimon Peres would be the minister for foreign affairs. I was familiar with their positions and views on these matters and I knew that the worry that swept over me has a solid basis" (*Yediot Ahronot*, January 28, 1994). According to Shamir, his first thoughts and concerns were solely about the Israeli-Palestinian conflict and the fear that the ideology and politics of the Greater Israel would be replaced by state politics of peace and coexistence without all, or most, of the West Bank, Gaza, and the Golan Heights.

Women's Transgression: A Forecast of the Turnabout

Israelis called the elections a turnabout, an upheaval, because they knew that the elections marked a sharp turning point in the state's Middle East policies. Just how far or how quickly things would turn about was yet to unfold, however, and few people on either the Right or the Left could have imagined a peace agreement with the PLO—from the Likud's perspective, a pariah organization—within a year after the elections. Signs that the upheaval would affect the proscription on communication with the PLO were in the political air, however, shortly after the elections. An indication that a change on this position was within the realm of possibility, and thus a sign of the turnabout, was displayed by two women peace activists who transgressed the law that prohibited Israelis from meeting with the PLO. The women, Naomi Chazan (Meretz) and Yael Dayan (Labor), who became members of the Knesset in 1992, went to Europe at the end of August 1992 to meet with a PLO representative. In political tandem with Rabin's emphasis in his inaugural address on peace as the government's position, Chazan and Dayan publicly announced that they had gone to the Netherlands to meet with Nabil Shaat, a leader of the PLO and one of Arafat's chief advisors. The media reproduced this public event; *Haaretz* revealed that, because Chazan and Dayan belong to parties that constitute the government (Meretz and Labor), their act was a historic upheaval: "This is the first time that members of Knesset from the government are meeting with an official representative of the PLO, which is against the law" (August 26, 1992).

The opposition's reaction to members of Knesset meeting with Nabil Shaat in 1992 expressed the Right's dismay at the political upheaval that was rapidly taking place before their eyes. The right-wing parties in the Knesset expressed rage *(zaam)* and displeasure *(morat ruach)* and called for legal measures against Chazan and Dayan (ibid.). The women's illegal yet very public act, and the intense reaction from the Right, revealed the scope, the direction, and the swiftness of the upheaval. Yael Dayan underscored the upheaval when she correctly predicted upon her return that the law would soon be struck down. The meeting with Shaat, which signaled the beginning of an unofficial dialogue in 1992, turned into official talks in 1993 between the new government and the PLO. Whether Rabin had been notified of the women's meeting in advance, their act dovetailed with his public call for peace in the Knesset a month earlier; it also went beyond what he said in his Knesset address. Dayan established a political fact of peace when she talked publicly about the meeting and stated that "the significance of the meeting is in deepening the ties between the two nations who must live side by side." In late August the two women, while breaking a law, established a fact on the ground of elected Israeli leaders from parties in the government talking to the PLO, a political act that foreshadowed the official meetings in Oslo in 1993.

Dayan and Chazan's trip to Europe to talk to a PLO official was a historic event, the first time that members of Knesset who are from the government's political parties had met with an official representative of the PLO, and it was predictive of the direction that the state would eventually take. Several months after the women's journey the Knesset repealed the law. The language of turnabout that permeated the national discourse in 1992 was used again by politicians and the media to describe the removal of the law as one of the major indications of new state policies. *Yediot Ahronot* noted: "Haim Ramon [Labor] was right when, after the Knesset overturned the ban to meet with Palestinians, he said: 'Tonight there was proof that there was a turnabout/upheaval, *mahapach*.' At least on this issue the alliance between Labor and Meretz maintained consistency and loyalty to its promises. Abolishing the law, a law that had no place in our book of laws, is a symbol of a meaningful *mahapach*, and signifies our hope that a new era is here in our attempts to negotiate/discuss with the Palestinian nation and its leadership in order to bring peace to both nations" (*Yediot Ahronot*, January 22, 1993).

While the striking of the law had the enthusiastic blessing of the Left, it clearly received strong condemnation from the Right and the ultra-Right. This reaction to the government's policies indicates the depth of the turnabout from the Likud's position. Rage, as a collective emotion expressed by the extreme Right in response to the Women in Black, also characterized the reaction of the Right to the meeting Chazan and Dayan had with the PLO. The magnitude of the turnabout is revealed in a collective response of "rage in the Right," which would surface at every step that Rabin's government would undertake, including the 1993 Oslo agreement and the 1994 agreement in Cairo.[1]

In August 1992, barely two months after the elections, the women's act was either audacious or shocking, depending on one's political position, because the government had not yet made this turnabout regarding the PLO official policy. In Rabin's peace address to the Knesset in July 1992 neither the PLO nor its chairman, Yassir Arafat, were mentioned. In retrospect, though, after the signing of the agreement in Washington, D.C., it is apparent that women peace activists, before and after the 1992 elections, have been a few steps ahead of the government regarding the PLO. Whether they have been acknowledged by the government (or by political commentators), they have emerged as political trailblazers. For a number of years, in peace conferences and in some vigils of Women in Black, women have called first on the Likud government and later on the Left government to talk to the PLO.

A Political Upheaval/Turnabout: Reimagining Jewish Nation-ness

For Israelis an upheaval signaled a reimagining of Jewish nation-ness that would move away from an image of a nation under siege (in the Middle East) and alienated from the world. In 1992 Israelis who did not vote for the Likud have stated that there was a desire to change the official image of Jewish nation-ness: "The nationalist camp was dealt a heavy blow and this is evident in the disappearance of Tchiya [a defunct ultra-Right political party]. The fanatics with the insane gleam in their eyes have remained outside" (Yoel Marcus, *Haaretz*, June 24, 1992). The Likud's image of the Jewish nation as indivisible from the Greater Israel would be reimagined by the new government as nation-ness severed from territories-as-land (the West Bank and Gaza as sacred, biblical patrimony). In his inaugural address to the Knesset, Rabin offered a reimagined nation when he said that he would redirect funds from settlements to fighting unemployment, creating jobs for new immigrants, and closing the gap between the Israeli-Palestinian and the Israeli-Jewish communities (Rabin 1992). The new government thus clearly offered a reimagined Jewish nation-ness that included social justice and space for another nation.

Nation-ness becomes politically significant in Israel when it can be transformed into state acts. Three months after the elections and shortly after the two new women members of Knesset met with a PLO representative, Rabin demonstrated the fact that the Left has taken charge of reimagining Israel's concept of the nation, a concept that is intimately bound with government politics. On September 3, 1992, Rabin publicly outlined the nation as one that calls on Israelis to "abandon the concept of a 'Greater Land of Israel' and to give up that land for peace. We must cut ourselves off from the religion of the Greater Land of Israel and remember that the strength of the nation is not measured in the territories it controls, but by its beliefs and its ability to develop social, economic and security systems" (*Democrat and Chronicle*, September 4, 1992). Rabin publicly announced the state's turning away from the Right's image of the nation as indivisible from the Occupied Territories as sacred land; a reimagined Jewish nation that accepted coexistence with Palestinians would now underline Israel's official position. Serri's epigraphic phrase, "it is imperative to change direction," captures the need to reimagine the nation that Israelis on the Left saw. In 1992 the prime minister and Serri, a woman peace activist, seemed to speak in unison, as Rabin's public statement outlined an Israeli nation-ness no longer defined by land or territories.

In discussing competing ideologies of nation-ness, Richard Fox (1990) identifies a key element of the "winning ideology," or what he calls "national culture"—the ability to put a set of ideas into action. A turnabout from the Right's vision of nation-ness of a Greater Israel to a vision that includes peace and coexistence is significant not because all Israelis would adopt it but because the Left's ideology will become official state policies. The elections were a fact of political parties that had acquired the power to implement their vision of the nation as the official state version of nation-ness. The turnabout in government meant having the power to transform an ideology of nation-ness (mere talk) into political action of peace and coexistence.

The 1992 elections promised an upheaval in the official nation-ness that people on the Right feared: land (the Occupied Territories) would no longer constitute one of the nation's defining features, and settlements would no longer constitute the linchpin of state policies. A Jewish-Israeli nation defined by an inalienable right to the land (of the West Bank and the Gaza Strip) would be reimagined as an Israeli-Jewish nation defined by peace and coexistence in the region. In his inaugural address to the Knesset, Rabin clearly outlined an upheaval of an official nation-ness that was a sharp departure from the Likud's understanding of the nation: "No longer are we necessarily 'a people that dwells alone,' and no longer is it true that 'the whole world is against us'" (1992, 5). For the Left the election victory promised to transform an ideology of peace and coexistence into political acts—and no longer from the margins against a government position but as its official policy. In his inaugural address Rabin drove the point home when he emphasized a shift from peace as mere talk to political action: "From this moment forward the concept of 'peace process' is outdated. From now on we shall not speak of a 'process' but of making peace" (Ibid).

From Exile to Homecoming

After the elections the media reported a sense of euphoria in the Left, in which the phrase "return from exile" was prominent. In Israel *home* and *exile (galut)* express more than spatial boundaries: *home* means power, while *exile* means powerlessness. Israel as a state is seen as home, but people who are alienated from government policies are no longer "at home" and consider themselves as living in exile. To be in exile at home (in Israel) means an inability to transform ideologies of nation-ness into state policies;

"coming home" politically means possessing or sharing the power of state. People in the Left spoke of a return from a long and painful political exile from the center of power—from state policies. Yoram Harpaz, a thirty-four-year-old Meretz activist, described the elections: "It is a homecoming. Fifteen years ago, after Begin's victory, a whole generation of us went into political exile. When the Likud won time and again, saturating Israel with what we considered to be an ideology of unreason—the redemptive politics of the whole of Israel—we cut ourselves off, as much as we could, from the public sphere and went about building our own private lives in a process I call 'emigration into inner space.' But since you cannot really escape politics here—in Israel politics is everything—we sank into a deep unconscious depression. And on Tuesday night, when we heard the election results, that depression finally lifted" (*Forward,* July 3, 1992).

Political marginality that is expressed in the language of exile of the Left meant a sense of political powerlessness. Harpaz's choice of words such as *home, exile,* and *emigration* is significant because they are linked to historical issues of political power or powerlessness. Exile signifies a history of powerlessness and laces Jewish history from ancient times; it permeates Jewish literature and liturgy and is still part of Israel's public discourse. Home(land) meant political power.

While in Israel's collective narrative exile and powerlessness are dreaded, home (power) is exalted, and Israel is seen as "the home" of the nation, politically, spatially, and spiritually. To live in Israel means to have a sense of political power even for those on the political margins; the country *is* a home, and Israeli Jews outside of the country often describe going back as "returning home." For contemporary Israelis, not to return home physically—to "emigrate" to another country—has negative connotations of living in exile and is expressed in the term *descenders,* which describes Israelis who leave the country and settle elsewhere and symbolizes the diminished power that is implicit in exilic living. But the loss of power applies as well to the kind of internal exile that Harpaz describes. Israelis, according to Harpaz, can be "in exile at home" when they have little political power. For the Left the 1992 elections and the terms *upheaval* and *turnabout* have meant a homecoming in terms of regaining political power.

After the Cairo agreement, in February 1994, Peres, who was in Cairo as the state's official, described his mode of consulting with Rabin throughout the negotiation as "keeping in touch with home" (*Yediot Ahronot,* February 11, 1994). Beyond winning the elections, this homecoming, this return from political exile, is seen as a legitimated collective wish. Individual hopes are submerged in a collective of people who want to change the center of power. Haim Ramon, who became minister of health in 1992, said: "For 15 years I have had this dream and it became a reality. Along the way we had disappointments. It turned out that the people want a different government, a different leader. Now the state of Israel will have a responsible government" (*Haaretz,* June 24, 1992).

As the Left and the Right exchanged positions of power, the elections meant, for both, a profound turnabout in terms of the Israeli-Palestinian conflict. For the Likud the upheaval signaled a turnabout from state policies of the Greater Israel that the Right has inscribed and a change in Israel's conflict with Palestinians. The meeting of two women members of Knesset with Nabil Shaat signifies this change of political ideology, of homecoming, and of power. Chazan and Dayan's meeting with a PLO official could have been dismissed as an unofficial act, a minor rebellion within the Left. But the rage expressed in the Right indicated that the meeting signaled a major political upheaval. Shamir's fear that Rabin would include new (and drastically different) images in Israeli nation-ness and forge state policies of coexistence with Palestinians was well founded. Moreover, social issues, the hallmark of the Yishuv, prestate period, and the early years of the state, were once again inserted into the concept of the nation.

In this struggle over the meaning of nation-ness the turnabout is also a shift in focus from the past (biblical patrimonial promises) to the future (a better one for the children, for future generations). Without rejecting the past, the political vision has turned collectively forward. In the signing of the agreement ceremony in Washington, Rabin deployed the past to legitimate the act of peace: "Our inner strength, our higher moral values, have been derived for thousands of years from the Book of Books, in one of which, Koheleth [Ecclesiastes], we read: 'To everything there is a season, and a time to every purpose under Heaven; a time to be born and a time to die; a time to kill and a time to heal; a time to weep and a time to love; a time to love and a time to hate; a time for war and a time for peace.' Ladies and gentlemen, the time for peace has come." Rabin's public address in Washington, D.C., at the signing of the agreement, stated that the question would no longer be what Israel is compelled to do for the past but that the past will be deployed to imagine what the nation must do to ensure life and peace for its future generations.

While Israel's security still defined the nation, it was now reconstructed on different grounds from a Greater Israel ideology, as it is no longer dependent on occupying territories. "The strength of the nation is not measured in the territories it controls" has become official policy. Rabin's act demonstrated that for the Left (and the Peace Camp), a turnabout meant a dramatic shift from engaging in the politics of protest to having the power to redefine both the meaning of nation-ness and the direction of the state's politics. The turnabout has taken place, according to some Israelis, because "the people were not apathetic, but have matured. They got fed up with the dead-end situation, with the corruption, and with the insane nationalism" (Yoel Marcus, *Haaretz*, June 26, 1992). The 1992 elections thus seemed to constitute both an epilogue to a political chapter in Israel's history (of the Likud and the Greater Israel) and a prologue to a new era marked by a government's policy of coexistence *(du kiyum)*, a policy long advocated by women peace activists.

Women Facing Their Own Comrades in the Government

The meeting between the two women members of Knesset and a Palestinian official had appeared to signal a profound turnabout regarding contact with the PLO. In the summer of 1992 it seemed that the Left had finally returned from political exile and that women peace activists could give up the politics of protest and support the government—in effect, a return from exile, since an ideology of the Greater Israel had come to an end. Yet for many women peace activists the 1992 elections have not been "a homecoming." Talma, one of the activists in Women in Black in Jerusalem, said a few days after the elections: "The Women in Black will continue to demonstrate until the government grants Palestinians autonomy. We did not stand here every Friday for the last four years to get Labor into the government. We are standing here to end the occupation, and we will go on standing here until there is an end to the occupation. We have added a new slogan, which says: 'Today more than ever: Stop the Occupation.'" Remaining on the political margins in 1992, the Women in Black continued to stand in the Friday vigils, despite the Left's victory.

In January 1993 a Women and Peace coalition conference in Jerusalem questioned the meaning of the term *turnabout;* rank-and-file women peace activists reconstituted themselves on the margins as they took a critical view of the government's policies regarding Palestinians. Thus, while all previous women's public events described so far took place during the Likud government, the 1993 Women and Peace conference in Jerusalem confronted a Left government with whom the women had shared a peace and coexistence ideology. The Jerusalem conference exposed a rift in the Left that questioned whether a political turnabout had in fact taken place. Several months after the elections the *Women in Black National Newsletter* provided its own perspective on the election results and revealed that some people in the Left are still on the political margins (protesting government policies) because they do not see that a turnabout has occurred: "It is a hard winter: little progress in the peace talks, more Palestinians killed and maimed, more Israelis killed and maimed, more [Palestinian] homes destroyed, more families shattered. One wants to shake the shoulders of politicians, generals, and terrorists of both sides—to shake them out of their madness, shake them into comprehending the tragic futility of their efforts. When will all this man-made violence cease?" (no. 4 [Winter 1992–93]: 2).

The women's questioning a turnabout highlights their own political hopes and expectations that followed the elections. The meeting in the Netherlands in August 1992 between the PLO representative and two women members of Knesset clearly indicates that not only men had high hopes. Orah Namir, who became a minister in the Labor government in 1992, said after the elections: "I am very happy. I did not believe that it would happen. We are doing very well now. This is a beginning of true change in the country" (*Haaretz,* June 24, 1992). In January of 1993, however, from the women's perspective the hoped-for "true change" had not materialized. Women's peace activism in 1993 reveals that what seemed like one position—peace and coexistence when the Left was in political exile—is now turning out to take on at least two different meanings and two distinct constructions of nation-ness. The government sees giving up land (in the territories) as the core of the peace and coexistence agenda and, unlike the Likud, constructs nation-ness and land in the Occupied Territories as divisible. While women agree with this ideological position, they also go beyond it, as they see nation-ness and justice to Palestinians as indivisible.

Illith Rosenblum, a member of Women in Black, notes the silence that still surrounds the act of occupation now under a Left government: "Occupation is the fundamental issue that has faced Israeli society for the past 26 years, and Women in Black are unique in addressing this issue in Israel. . . . One fact has not changed: Israeli military occupation still continues. All other issues that are thrown into the public arena are smokescreens. There is an all-out denial of the occupation by a majority of Israelis. 'What occupation?' is a common question heard from passers-by of the vigil. It is against this thick denial that Women in Black stand alone and, like so many Cassandras, speak out the truth to the public for one hour every week. I would like to suggest that 'The very basis for the survival of the vigil' is the need to speak the truth in the face of denial; that the political-social changes have not been 'significant' when the occupation continues; that, although researchers have exhausted the topic, it is the continuous occupation in its deadly routine of violence that is 'the very basis for the survival of the vigil'" (1993, 5). Women in Black continued the vigil, and the Women and Peace coalition held a conference in Jerusalem in 1993 because the occupation and its attending oppression for Palestinians have not come to an end.

A political position that peace and coexistence entails justice for Palestinians was expressed after the 1992 elections by women such as Maya Rosenfeld, a peace activist and a member of the Jerusalem vigil of the Women in Black: "Our vigil has always had another layer of meaning beyond 'end the occupation,' and that is the statement that a new situation exists, that the struggle of the Palestinians must lead to real progress for them. We stand in the vigil as a public reminder to the citizens and the government until such change comes about" (*Women in Black National Newsletter,* no. 6 [Fall 1993]: 5).

To speak of a political turnabout in terms of peace and coexistence depends, therefore, on whether the Left government faces the Likud or women peace activists. The government position differs fundamentally from the Likud in that it is willing to give up land for peace. The implications of this crucial difference were publicly acknowledged by people on the Right. Yuval Neeman, a leader of Tchiya, one of the extreme right-wing political parties that lost in the 1992 elections, said: "We have made significant contributions to Israel's political life in that we have revived the ideology of the Land of Israel" (*Haaretz,* July 3, 1992). Rabin's public statement thus signified that Greater Israel ideologies defining nation-ness as indivisible from land would be replaced by those of the Left. From the women's perspective, however, a turnabout meant far more than getting away from an ideology of the Greater Israel: it meant reinscribing justice into nation-ness and a policy of an immediate end to the occupation and to the violations of human rights.

The women's position should not be read as an isolated feminist agenda of justice, different from that of the rest of the (male) Left. The women's emphasis on justice reflects a contestation within the Left, a position that is different from the one that Rabin emphasized and a political agenda for which the Meretz Party was, until the elections, its official proponent. A few days after the 1992 elections and shortly before a government coalition was formed, *Haaretz* delineated the difference within the peace and coexistence position of land versus justice: "The people who voted for Meretz did not do it to strengthen Rabin . . . their main consideration was the wish to get rid of the occupation of the territories. The former defense minister, Rabin, carries much of the blame for what is happening today in the territories, but as prime minister he will have the power to put an end to some of the worst violations of human rights. As prime minister he can for example, order the SHABAK [an acronym for the secret security service] to stop the tortures. Meretz needs to carefully consider whether to join Rabin's government . . . it should also not be contingent on 'continuing the peace process.' It is hard to believe that Rabin will bring peace. The support for his government should be linked in the first place to his willingness to stop the abuse of the people in the territories" (June 21–26, 1992).

Uninvited Women: Reimagining Nation-ness and Justice

A vision of Israeli nation-ness that includes justice to people of another nation is clearly a position within the Left that is supported by both men and women. Women's peace groups, however, deploy gender solidarity to participate in imagining nation-ness indivisible from justice. Justice for Palestinians is at the center of the women's understanding of peace and coexistence. Women's groups thus highlight a dissenting position within the Left and display ways in which gender provides a ground for reimagining the nation. Differences within the Left in defining nation-ness—divisible from land, indivisible from justice—emerges not only between Women in Black (calling to end the occupation) and the government (giving up land for peace) but also in the wider context of women's peace activism. A gendered collective of women who protest the state's position regarding the occupation emerged as "We Women and Peace coalition." The Women and Peace coalition is an umbrella organization that includes Women in Black, Women against the Occupation, Women for Women Political Prisoners, Peace Quilt, Bridge for Peace, Haifa Women's Group, and Women's International League for Peace and Freedom. It created a political fact of a reconstituted margin that insists that "the protest must not die" despite the change in government. A turnabout/upheaval for the women means severing the link between the state and the occupation. Their position on nation-ness and state policies is seen in the fact that the women, once again, are protesting against the state because "the occupation, violation of human rights, violence, and killing continues" under the Left government.

On January 8, 1993, the coalition organized a National Women's Conference in Jerusalem. The theme of the conference, "Are We Really on the Brink of Peace?" indicates that the closing of a chapter of what Rabin described as "the religion of the Greater Land of Israel" and Harpaz described as "an ideology of unreason—the redemptive politics of the whole of Israel" is only part of what the women include in a peace and coexistence position. The conference organizers established a transnational space [Israeli and Palestinian women from Israel and the Occupied Territories] of women and presented the peace position to include justice that is beyond land and includes deep concern regarding "the occupation, violation of human rights, violence, and killing."[2]

The category "peace" took on a different meaning in this conference as the women noted that the oppressive nature of the occupation had not changed despite the change in government. Rabin's inclusion of "security" in redefining the nation (security as detachable from land of the Greater Israel) parallels the women's different imagining of the nation (detached from occupation) as one that includes justice for Palestinians. While Rabin emphasized the need to give up land for peace (land and nation-ness are divisible), the women objected to the occupation itself and emphasized the nation as an ethical and just imagined community. Tikva, one of the panelists at the conference, highlighted the differences between the women and the government: "I want to tell you of a meeting with Prime Minister Rabin after the deportation. The purpose of the meeting was to try and talk to him about it. I am telling you about the meeting because it symbolizes the government's rigidity and closed-mindedness. It was shocking to see that it was impossible to talk to the prime minister about a topic like human rights. It was impossible to have a dialogue about the political price of the deportation. I came out of the meeting frustrated, pained, and shocked. Things are rapidly deteriorating in the territories, of which the deportation is symptomatic. I think that in the deportation the government has committed an ethical crime, that it broke international conventions, and that it made a major political blunder."

The Jerusalem conference reveals some serious disagreements in the Left on the meaning of nation-ness and, consequently, for state policies: for the Labor government, the nation, and the land are separable; for the women the basic inseparability is the nation and justice. For the women the promise of giving up land for peace is a necessary but insufficient element in the state's position on the Israeli-Palestinian conflict. The Labor government has been willing to give up land, which the Right refused to do, but the women are concerned with the occupation and the treatment of Palestinians as well. Women at the Jerusalem conference stated that under the Left government there is still more of the same state policy that characterized the Likud government. In choosing to stay on the political margins, protesting a Left government, the women's conference reimagined nation-ness to include justice for the occupied.

Israeli-Jewish women peace activists are reimagining nation-ness that is different from the official version of the nation. Yael, one of the panelists in the 1993 Jerusalem conference, sees the task of women to take an active role, invite themselves into the nation, and affect government policies: "I am convinced that what we do strengthens the peace element in the government, supports coexistence and talking to the PLO and the idea of two states for two nations. We fight for the future and for the present; we fight for the Palestinian people and their rights as human beings; but we also fight for us as citizens and as women. It is impossible to expect that Israeli society will be better, more tolerant, and more understanding to women if it will not get rid of this terrible thing called occupation." While differences within the Left are acknowledged, nation-ness is seen as shifting and amenable to changes to include justice for Palestinians and for women.

Nation-ness as indivisible from justice is a key element in the women's ongoing protest, despite the 1992 elections and political upheaval. Women peace activists have repositioned themselves on the political margins (of protesting), facing a Left government because they want publicly to inscribe their understanding of a peace and coexistence ideology. These women peace activists have chosen to make room for their understanding of nation-ness on what Rosaldo (1988) calls the political marginal land of their own people. Gupta and Ferguson (1992) and Rosaldo (1988) note that Anderson's (1983) discussion of the nation attends to the center of power but that much more needs to be said about nation-ness as imagined by groups on the margins. Mary Louise Pratt, who includes women in the silenced marginal groups, says that "women inhabitants of nations were neither imagined as, or invited to imagine themselves as, part of the horizontal brotherhood [of the nation]" (1990, 51). But women can and do invite themselves, individu-

ally and/or collectively, as elected officials or as rank-and-file women to construct their own understanding of the nation.

There are numerous instances in Latin America (and in other places) of
women who, uninvited—collectively and daringly—insist on redefining the
nation, often in surprisingly effective ways (Jaquette 1989). Women reimagine the nation as different from the official version; "in Argentina, Chile and
Uruguay, for example, women were among the first to protest against the
mass imprisonment and disappearance" (4). These military governments,
which "depoliticized men and restricted the rights of 'citizens'" (nation-ness
divisible from civil rights), faced "marginal and normally apolitical" (uninvited) women, who challenged the official version of the nation (5). The
protest of the Madres of the Plaza Mayo of Argentina, Jaquette notes, "came
to symbolize the moral outrage of civilian society against bureaucratic
authoritarian regimes for the regions as a whole," so that specific imaginings
of official nation-ness were shown by (uninvited women) to be unacceptable
and alterable, whereas nation-ness and justice were seen as indivisible.[3]

A Return from Exile (for the Left) Prompts Another Exile
(of Palestinians)

Whether or not justice is indivisible from nation-ness marks the difference
between the Left government and women peace activists. The meaning of
nation-ness, as I noted earlier, underlines the government's policies toward
Palestinians, and the latter came up as unacceptable to women. Panelists
and participants protested the state's deportation of 415 Palestinians to exile
in Lebanon in December of 1992. The questions raised in the conference
were about acts and claims: How does the deportation speak of a political
upheaval? Does exiling such a large number of Palestinians negate a turnabout? Is it consistent with what the women imagine as nation-ness, as
redefined by the Left? Does the deportation of 415 Palestinians described as
Hamas activists constitute a fact of coexistence?

The Jerusalem 1993 conference revealed that from the women's perspective Rabin's deportation of Palestinians transformed his earlier act of
peace and coexistence (turning away from the Greater Israel position) into
mere talk. Sending Palestinians into exile, which further disempowered an
occupied people, seemed to the women a political act that contradicted a
peace and coexistence position as they construct it. Shifra, one of the panelists, said: "We are not talking about great expectations of changes in poli-

cies; there has been no major change, despite the fact that there was a political change as a result of the elections. After fifteen years [of the Likud] there
is another political party; different people occupy the government. But the
nature of the policies has not changed. The Right was shocked, as we all
were, by the deportation. But it was shocked because the [Left] government
did what the Right government did not dare during all these years. What is
very serious is that there is no significant change in government policies and
that the peace process is not a peace process. The continuity between the
former government and this one is stunning. In the face of the deportation
the Right does not have to do much. It needs to sit and wait until the Left
will do the work. Why should the Right make an effort? The Right is not
unified and faces internal conflicts. It is not a strong opposition, but on the
other hand the [Left] government is doing the job, so why try?"

A divided Left was revealed as some women saw the deportation as not
more of the same (implementing the Right's policies) but, rather, as a sign
that the Left has made a turnabout, only in the wrong direction. Ruth, one of
the panelists, said: "The question is how is it possible that a government that
won the elections on a slogan of change, of an interim agreement [with
Palestinians], within six to nine months has reached such a low point of cru-
elty and myopia, and I would add of political stupidity. It is not that we have
not seen in the past horrible and awful acts; it is not that we did not witness
in twenty-five years of occupation oppression, arrests, demolition of houses,
deportations, etc. But, when we wait for a change for the better and we get a
change for the worse, the shock and the anger are much greater."

For these women, being on the margins now was different than during
the preelection period, because they now face not a clear opposition, the rec-
ognizable opponent (the Right), but, instead, a government that seemed to
constitute "one of us" (mishelanu). The women, still on the margins, were
now confronting a government that they hoped would engage in the politics
of peace as they define it. Yael said: "In its latest acts the government has not
demonstrated the slightest desire for peace. People that I talked with lately
have been surprised. No one would have imagined that deportation; it was a
dramatic turning away from everything that this government could include
in its definition of its goal to achieve peace."

The Left Government as Occupier Produces Questions for Women
Precisely because in 1993 there was a Left government, the occupation, for
the women, became less tolerable. The gap between the women and the gov-

ernment was more acute and more painful than when the Right was in the center of power. The women had few expectations in the past to share a position on human rights with the Shamir government, but they had expectations after the upheaval that a Left government would be closer to the women's peace position. Because women now faced a Left government, action turned into mere talk was readily apparent. After the elections state officials seemed to establish political facts of peace and coexistence that the act of deportation turned into just talk. Ruth, one of the panelists in the 1993 conference, said: "The message to Palestinians is: 'Don't hope for anything. Because even this small thing that has been offered to you, namely to be able to live in your own country, has been denied.' This is a terrible message. I remain unconvinced when the government says: 'But it is only 415.' There is a major difference between deporting 1 or 2 people and 415. There is also a difference between deportations when there is no peace negotiation and when we are in the midst of it. The message of the deportation is: 'Talks are talks, but in actions don't expect a thing.' It is also a terrible message to Israelis and to us women who work for peace because all of a sudden there is a hidden national consensus. This dreadful deportation has gained almost total support in the government and congratulations from the Right opposition. A bad political situation has emerged in which there is a consensus in the Knesset from the extreme Right, Moledet and Tzomet, to Labor and Meretz on the Left."

Women talked about facts (peace talks) contradicting facts (deportations), revealing that for them peace and justice are not only indivisible but are the ground on which they stand together with Palestinian women. Not only gender but justice as well provide the ground for sororal solidarity. Justice in this case takes on a transnational turn: it means not only calling for civil rights within one's own community but also acknowledging the suffering, the claims, and the needs of other communities, including those of Palestinians. Susan Moller Okin's argument that one of the crucial components of justice is "thinking of the interests and well-being of others who may be very different from ourselves" takes on a local shape as it involves Israeli and Palestinian women (1989, 15). The women in the 1993 Jerusalem conference faced a situation in which, as a result of the deportation, they could be separated from Palestinian women. Because the government now included peace activists, the ground for transnational solidarity paradoxically became shakier. Galia told the women at the 1993 Jerusalem conference: "A delegation went to Gaza and met with those who now represent the deportees and visited families whose sons were killed this week. I want to share my feelings of this visit with you. I knew that I came as a representative of all Israelis who opposed the deportation and of those who seek peace. In one home a fifty-year-old mother was mourning two sons who were shot and murdered. There were two widows in that house and twelve orphans. Facing them, I want to say that no demonstration, no act, and no struggle that we women engage in can give us a cover as we stand there. We stand there naked, *arumot,* as part of Israeli society. I say that because there are norms of atrocities that we have become used to. These atrocities have become a barrier to dialogue."

Precisely because there is a Left government that expresses an ideology of peace and coexistence, solidarity with Palestinian women has become more difficult for peace activists after 1992. The black clothes of the vigils, which veil differences but unveil the injustices by protesting the occupation, are now seen by women such as Galia as no longer offering the same ground for transnational solidarity. A Left government holding an ideological position of peace and coexistence makes it much harder for women peace activists to distance themselves from the occupiers. The occupiers, for some women, have become more clearly "us" (the Left), not "them" (the Right). The space that women now occupy on the margins no longer has the obvious distancing from the center that it did during the Likud government. In public events such as the vigils and conferences in 1993, women needed to clearly define their own reimagining of nation-ness that is indivisible from justice. Whereas during the Likud government the women's dissenting position was clear, since the 1992 elections they had to demarcate a less readily obvious dividing line between Left protesters and a Left government. One of the ways that lines were drawn and differences noted in the 1993 Jerusalem conference was when women urged a Left government to talk to the PLO.

A Discourse in the Left about the PLO

The women's struggle to include the PLO in the peace negotiations as part of a meaningful turnabout is not a gendered position and is reflected in a position within the Left.[4] Several months after the 1993 Jerusalem conference this position was reenacted in the Knesset. This time it was a male member of the Labor Party, Hagay Merom who "broke the rules" *(shavar et hakelim).* "On the labor benches they were stunned: Merom named seven ministers, who, he said, 'I know are in favor of direct talks with the PLO. He urged them to express their position openly, and to come out of hiding and to join with Meretz ministers to exercise their majority in the government to bring about a breakthrough. The time has come.' Merom said: 'There is among the Ministers a majority for new solutions. This is the place, *ze hamakom*, and this is the time, *ze hazman*, to talk to the Tunis PLO. The government of Israel should send a minister from the Labor party to talk directly with the PLO. It is necessary to be liberated from saying that there is no room for a Palestinian state in the territories. . . . In view of the current deadlock [in the peace talks] the time has come to end the public lie, originated by the Likud government, that there is no talk with the PLO.' " Labor members of Knesset were stunned, and the opposition began to interrupt the speaker (*Yediot Ahronot,* July 9, 1993).

Yediot Ahronot participated in the discourse about the different positions in the Left regarding the PLO as it informed its readers that "Meretz Ministers Demand: To Talk to PLO-Tunis" (ibid.). But in July of 1993 Merom's political act in one of the most public spaces, the Knesset, was still seen as a dissenting position that did not reflect the Labor government's policy. The disagreement in the Left regarding the PLO was revealed not only in women's conferences but in the fact that the government was seen to oppose such a position, despite the support for it among elected officials. Merom's statement was considered to be so far removed from the government's position that it was described by some as "frankly a case of a regular ritual, in which Meretz ministers propose—with support from [several Labor ministers]—to talk directly with the PLO on the future of the territories, and demand new proposals to bring closer the negotiators' different positions. According to this regular ritual Meretz ministers 'release steam' and [Prime Minister] Rabin, supported by a government's majority, summarizes the debate in preserving the current position without change" (ibid.).

In 1993 there were people on the Left who, like the women at the conference, thought that the time had come for Israel to accept the fact that the PLO represents the Palestinians and that fruitful negotiations must include its leaders. Women panelists in the Jerusalem conference expressed what Sarid, then a member of Knesset and now a minister in the government, said a few months later: "This government sits on one branch—the peace branch—if this branch breaks, we will all fall" (ibid.). Sarid's interpretation of peace was parallel to one taken by women like Hassan: "The government must open the gate for Tunis-PLO and to Yassir Arafat, because he is the true 'homeowner' among the Palestinians" (ibid.). Several months after Hassan said publicly in the Jerusalem conference that "letting the PLO participate in the peace talks would accelerate the negotiations. Everyone knows now that PLO is here, and is part of it," Sarid said, "To talk or not to talk to the PLO, this is the only decision this government now faces and it cannot, forever, get away from making the decision" (ibid.)

Talking to the PLO eventually became public government policy, which culminated in the signing of the agreement in Washington and the ongoing negotiations in 1994 between Israel and the PLO. But for the women the issue of justice goes beyond inclusion of the PLO in the peace talks. After the 1992 elections it was all too easy for people in the Left, particularly in a wave of euphoria on the return from political exile, to be co-opted or included in what seemed a single peace and coexistence position. Women who call for justice, however, realize that they need to chart some distance from the state and to elucidate the differences that they have with the government. It was important to them because the similarities between those who hold a peace and coexistence position are clear and because they share with some members of Knesset, such as Merom and Sarid, a position that there needs to be talks with the PLO.

A national meeting of the Women and Peace coalition held in Haifa on November 7, 1992, revealed the parameters of the similarities and the lines drawn between elected officials and rank-and-file women on the issue of justice: "The discussion focused on the effect of the political changes in Israel and the world upon the Israeli-Palestinian conflict. Although Meretz has joined the government, there was agreement that we must continue our role as an extra-parliamentary movement which opposes the occupation and is committed to a just solution that brings peace to the two nations" (Deutsch, 1992–93, 3). A year after the 1993 women's conference Peres said that he saw the Cairo agreement as good mostly because "we can liberate ourselves from the need to rule over another people, liberate ourselves from the need to police the life of other people. Without it there is no sense to this negotiation." He reiterated that "we will be free from a thing that we could not go on doing: ruling another people, in a very narrow country. Today there are here 4 million Jews and 3 million non-Jews. This is a situation that could easily turn into a tragedy if there will not be leaders who will see the dangers" (*Yediot Ahronot*, February 11, 1994). The women at the Jerusalem conference would probably disagree that "it could easily turn into a tragedy," however, because from their perspective the tragedy has already taken place in the very existence of the occupation.

Residents at Home and (Powerless) Homeless Inhabitants

While there may be a political commitment by leaders such as Peres to end the occupation, there is a difference in what aspects of it people decide to emphasize. Unlike the women, Peres did not use the word *occupation* but chose *rule,* a more ambiguous term. Enfolded in the different terminology are acts of disguising (using *rule*) or revealing (using *occupation*) the powerlessness inherent in the disunity between nation and state for Palestinians. Underlying it is an implicit or explicit Israeli sense that Palestinians are in "exile" in their home. While Israelis do not necessarily quote Herzl's argument for a Jewish homeland, they share his position about home as a sign (and a fact) of power and exile as a condition of powerlessness. Israelis are well aware of the consequences of powerlessness (even for citizens) and of not having the rule. People on the Left saw themselves "in exile" during the Likud government because they felt politically powerless in their own country. The argument between the Left and the Right, as their different ideological positions indicate, is about whether Palestinians can have a home in the West Bank and the Gaza Strip. The differences within the Left, as expressed in the division between women in the 1993 Jerusalem conference and the government, are about what kind of a home Palestinians can have or how much political power.

To speak or not speak of occupation is to reveal or disguise power differentials between Israelis and Palestinians. Women who make constant reference to, and use, the word *occupation* speak of the powerlessness of Palestinians and of the disregard for their rights. Behind and within their discussions on the occupation and the deportation is the indication of the powerlessness in the absence of a legitimated nation and of a state, revealed in women's frequent insistence on two states for two nations in their public statements. The women in the 1993 Jerusalem conference focused on the oppressive nature of the occupation. The deportation of 415 Palestinians is both the reality and a symbol of Palestinian powerlessness of not having a home they can call their own. Nabiha, a Palestinian panelist in the Jerusalem 1993 conference, noted the link between forced exile and powerlessness: "Israel is dealing with the people who are sitting at the negotiation table as inhabitants of the land but not the residents of the land. And there is a big difference when you are inhabitants. The government can tell you to leave the country, and you leave. But when you are a resident it is your right to be in the country, and this is our country. We have a right to stay in it."

Solidarity between Israeli and Palestinian women from the Occupied Territories is forged on the ground of gender and justice and its entailed implications of home (power) and exile. In women's public events the participants attempt ceaselessly to construct not only gender but also justice as the ground on which they forge transnational solidarity: "We Women and Peace coalition know that as long as the occupation, violation of human rights, violence, and killing continues, the protest must not die." Women's conferences during the Likud government recognized that atrocities have been committed in the Occupied Territories and often called on the government to put an end to them. But during the Likud government women peace activists did not appear to themselves, as Galia called it, politically "naked," because they stood in ideological opposition to the Right government. In 1993, however, they seemed to stand in the same ideological space as the government, but that was only partially the case. In all previous women's public events described so far, which took place during the Likud government, gender solidarity was seen as a major theme, and women ceaselessly tried, with varying degrees of success, to construct female unity. In the 1993 Jerusalem conference, when women peace activists faced their own comrades in the government, justice as well was prominently constructed as a space on which Israeli (Palestinian and Jewish) and Palestinian women from the Occupied Territories could stand together.

At the same time that women peace activists called upon justice and gender to make a common space, acts such as deportations took on personal dimensions for Palestinian women; the deportees could be their relatives or friends. The dilemma for these women was: to come or not to come to a peace conference. Hassan, a Palestinian woman, said in the conference: "When I got the invitation for the conference, it was after the deportation, and it was a question for me to come or not to come." A ground of solidarity has been forged in the past; conference participants hoped that solidarity could be reconstructed in the midst of crises and potential divisions between women who are either the occupied or the occupier: "I decided to come because I believe in people, and I believe that people are the ones who could make the change. . . . The conditions that are imposed on us as Palestinians are such that we are forced to enter the negotiations whatever the conditions are. We believed that the negotiations themselves will change the conditions. But now after more than a year of negotiations we find that things are not proceeding in order. At first with the Likud government things did not progress. We believed that with the change in government, with the Labor and Meretz parties, things would change in the negotiation. . . . But the negotiating Israeli team is the same as it was during the Likud government, and the agenda is still the same. So, this is not an encouraging situation. But, if it is still at that level, we say we could go on not for an unlimited time but to see how it is developing. What we have is the situation on the ground that is not hospitable, while it forces us to go on with the peace talks. As one who really believes in peace and supports the peace process, as well as other Palestinians who support the peace process, we find ourselves in a very difficult situation."

Justice: A Fragile Transnational Solidarity

Women's accounts in the 1993 Jerusalem conference reveal that the issue of justice unites women of two nations. Randa, a Palestinian panelist, revealed a transnational solidarity with Israeli women peace activists; at the same time, she challenged the Israeli government and the occupation: "I am very glad to be here today because I have no doubt that I am with women from the peace movement who are already converted, so I don't need to convert anybody; that relaxes me and makes it more easy. I did not have a dilemma being with you, because I was sure that I was coming to be with friends, and so it was not a problem for me. And I am among friends.

"I will speak today on the human rights issue with the specific focus on the Labor Party, the Rabin government coming to power with all the optimism that it had brought to some of you—maybe to some of us Palestinian people too. I am a human rights activist, and I know what is going on in the Occupied Territories, and I don't see a reason for optimism—after seeing what has happened after the Madrid peace talks in the Occupied Territories: full restrictions still continuing, closures of areas, deportations, killing of people by the Israeli undercover units, prisoners under administrative detentions, and the torture that continues in Israeli prisons. I don't want to name and count all the human rights violations that go on daily because it is not the purpose of what I am doing here today. But this continues, and, as a human rights activist, I want to note that since the peace talks have started the attention of the international community has shifted from human rights violations to the peace talks; there is not enough attention on what is happening on a day-to-day basis in the Occupied Territories. The new government coming into power seems not to have enough votes [to feel secure] and that may explain the deportation [of 415 Palestinians]. But I consider it completely illegal; I don't accept the deportation as anything else. There has been talk by the government in the middle of July [1992], immediately after it came to power, about the building of confidence of the Palestinians to make progress in the peace negotiations. But there have not been changes in terms of human rights. There have been no improvements, although there was a change in government."

Palestinian women did come to the 1993 Jerusalem conference, but their accounts revealed the fragility of transnational solidarity. Israeli-Jewish and Israeli-Palestinian women know that in times of crisis, such as a deportation, the Palestinian women from the Occupied Territories face the question of whether to engage in any joint activities. Crises of this dimension bring to the fore the difference between belonging to the occupying community (albeit in opposition to occupation) and living under occupation. Acts such as deportation elicit for Palestinian women existential anxieties and the question of collective survival. In some ways each nation's anxieties are familiar to the other; they speak the same language of anxiety concerning collective survival. Parallel to Israeli-Jewish anxiety about exile (political powerlessness) is the Palestinians' dread of exile. They have heard people on the extreme Right advocate a policy of "transfer" as well as people on the Right who refuse to acknowledge the national aspirations and identity claims of Palestinians and who made arguments for the transfer of what they call "Arabs" to other Arab countries. The deportation raises Palestinian collective anxieties of survival as it touches on their themes of home and exile. Nabiha said at the conference: "We can see that the people who were deported are living in very bad conditions. Lebanon is not Israel, and Israel wants to deport these people to Lebanon and to show that Lebanon is sharing the decision of deportation—but it does not. This is Rabin's mentality; he believes that he could achieve things by force. I cannot understand how the head of the Israeli team could say yesterday that there is no relation between deportation and going on with the negotiation. I don't know how he thinks that. The expulsion was of 415 people directly, and, if you take into account the families of the deportees, it has directly affected thousands of people. Neighbors and communities are affected, for we live in very close proximity. So, what can we do in this situation?"

The Palestinian anxiety of exile, which was high during the Likud years, did not go away despite the promise of peace and coexistence by the Left government. The distinction that Nabiha makes between Lebanon and Israel indicates that for Palestinians other Arab countries represent diaspora and exile. Home for Palestinians is where they live: East Jerusalem, the West Bank, or the Gaza Strip. But the deportation to Lebanon questions Palestinians' right to be in their own home on their land and their Palestinian nationhood. The significance of homeland and its indivisibility from Palestinian nation-ness was expressed by Youseff Ibrahim a day before the signing of the agreement in Washington, D.C., in 1993: "Whether or not the mutual recognition agreement between the Government of Israel and the Palestinian Liberation Organization leads to Palestinian statehood, it nonetheless enshrines the principle that the Palestinians are, in fact, a distinct people [a nation], defined by the land they call home" (1993).

In the 1993 Jerusalem conference Palestinian panelists from the Occupied Territories spoke of the concept of home for Palestinians. Home under occupation, they said, is not a safe place, because human rights violations, such as deportations without trials, continue, despite the change in government in 1992. They noted the absence of legal justice as contributing to the sense of danger. Hannan said: "The deportees have not been tried. If these people have done something, let them be charged and be brought to trial. Occupation cannot be a nice occupation. We understand that the violence is on both sides, and it is action and reaction every time. We see that the deportation happened, and still bloodshed continues on both sides. So, deportation does not stop anything. The only thing that could stop it is the end of the occupation. This is the only thing that will stop all the suffering. We want to put an end to all the sufferings of both Jews and Arabs. It can be done only by ending the occupation and reaching an agreement, a real agreement."

The Meanings of Real Agreement

Hannan raised the theme of "a real agreement," but, like the ideology of peace and coexistence, the term takes on different meanings in different contexts. A real agreement for the women, Israelis and Palestinians, in the 1993 conference meant a turnabout that includes justice in the Occupied Territories. For many participants it also meant two states for two nations as a Left peace position. The 1993 women's conference exposed some differences within the Left between the conference participants and their own comrades in the Peace Camp who were now in the government. To make an agreement real for Israeli women, those who participated in the 1993 Jerusalem conference, justice and the end of the occupation would have to be included. In this political position, as the 1993 Jerusalem conference revealed, they stand closer to Palestinian women than they do to their Left government—even as that government makes its own upheavals in its policy regarding Palestinians.

In September 1993, ten months after the women's conference, some of their claims and hopes materialized: the government made its dramatic agreement with the PLO and signed partial agreements on Jericho and Gaza with Arafat. In 1994 Israeli officials publicly made an upheaval by talking with the PLO in Cairo. But from the Palestinian side the very same agreement was viewed differently. In the Occupied Territories it was met with skepticism and indifference because, as the Jerusalem conference revealed, justice and occupation—as facts on the ground—define whether an agreement is real. Palestinian leaders said that "what is important from their perspective is to see a sign of withdrawal, the end of occupation, an improvement in human rights; not a piece of paper. Releasing prisoners before the month of Ramadan fasting would have been more effective for [Palestinians'] morale" (Gilat, *Yediot Ahronot*, February 11, 1994). One Palestinian leader said: "We have given concessions in a most painful way. Our credibility has been damaged."

From the Likud's perspective a real agreement seemed similarly alarming but precisely because it believes what the Palestinians doubt: the direction, the turnabout, in reaching an agreement. Shamir's response to the agreement was that "this is the beginning of the surrender and withdrawal"; he emphasized that "it is necessary to continue the war and not put up hands in surrender." His fellow party member Netanyahu said that "the government is implementing the first stage of a Palestinian state on the 1967 borders" (*Yediot Ahronot*, February 11, 1994).

Clearly, the terms *peace, a real agreement,* and *turnabout* take on different meanings depending on the speakers' political position. What seems an upheaval (and a political disaster) to the Likud Party or a historic achievement to the government may be viewed very differently by Palestinians or by women peace activists. One version of peace and coexistence was outlined in Rabin's inaugural address in 1992, when he said that Israel will take "vigorous steps that will lead to the conclusion of the Arab-Israeli conflict"; furthermore, he called on the leaders of the Arab world to follow the lead of the late president of Egypt, Anwar Sadat. Rabin did not leave the Palestinians out. He invited the members of the Palestinian-Jordanian delegation to meet with him, "so that we can hear their views, make ours heard and create an appropriate atmosphere for neighborly relations" (*Forward,* July 17, 1992). Rabin spoke directly to Palestinians as well in his address: "To you Palestinians in the territories, you who have never known a single day of freedom and joy in your lives, listen to us, if only this once. We offer you the fairest and most viable proposal from our standpoint today: autonomy, with all its advantages and limitations. You will never get everything you want. Neither will we. So once and for all, take your destiny in your hands. Don't miss this opportunity that may never return" (*Near East Report,* July 20, 1992, 5). But the Palestinians were cautious in their response to this invitation. Abdel-Shafi Haidar, the head of the Palestinian delegation to the peace talks, noted that "the fact that he [Rabin] said that there would be no withdrawal from the territory and his failure to halt settlements throw a negative light on talks" (*Forward,* July 17, 1992).

The difference between an agreement to give up land for peace and an agreement that calls for an end to the occupation (withdrawal from the territory) was revealed in the Jerusalem conference in 1993. Nabiha, a Palestinian woman panelist, like Israeli-Jewish women panelists, engaged in the debate on the meaning of a turnabout: "People do not perceive peace progress around the negotiation table or on the ground. There is a lot of violation of basic human rights that was made worse by the deportation of 415 persons. Deporting them is a very bad situation. The number of deportees shows that Israel is defying all international conventions and is not considering the people. With this deportation the acceptance by Left government members of the vote for the deportation is a depressing situation. We ask ourselves: Are there Israelis that you could talk with and really work with for a just peace? This is the question asked by our people. We are really in a very, very difficult position, in which there is not much room to move. And who is responsible for moving first? I don't think it is the Palestinians. The Israeli government must realize that something serious has to happen." Like Israeli-Jewish women in the Jerusalem conference, Nabiha raises the question of what is the meaning of peace and coexistence. Dissimilarities with the Left government are expressed when she puts together what the government has sundered: occupation/deportation and peace talks. She speaks about the inseparability of Palestinians from their land, the Occupied Territories, and the indivisibility of pursuing peace talks and human rights for Palestinians.

Producing a Position Statement in the Jerusalem Conference

In facing their own comrades in the government, the women at the 1993 Jerusalem conference were divided on how to deal with what they saw as the abdication of a political position of justice by elected officials (peace activists) who voted for or did not protest against the government's deportation of 415 Palestinians. The division was revealed as Amal, the conference moderator, read a statement prepared by some of the women and brought for confirmation as the conference position. The statement said: "We women from all over the country, who work and struggle in extra-parliamentary activities for a just peace in our region, insist on a struggle outside the government. Our demand is to change the system and not to make revisions in the existing one. The bitter experience of the last few weeks has demonstrated to us that Meretz women who joined the government with a mandate to work ceaselessly for peace have become a rubber stamp for the largest transfer by an Israeli government since 1967. We are steadfast in our belief that no goal justifies the death of one man or one woman. The massive deportation proved to us that this government, like those that preceded it, disregards state laws as well as international law. We call on the government to return the deportees immediately. It is clear to us that deportation not only does not bring about peace between Israel and the Palestinian nation, *haam haphalstini,* but it removes any possible dialogue between the two nations. The Palestinian people/nation have chosen the PLO to represent its aspirations for national liberation. We call on the Israeli government to negotiate directly with the PLO for a peace agreement between Israel and Palestine."

This proposal of the conference position, however, met with protest. Women objected to what they saw as a rejection of a Left government and/or of their comrades in the Knesset and to the criticism leveled at women in particular. Even if there would be a majority vote, these were strong objections, and the conference organizers wanted to arrive at an acceptable consensus. Karin expressed this reaction by calling on democratic principles that, in her opinion, the statement contradicted: "The statement calls for changing the system, and I don't want to change the system. It is an undemocratic statement because we have an elected government. Just as the Palestinians chose their representatives, Israelis have chosen their leaders. We may have differences, but I refuse to come out of this conference calling to change the government. Reservations—yes, disagreements, yes—but to change the government I say: No." Rachel offered a compromise position that would not involve a rejection of Meretz: "Just as we say 'stop the occupation' we can take out the words 'condemning Meretz.'" Gila, who revealed a sense of already being on the political margins as a peace activist, did not want to further exile women politically by requiring them to sever ties with their comrades in the government: "I don't like the phrase 'extra-parliamentary activity' to describe peace activism. True, we feel let down by the women who represent us in the government. But we need not paint a totally black picture and reject them. They slipped." Naomi feared that the disagreement would not be resolved and that the conference would be a "mere talk" event; she urged women to act by coming out publicly, and to the press, with a statement: "The women who are here today are genuine—when they say that the Palestinians have a right to self-determination, they mean it. And, when say that they are for negotiating with the PLO, they really mean it. These things are tested in deeds, not in talk. I therefore think that we should come out from this conference with a clear statement. We must include our position on the deportation and make it clear that the topic will not be silenced until all the deportees come back."

Yael resonated a similar concern that the event would lose its political potency and turn out to be mere talk, lacking in substance, rather than a public event: "We have a problem here, and we need to address it. One of the reasons that we organized this conference is to stir up the peace movement into intense action. Our goal was not to have a once-a-year conference. I don't want to spend the rest of our time on the statement, but I don't want it to turn into a conference in which we met, we talked the same language more or less, we hugged, kissed, were happy to see each other, and then go back home to return to the same activities." The women agreed that a few women would leave the conference hall to rewrite the statement. When they returned Tamar read the amended statement, indicating the actual changes: "'Women and Peace conference, January 1993. We women from all over the country work and struggle for a just peace in our region in all possible ways.' We have made a change not to exclude women who are in the Knesset and who are part of us, and we say: 'we insist on a fundamental change in the policy of the Israeli government toward peace,' and we took out the words 'working outside the government and changing the system.' We say: 'the bitter experience of the last few weeks demonstrated that people who sit in government, and the women in particular, who were entrusted with a mandate to ceaselessly work for peace, provided a rubber stamp to the largest deportation by an Israeli government since 1967.' The rest of the text is the same as in the original version, except that we say that 'the deportation prevents a dialogue' and not any dialogue. We also changed the words 'call on the government' to 'we demand that the government negotiate directly with the PLO.'" When Tamar finished reading it, she said, "We all agree to accept it as our official statement, and yet I would like to call on the women from Meretz in the Knesset and the government and let them know in writing what we think about their vote regarding the deportations." There was a clear sense that women at the conference saw Meretz as the political party representing the Peace Camp position in the government and focused their attention on women in that party, saying much less about peace activists in the Labor Party.

The compromise statement was accepted with no voiced dissent in the conference. It revealed most of all that gender solidarity was important and that women did not wish to cut themselves off from elected women peace activists. Tamar's call to let their comrades in the Knesset and the government know that women feel let down was a solidarity gesture that meant gender unity among peace activists. Women are seen in this context as unified in their peace position. Yet it is important to note that, while women construct a justice/gender solidarity, their position on justice as inseparable from peace reflects a wider concern in the Left. Regarding Israeli-Palestinian relations, differences within the Left usually are constructed around Rabin, who was viewed in his first year as prime minister as more center than Left. Some Israelis saw him as closer to the Right than to Meretz. This, as I noted earlier, was obviously not at all the way in which the prime minister was viewed by Shamir, who made no distinction between Rabin and Peres's positions. But until September 1993, some people questioned just how much of a "Left," a dove, Rabin actually was—or, in the women's framework, how much his administration was concerned with justice as indivisible from a reimagined nation-ness. Rabin's actions at the onset of the Intifada in 1987 when he served as minister of defense were mentioned when questions about his peace and coexistence position come up. *Haaretz* noted, after the election results became known in 1992: "The former Defense Minister, Rabin, carries much of the blame for what is happening today in the territories, but as prime minister he will have the power to put an end to some of the worst violations of human rights" (June 21–26, 1992). The division in the Left, however, goes beyond the way that Rabin was perceived in 1992. It is seen, rightly or wrongly, in a difference between Meretz and Labor in terms of linking justice to a peace and coexistence position and, consequently, to a different vision of nation-ness and state policies. *Haaretz* addressed such differences: "Meretz needs to carefully consider whether to join Rabin's government . . . it should also not be contingent on 'continuing the peace process.' It is hard to believe that Rabin will bring peace. The support for his government should be linked in the first place to his willingness to stop the abuse of the people in the territories" (Ibid.).

Some Israelis, however, make no distinctions between Meretz and Labor, as both are seen currently as making state policies together. After the Washington peace agreement Stan Cohen, an Israeli scholar and peace activist, reflected on the degree to which justice is indivisible from peace for the Left government: "Soon after the June 1992 elections, it became apparent that Meretz and Labor doves would, in the name of political expediency, refrain from opposing human rights violations. Their continued refusal to denounce the work of the undercover units (Shulamit Alon's only concern was that the killers in these units were too young to be exposed to such demanding work); their support for the mass deportations of December 1992 and for (continuing) closure of Gaza and the West Bank—all this was justified by the argument that we should not rock the boat, that a secret deal with the Palestinians was on the way" (1993, 16).

Women in Black and the Question of a Turnabout/Upheaval

Women peace activists have a hard time sorting out what direction to take when the government acts in ways that seem to support a peace and coexistence ideology. It is hard for women to reject such acts because they express a peace position, and it is difficult for women to accept acts that they see as necessary but partial in terms of justice. The signing of the agreement in Washington presented this dilemma to the Jerusalem vigil of the Women in Black. The question was whether the agreement signaled the end of their struggle and, in that case, whether they should disband the vigil. Before deciding, the women met to discuss whether the signing of the agreement constituted a sufficient turnabout from their perspective. Ruth Cohen, one of the founders of Women in Black, noted: "The first of these meetings was an ad hoc gathering of fourteen women who met after the announcement [of an agreement between Israel and the PLO] but before the signing of the agreement. Only one woman took what proved to be a prophetic view of what lay ahead for Women in Black. She believed there would be a steady decline in the number of vigil participants, which would gradually weaken the impact of Women in Black. The rest of us were in favor of continuing the vigil while adding some sign acknowledging the new political situation. We made a hasty decision to provide a white sash saying: 'Yes to Peace' for any woman choosing to wear it." A month after the signing of the agreement, however, "on Wednesday, October 20, Women in Black of Jerusalem made a historic decision to end the weekly Friday vigil. I doubt whether a single one of the women who have stood in Paris Square for the past five-and-a-half years did not feel a sense of emptiness and regret on Friday, October 22nd, at one o'clock" (1993, 11).

Women in Black and other peace activists face a dilemma of wanting to support the Left, which confronts strong opposition from the Right in the Knesset and the settlers on the streets, but at the same time wanting to hold on to justice as the center of peace and coexistence. A few days after the first meeting, on the following Friday, "it was clear that the majority of women who participated did so in the kind of celebratory mood that was prevalent elsewhere after the announcement of mutual recognition and the signing of the agreement between Israel and the PLO. Without any need for a formal decision, all the women, apart from the 30 core activists, were bidding their farewell to Paris Square on Fridays. Nevertheless, two subsequent discussion meetings were held, during which the dilemma over whether or not to continue the vigil became clear. Without exception, every woman at the meetings understood that the agreement would not mean an immediate end to the occupation, nor to human rights abuses. The few women who, from the start, were in favor of ending the regular vigils were equally certain that events, in the coming months, might prompt them to stand again" (ibid., 11, 13).

Women in Black understood that when the euphoria of the agreement, like the euphoria following the 1992 election, subsided, political facts would be sorted out from mere talk, and justice once again would be at the center; the question of whether justice is indivisible from the peace agreement would confront them again. Some of the women were not certain that the agreement signed in Washington, D.C., was in fact an epilogue to their protest against the occupation. "Whether this is a permanent or a temporary change hinges on what kind of change the government will initiate. . . . If the current attempt to find a just solution to the Israeli-Palestinian conflict does not measure up to expectations, we will, one by one, resume our weekly stand against the occupation" (ibid., 13). To stand against the Left from within the Left was especially difficult right after the signing of an agreement with Palestinians. Renate Wolfson, a member of the Women in Black, expressed this predicament: "I was not happy about the decision, I thought that there were many reasons for a protest. But the situation is so complicated now that it is impossible to convey it in a few words—'end the occupation.' People could not understand why we were still standing there" (*Hadashot,* October 28, 1993).

Home Again?

A few days after the Women in Black decided to relinquish the public space in Jerusalem, home as a domestic/familial space was invoked, as Yael Kopelman published an interview with several members of the Women in Black in *Hadashot* under the title "Going Home." She said: "After the signing of the agreement with the PLO, Women in Black have vacated their headquarters in Paris Square, and in the coming Fridays, if no one will make them angry, they will stay home" (ibid.). Going home, however, it was noted by Kopelman and by the women she interviewed, was in its political sense only a partial move. It was unclear just how politically appropriate the term *going home* was for peace activists. Kopelman's phrase "if no one will make them angry, they will stay at home" means that the women will have to see if justice for Palestinians follows the signing of the agreement. The ambiguity about whether this was a real homecoming was expressed when the women did not give up their political voice but decided to suspend judgment to see whether a turnabout in fact takes place. Anat Hofman, an active member in Women in Black, commented on the vigil's decision and used one of Rabin's keywords, *security,* to convey the sense that these women's home was on the map of Israel's political life: "There was nothing passive about the vigil. It was our nonviolent way to convey our message about security, an area that has been ordinarily closed to women" (ibid.).

Just how partial and premature this homecoming was could be seen when on December 10, 1993, Women in Black stood again in Paris Square in Jerusalem. "After a nearly two-month hiatus, 104 Jerusalem Women in Black renewed their vigil with slogans supporting peace and condemning settler violence. The weekly vigil is scheduled to continue until the promised IDF

[Israeli Defense Force] withdrawal from Gaza and Jericho takes place" (*Challenge,* no. 23 [January–February 1994]: 32). The women displayed signs such as their traditional "Stop the Occupation," "Stop the Violence," "Stop the Bloodshed," and "Bring the Soldiers Home." *Home,* in this case, means delineating the boundaries of power. The use of excessive power and violence by settlers is seen by peace activists as transgressing geographic and ethical limits of home for Israelis and making home unsafe for Palestinians. *Home* is redefined by peace activists as Israel's homeland without the Occupied Territories. It was expressed when the Israeli Peace Bloc demonstrated in Tel Aviv, where Rabin met editors carrying signs "calling for the settlers to return inside the Green Line" (ibid.). Home emerges not only as linked with power but with justice. Homeland's boundaries, drawn on the Green Line (the 1967 border), are defined by justice. For peace activists justice requires that the settlers "return home." Questions about the government's interpretation of peace revolve time and again around the question of whether coexistence is divisible from justice and from the construction of home.

While the Jerusalem Women in Black was reconstituted, some members have decided not to return to the vigils and to seek new ways of political activism. In a letter of January 23, 1994, Yael, who was active in Women in Black, wrote: "As you know in October Women in Black in Jerusalem have decided to end the vigils. In the last month, however, because there was no Israeli withdrawal from the territories about 20–30 women went back to demonstrate. I was not among them. It seems to me that the time has come to act in different ways. I believe that there will be a withdrawal, but it is natural that it takes some weeks or months. In Tel Aviv as well the Women in Black continue to demonstrate but it is a smaller more militant group." Some women see silence as complicity in the occupation and regard the vigil as a constant breaking of the silence on the occupation and injustice to Palestinians. Tamar, who stood in the vigil of the Women in Black in Jerusalem from the beginning, said: "I stand there not because I think that I can change other people's minds. I stand there because one day when my children will ask me: 'Where were you when the occupation took place?' I will say: 'I was in Paris Square every Friday afternoon between 1:00 and 2:00 P.M.'" Women peace activists such as Tamar illuminate a reimagining of nation-ness indivisible from justice and inscribe themselves in the nation. For these women, coming home would mean a turnabout in state policies to include justice not only within the Israeli-Jewish community but transnationally—for Palestinians.

In the Jerusalem 1993 conference Ruth, an Israeli-Jewish panelist, saw an official reluctance to redefine home within the Green Line as a space bounded by justice as the government's political fear (of the Right, of the settlers and their supporters): "In light of these events [deportations] I am asking myself: What is happening to people? How do people come to surrender to pressure? It has political implications because members of Knesset yell and scream because the Labor Party wants to get out of the territories and act as if the government has no legitimate right to do so. I ask them: 'When Begin was elected, did he tell the voters that he would return Sinai to Egypt in return for peace?' To my knowledge Begin has never told the voters that this was his intention. I am saying it because I don't want people from the Left to come later on and say that they could not take the pressure, that they could not face the mob that wanted revenge. If leaders cannot refuse a mob that wants revenge, I have serious questions about their role, their status, and their methods."

Beyond commenting on the government's degree of courage, accounts of women such as Ruth touch on the complicated history of the Left during the Likud government on the theme of home and exile. It is a history that included "emigration into inner space"—abandonment of the public sphere—by some people on the Left, on the one hand, and women's increased public activism in the last few years, on the other. Some people who hold a peace and coexistence position prefer silence, while others act publicly. Becoming political, speaking up, or choosing silence have divided the Left. The temptation to emigrate from the public sphere and from political dissent and to retreat to the private sphere is still an issue after the 1992 elections. In the 1993 Jerusalem conference women stated the need to act publicly. Yael said: "As the means of oppression in the Occupied Territories grows, our ability to act as women does not diminish, but we go more into a private domain, we feel more helpless, ineffective, and we don't raise our voices enough. There are tens and hundreds of women, all the women who are today very upset by it and would like to invigorate the peace movement."

During the fifteen years of the Likud government many peace activists believed that meaningful change—that is, resolving the Israeli-Palestinian conflict in a peaceful and just way—would not take place. Some women said to me in 1990 that in their darkest moments they fear that it will not happen in their lifetime. A number of people in the Left escaped into what they described as an "inner exile"—the domestic sphere—retreating from political action that seemed to be spinning its wheels. Others, like women's peace activists who refused to accept exile and chose to act politically, faced a right-wing government that seemed unwilling to bring about the kind of political change that the Left wanted. While the Likud government had agreed in 1991 to undertake activities toward resolving the conflict, such as the Madrid Peace Conference, women peace activists and people in the Left saw these as false gestures, as mere talk (of a government bowing to American pressure) while the government was building settlements in the Occupied Territories. As it turned out, their perception was not far from the way that Shamir himself saw his government's participation in the peace talks; he declared after he lost the elections that he intended to drag out the talks while creating massive settlements, hoping to make the return of the Occupied Territories to the Palestinians practically impossible. During and after the Madrid Peace Conference women's peace activism, as I noted, took place in what seemed the politics of negatives: no peace negotiation, no talks with the PLO, but more of the same occupation, conflict, and bloodshed.

In 1990 few people in the Left believed that a change in government was imminent; many women peace activists did not believe that Labor could win the elections, and it seemed that the Likud was there to stay. This sense of powerlessness to bring about meaningful change drove many peace activists into political exile. But not everyone emigrated into inner space. Women peace activities took the opposite direction; they emigrated from the domestic home to the public space to reclaim a homeland for Israelis and for Palestinians. Women, and other peace activists, aimed to transform their understanding of the ideology of peace and coexistence as political facts of justice in public events.

How Political Acts Dissolve into Mere Talk

The Women and Peace public event in 1993 highlighted ways in which political facts of peace and coexistence are exposed as mere talk (rak diburim). Rabin had publicly established facts of peace and coexistence, such as his inaugural address to the Knesset. Women confronted the Left government because they perceived that these facts were exposed over time as insubstantial when the government deported Palestinians. Political facts, once established in a public event, are tested time and again; political facts must be reproduced to be seen as having substance, or they can revert into mere talk. Beyond the obvious act of protest, women's vigils and conferences are public events in which these women's version of peace and coexistence is produced and reproduced. Precisely because of the fine line that separates facts from talk, women peace activists have to create conferences and reproduce political acts. The phrase used in the Women and Peace statement, "peace talks—yet the bloodshed continues," reveals that when these two arc placed side by side the political fact of ongoing bloodshed and occupation exposes peace as mere talk.

The state official position of turning away from the Greater Israel to giving up land for peace is, from the women's perspective, a necessary but not sufficient act. For the women to agree tacitly or explicitly to the government's peace position is to lose their own collective identity as women who struggle for justice for Palestinians. The women's conference in 1993 is, among other things, linked to delineating the boundaries of their collective, so that it does not disappear into a generalized peace and coexistence position. It was important for the women's conference to highlight the government's wavering between an epilogue to the politics of the Greater Israel and a prologue to what Rabin described as a new era of peace in the Middle East. To highlight this wavering also points out the boundaries of the women's collective as peace activists who struggle to inscribe justice as indivisible from nation-ness.

In the Jerusalem 1993 conference three political acts took place: the women transformed their ideas of peace and coexistence into a political act; they exposed the government's peace position as mere talk; and they reaffirmed the survival of women peace activists as a collective. The deportation was an act that exposed peace and coexistence as divisible from justice and therefore, as the women saw it, exposed the government's position as insubstantial mere talk. Nava, an Israeli-Jewish panelist, gave her version of what does not constitute an act of peace in the 1993 Jerusalem conference: "The message of the deportation to Palestinians is: you live under our patronage, and we give you what we want to give you, and by the same token we take what we want. The agreement between us will constitute what we are willing to give. There is no real dialogue; there is no real give-and-take. There is an attempt to create a more sophisticated system of occupation with a few adjustments that would make it less obvious and less painful, but no more than that. The deportation, however, was a shock even to those who had few expectations from this government."

The women's 1993 Jerusalem conference highlights the complex relationship between mere talk and political acts. The conference unveils public events as spaces for making and unmaking political facts, including political acts of peace and coexistence and political facts of collectives. But political acts and facts require substance, and the evidence for substance is lodged in producing and reproducing them in public events. Silences, inner exiles, meetings behind closed doors, or, worse, contradictory acts, expose the insubstantiality of previous acts and, therefore, revert back to ideology, to mere talk. "Emigration" to the domestic home, a retreat from the public sphere, is also a sign of a threat to a collective existence. This is the case not only for collectives that are directly involved in the Israeli-Palestinian conflict, such as the settlers on one side and women peace activists on the other. It is also the case, as I noted earlier, for Israeli religious Jews, mizrahim, and Israeli Palestinians. To retreat voluntarily or involuntarily from the public sphere is seen as a threat to collective survival. Women's peace conferences underscore the fact that political acts (in this case, for justice) must be reproduced to maintain their substantiality.

Public events such as the 1993 Jerusalem conference illuminate the significance of justice for women's peace and coexistence position and its absence from the state's policies. Clearly, women who are concerned with justice for Palestinians are not alone in the Left, and it would be against this local fact to argue that justice is precisely women's concern. It would be equally contrary to the facts on the ground to claim, however, as Carol Gilligan does, that women are not concerned with justice or with the social good (Gabriel 1992). For some women and men in the Israeli Left intercommunity justice is transgendered, transnational, and indivisible from peace and coexistence. Justice and peace cannot be construed, globally or locally, as gendered. In women's public events justice and gender are employed by women to forge solidarities. In the 1993 Jerusalem conference the Women and Peace coalition stated, "we women from all over the country work and struggle for a just peace in our region." They constructed a transnational territory of gender and justice on which women of two nations could stand together, in turbulent times and in less stormy days, to transform ideologies into political acts of peace and coexistence.

CHAPTER 6 · When Locals Meet the Global

A Discourse about a New Global Era

Women's peace activism in Israel illuminates more than the various contours of Israel's political life. The spread of the Israeli Women in Black to places around the globe and the employment of Western feminism by women peace activists offer critical insights to the riveting recent phenomenon of a discourse about reimagining a global community. In 1991 President George Bush spoke of "a new world order" and used the Gulf War as a sign of an international community united against border invasions. A number of political events were featured in the discourse of a new world order and included the end of the cold war, the unification of Germany, the defeat of apartheid in South Africa, and the international community's claim that it will not tolerate aggression (Iraq's invasion of Kuwait) and that it will no longer ignore massive hunger in places such as Somalia.[1] The discourse offered a version of an altered and more caring globe and about a new era of a world without boundaries.[2] The demise of the Soviet Union was accompanied by economic, political, and cultural discourses of the globe as a new (more peaceful, less threatening) world order, new trade agreements, a more congenial, "kinder" "family of nations."

While anthropology also participates in this new discourse, it has always paid attention to the relationship between the local and global. Much of the recent focus in anthropology is on identifying numerous global-local changes and the implications that these have for the anthropological project. Anthropologists such as Appadurai have paid close attention to the shifting boundaries between the local and the global as it affects group identity. Appadurai argues that "the landscapes of group identity—the ethnoscapes—around the world are no longer familiar anthropological objects, insofar as groups are no longer tightly territorialized, spatially bounded, historically unselfconscious, or culturally homogenous" (1991, 191). Anthropologists such as Hannerz pay attention to a growing globalized culture: "Cultural interconnections increasingly reach across the world. More than ever there is a global ecumene. The entities we routinely call cultures are becoming more like subcultures within this wider entity, with all that this suggests in terms of fuzzy boundaries and more or less arbitrary delimitation of analytical units (1992, 218).

Both Appadurai and Hannerz urge anthropologists to confront this altered globe. "To grasp this fact of globalization," argues Hannerz, "is the largest task at present confronting a macroanthropology of culture" (ibid.). My own anthropological interest is with the ways that the locals, very much like "us" who write about them, are aware of the facts of global changes and of the international conversations about a changed globe; my focus is not on how much or in what ways global changes are actually taking place but, rather, in how locals employ international discourses about a changed globe for their own local political purposes. This is evidenced when locals in the Middle East politicize ideas of a changed globe to engage in the Israeli-Palestinian peace agreements. They give local substance (coexistence) to the global discourse (a kinder world); in public events they transform their versions of local/global peace images from mere talk into political acts and facts.

The new discourse on "international community" did not elude the new government in Israel in 1992. In his address to the Knesset on July 13, Yitzhak Rabin, then a newly elected prime minister, employed the discourse about a changed world to create drastic local political changes and to establish a fact of a turnabout in state policies. Rabin urged Israelis to join the international community, to dismantle some old boundaries, and to embrace (local) change because the globe has changed: "We must overcome the sense of isolation that has held us in its thrall for almost half a century. We must join the international movement toward peace, reconciliation, and cooperation that is spreading over the entire globe these days" (1992, 5).

The ceremonial signing of the peace agreement between Israel and the Palestinians, on September 13, 1993, in Washington, D.C., illustrates a construction of a changed globe for political purposes. Locals from the Middle East and their hosts from the political global center participated in this act. In the Washington ceremony the discourse about an altered better globe, "the dawn of a new era," was used to forge an international legitimacy for the signing of a local agreement between Israelis and Palestinians. The locals from the Middle East employed the discourse to establish mutual recognition as a political fact (against some opposition) on the ground in their respective communities.

In his 1993 address in Washington, D.C., Israel's foreign minister Shimon Peres enjoined cities and people across the globe: "From the eternal city of Jerusalem, from this green, promising lawn of the White House, let us say together in the language of our Bible: peace, peace to him that is far off and to him that is near sayth the Lord." As the world was watching and listening, Rabin employed Washington, the political center of the globe, to inscribe a local political turnabout—peace with Palestinians. Rabin evoked the globe as "a family of nations" as he spoke of local parents and children: "Today here in Washington, at the White House, we will begin a new reckoning in the relations between peoples, between parents tired of war, between children who will not know war." Mahmud Abbas, PLO Executive Committee member, described the intertwined local/global relationship as "the support of the international community" for the local "journey that is surrounded by numerous dangers and difficulties." Warren Christopher, U.S. secretary of state, participated in the global/local discourse when he said: "We need the entire international community to join us in this work and to oppose any effort to subvert the peace." Yassir Arafat, chairman of the PLO, in his first appearance as an internationally legitimated representative of the Palestinian nation, made the local conflict a global concern. He spoke of the signing of the agreement as the "historic event which the entire world has been waiting for" and noted that, "without peace in the Middle East, peace in the world will not be complete." He called on "the international community in its entirety to help the parties overcome the tremendous difficulties which are still standing in the way." President Clinton's closing remarks summarized the vision of this new world peace order and its global magnitude: "Let us go from this place to celebrate the dawn of a new era not only for the Middle East, but for the entire world."

"Mere Talk" or "Political Facts": The Litmus Test of a New International Community

A closer examination of a discourse about the dawn of a new era of peace for the entire world, however—an international community seeking peace and reconciliation—contradicts political facts in places from the former Soviet Union to the Middle East. In fact, Andrei Kozyrev, the Russian foreign minister, put a political damper on the hopeful ceremony in Washington, noting that in many places around the globe and particularly in the Middle East, outside the Israeli-Palestinian conflict, there are other "forces of subversion, terrorism and extremism." Kozyrev expressed his hope that the international efforts will be directed toward "stability in the whole region." The facts on the ground in the former Soviet Union and in other places around the globe are that nationalisms keep coming out of the closets of postsocialist and democratic countries, and boundaries, rather than being removed, are drawn sharper and closer to home. European countries such as Germany consider local laws that would close its borders to all kinds of "others"; the international (imagined) community, for its part, witnessed (until recently quite passively) "ethnic cleansing" in Bosnia. There is an undeniable gap between a rhetoric of a "world without boundaries" on the one hand and the facts of swift mappings of old and new boundaries on the other. There is an obvious contradiction between mere talk about an international community, a family of nations (a concept used by politicians and the media during the Gulf War), and the determined rejection of "strangers" who take this imagined international community seriously in their attempts to move from the (impoverished) margins of the globe to its (privileged) centers.

It would be easy to dismiss the discourse about a changed globe as sheer hypocrisy and object to events such as the ceremonial signing of the agreement in Washington as mere sentimental talk. But the local context does not lend itself to this kind of convenient dismissal. The Israeli local understanding of public events as the contexts of making politics suggests that, while the discourse of peace is partial, it is nevertheless significant: mere talk *about* a global peace community is seen on the ground—in acts being actually performed, former enemies shaking hands, and agreements being signed. The local understanding of the relationship between mere talk and facts is thus useful in thinking about the newly constructed international community. Political refugees, illegal immigrants, local conflicts, and other events constantly test this new world order: Is it mere talk, or does it display real acts? The ceremonial signing of the agreement between Israel and the Palestinians is a fact on the ground, a historic event, but one that can turn into "a piece of paper," mere talk, if other acts do not follow to give it substance. Crises in the relationship between Israelis and Palestinians become the acid test: they tell whether the Washington ceremonial agreement is still a political fact or whether it has turned into mere talk. Political acts, global and local, must follow to give substance to facts and ensure that they have not evaporated into mere talk.

The relation between local and global is marked not only by the process of moving "from mere talk to political facts" that delineates this new world order but by a local ambivalence as well. Global centers both hold tremendous attractions and elicit deep collective anxieties. There is the lure of a friendlier globe that has all kinds of goods—material, political, and cultural—of which locals would like to partake. Then, politically, there is the attraction that the international community *can* bring about a long-yearned-for peace in the Middle East. But there is also an existential anxiety for collective survival that is threatened by the global centers. Israelis and Palestinians are anxious about their respective identities as authentically indigenous. Accordingly, women in Israel do not want their peace activism to become a mere shadow of global movements. Indeed, one of the hopes of the people of the region is that the peace agreement will transform the Middle East from a place on the margins to one of the global centers (Bialkin 1993).

Exporting to the Globe, Maintaining Local Authenticity

The lure of the global centers and the anxiety about survival of authenticity (cultural, economic, and political) it elicits for locals is revealed in the way that women peace activists are keenly aware of and deeply concerned with local/global interactions. In 1993, when the Women in Black knew that Israel and the PLO were on the verge of signing an agreement of mutual recognition and a preliminary agreement called "Gaza and Jericho First," the Jerusalem vigil noted its own global presence: "Women in Black have also sprung up in other countries, some protesting the Israeli occupation and others protesting war, militarism, and organized violence in their parts of the world" (*Women in Black National Newsletter,* no. 6 [Fall 1993]: 1). Yet to maintain indigenous authenticity the Women in Black did not "internationalize" its local activities in the sense that it did not adopt a general pacifist agenda. It has retained its indigenous goal, ending the occupation, and upholding a local meaning of justice.

Women in Black, however, became a transnational movement adopted by women across nations around the globe for various local peace agendas. In Europe vigils of the Women in Black express the Israeli women's political idea of peace and justice but transformed and translated into other specific local conflicts. Exported to Germany from Israel (and this fact is commendable, deplorable, or ironic depending on the point of view), the vigils have been transformed and translated into a European context. Hedwig Raskob writes to the Israeli women: "Dear Sisters in Black: First let me express great pleasure that Women in Black are spreading fast. In Germany alone we heard of a new vigil in Wiesbaden, and women of Nuremberg are preparing a vigil in their city. We hear of Women in Black in Zurich and Verona. Most of all, I am pleased to hear about Women in Belgrade. They valiantly and vigorously stand against the unspeakably cruel war on the Balkans. It is the time of the Women in Black!" (ibid.).

In its global representation, in Germany, the Israeli Women in Black also take on unexpected configurations of the meaning of peace: "In the light of Christmas, the festival of peace, I'm writing to you about activities in the city of Cologne. Here in the pedestrian mall, in the very center of the city, we stand every Friday from 3:30 to 5:00 P.M. Our little group of almost 12 women began our vigils in autumn 1990" (Butternweck 1993, 9). Christmas as a symbol of peace, however, is quite removed from the lives and experiences of Jewish women in the Israeli vigils; Women in Black has now been linked with a Christian holy day that has very different meanings for women peace activists in Israel. Butternweck's account from Cologne evokes some familiar features of Women in Black: the time, Friday afternoon; the place, a public space. There are also some parallels in terms of the reaction in Cologne to the vigil: "Some people are very aggressive and insult us with vulgar words and gestures, but most identify with our aims. This is a very encouraging sign for us! We are very glad that the groups of Women in Black are increasing all over the world" (ibid.).

While the Cologne importation of Women in Black is seen in the context of a globalization of a specific peace and justice vigil, women are also aware of historical complexities that the Holocaust experience brings to the relationship between Israeli-Jewish women and German women: "One of the most exciting and inspiring events prior to our existence was the great ceremony in Aachen in September 1991, when the Aachen Peace Prize was bestowed upon Israeli Women in Black. We greatly admired the courage of those women who accepted this reward although it came from German hands. We talked together about our experiences and sang together with much enthusiasm, 'We Shall Overcome'" (ibid.).

Butternweck's account almost suggests a new world order, an international community: a peace prize goes from the global to the local vigils and the ceremony includes yet another call for justice, by African Americans, by women singing "We Shall Overcome" in English, an internationalized language. The day after the ceremony in Aachen, a Jewish-Palestinian-German Festival of Culture and Peace in Cologne seemed to underscore a reimagined international peace community. Israeli-Palestinian efforts to bring about peace and coexistence thus foreshadowed an official political act by Israelis and Palestinians in 1993 in Oslo and later that year in Washington, D.C.

What links the local and the global for women is more than the fact of the Women in Black vigils in Israel and worldwide. What emerges as crucial in exporting the local idea is the survival of this political act (women's peace protest) in the future, beyond the life span of the Israeli vigils. A worldwide Women in Black ensures that, while the local vigils may diminish in size or disband, the cause will survive politically: it has a global future. The vigils, which have transformed its members into political agents in Israel, will survive in the future, "transformed" globally.[3] Women in Black is thus seen as a transformative phenomenon that will have a life beyond its original form.

The transformative aspect of the Women in Black displays how political ideas invented in Israel are adapted for European local concerns of recent overt racism. According to the German Women in Black, their government did not respond appropriately and swiftly to racist violence. Mechthild Shreiber, who has stood in the Munich vigil, describes the ways in which this imported product of peace and justice politics is reconstructed in Munich: "In Germany, especially, racist violence and the policies of our government—responding to racism drives me to action. Since the Gulf War, I continue my vigils in Munich with four other women as Women in Black. I stand, first, to mourn, but also to discuss with people the possibility of non-violent ways to end the war in ex-Yugoslavia, the psycho-social reasons for nationalism and anti-Semitism, and the need for peaceful cooperation throughout the world" (Shreiber 1993, 12).

Europe (Munich), representing one of the centers of global power, has become the recipient of a political phenomenon from the margins. In its transformed global configuration (its exported version), Women in Black takes on particular features and expresses different political agendas such as concerns about racism, anti-Semitism, and the war in Bosnia. A political position of peace and justice "made in Israel" (concerning the occupation) has been received in Germany and reincorporated into what these German women hope will affect local European issues of justice and the war in Bosnia. The idea of peace in its corporeal form of Women in Black is expressed by women in Belgrade as a local response to the war in Bosnia, but in some features it is remarkably similar to the Israeli vigil. Stasa Zajovic writes in the Israeli *Women in Black National Newsletter:* "Women in Black Against War began in the streets of Belgrade in October 1991 to express our disapproval of the ongoing war in Croatia. Ever since, with short breaks, the women stand every Wednesday, from 3:30 to 4:30 P.M.—the time of the local rush hour—in front of the Student Cultural Center of Belgrade." Zajovic notes that the opposition to the vigil has parallels with the vigil in Israel because, among other things, in both places the women are perceived as aligning themselves with Muslims: "The most unpleasant reactions come from nationalist women, who say: 'Idle whores of Izetbegovic and Tudjman,' 'Traitors to the Serbian nation!' 'Serbia is not at war; go protest to the Croats and Muslims'" (1993, 10). Whether members of Women in Black in places outside of Israel acknowledge the birthplace of this political idea, Israeli women see these satellite vigils as an extension of the Israeli vigils, a global political fact of the local women's peace politics.[4]

Women in Black has a future locally and globally. Its survival assumes global dimensions as it is transformed into "a model for women's political action adopted worldwide." Women in Black, in this sense, has transcended mere talk, solidifying the peace idea into a global political fact. That the group's political ideas are taking on broader meanings of generalized political empowerment indicates to its participants that Women in Black has an existence beyond local politics. The women in Israel have created a political phenomenon that is transnational (it travels across nation-state borders), that is global enough to be incorporated into other national local contexts, and that Israeli women can see as an extension of their own Women in Black. What the locals see is that the roots of Women in Black are grounded in the East (the Israeli-Palestinian issue), but its branches spread widely to the West, the global center.

"Cosmo-Local" Feminism

Women peace activists export a local product of Women in Black to other places around the globe; at the same time, these women are conscious of the fact that the "global" is coming home to them in its many shapes and forms, from material goods to feminist ideas. Women employ and reconstruct imported ideas, such as Western feminisms, in a local fashion; they make sense of these ideas in a local context and make use of them to suit local needs. Women produce what I call "cosmo-local" (universal and culture-specific) feminism in their peace activism. "Feminism," a Western product, like a multitude of other Western products, travels around the globe in accidental (or deliberate) mass media and in scholarly baggage. Feminism easily lends itself to be imagined as cosmic, universally shared, thus easily claimed and owned by women around the globe. Yet close attention to local use of feminism reveals that, when this global baggage is unpacked and claimed by women, it takes on cosmo-local features. In the 1993 Jerusalem

Women and Peace conference Tamar blended imported feminism in its cosmic version and the local peace position of ending the occupation, reconstructing an adaptable universal feminist motherhood: "Jean Elshtain, a professor of political science, was in Israel. She writes extensively on women and war, and we talked about the fact that there is a tremendous gap between what women feel when their children go to the army and what they do with this fact in political life. Elshtain said that the time has come to politicize motherhood. We must stop silently accepting what it is that makes our children go to the army and go to the territories."

Tamar invoked Western feminism at a point in the 1993 conference when solidarity among women peace activists was being questioned and revealed a gap between elected officials and rank-and-file women over the issue of the deportation of 415 Palestinians. The authority of global feminism (the American scholar) was marshaled for local purposes of both forging unity among women and exerting pressure on the government to end the occupation in the name of mothers.

Other women in the 1993 Jerusalem conference, such as Yael, saw gender as the linchpin of a political position of justice: "I want to say something about women's organizations, Women in Black, Reshet and other groups, who did not lose their heads after the deportations and who continued their peace efforts, in vigils, in conferences, in fighting and protesting. I am very glad that two Palestinian women are sitting with us today; this is a testimony to our continued dialogue." Western feminism is turned into a local product that women often use to forge gender solidarity. It is a blend of a notion that there are things that all women share, that there are "things only women can do" and, in the local context, that "only we [Israeli and Palestinian women] can do" for peace.

Salma, an Israeli-Palestinian woman, said: "When Amal [a Palestinian woman from the Occupied Territories] talked about her dilemma of coming to this conference in face of the deportations, I was reminded that two years ago during the Gulf War we faced a similar issue: Should we continue to meet with Palestinian women from the Occupied Territories? There was a big debate in the Israeli Left, and we said that our position as women was that we were against the war and we supported a dialogue between Israel and PLO. We came to Jerusalem, and the atmosphere was very special. Women from both sides came to make a statement. We needed a large hall to accommodate all the Israeli and Palestinian women who came. I see it as symbolic of what only women can do: take the first step. Only women could under these circumstances [of the Gulf War] continue the dialogue. We need power and willpower to continue to demonstrate our strength and determination. We need to come out of here with ways to act. We know what we need to do. We need to have more women in government and to have an impact in decision making."

Some women made explicit links between peace activism and feminism. Ruth Cohen writes about the decision to disband the Jerusalem vigil shortly after the signing of the peace agreement in Washington in 1993: "Does this really mean the end of Women in Black? Personally, I think not. What began as a local protest against the Israeli occupation of the West Bank and Gaza Strip has turned into a model for women's political action adopted worldwide. Five and a half years of putting one's political views on the line every week has been an empowering experience for every woman who has participated. In Jerusalem, the vigil has shown many women with no feminist background the effectiveness of a feminist model of cooperative action and decision-making. Each individual in Women in Black knows that she can voice her opinion and make a difference" (1993, 11, 13).

Peace activism is seen as a space in which women's politicization as feminists takes place. Yvonne Deutsch, a veteran peace activist, gave an account of a national meeting of the Women and Peace coalition that took place on November 7, 1992, a few months after the elections and shortly before the 1993 Jerusalem conference. Deutsch drew on a version of Western feminism that seeks to link practice and theory: "From the discussion on peace, feminism, and women's political power, it seemed as if women active for peace and for women's rights feel the need to strengthen the connection between the personal and the political. I believe that we must deepen our understanding of the theoretical and the practical relationship between the struggles on behalf of peace" (*Women in Black National Newsletter,* no. 4 [Winter 1992–93, 4]).

Feminism as a Fact on the Local Ground

Though they remain politically separate, women's peace groups, and groups such as the Israel Women's Network (IWN), a political organization that works for women's rights, converge as consumers of global feminist products; both express the recent politicization of Israeli women. Women peace groups and the IWN have taken Western feminism for local uses, but the construction of collectives as "we women" are distinct, revealing the divisibility of peace from feminism; the two do not necessarily go hand in hand.

Women's peace groups began to make their public mark in 1982 after the Lebanon War; the IWN came into being in 1985, after the Lebanon War and before the Intifada. This group, which has embraced a version of Western feminism, includes women from the Right to the Left of Israel's political spectrum. Some women in the IWN are members of the Women in Black or other peace groups; others are members of the Likud, and some have opposed peace activism. Yet the political turnabout of the 1992 elections has been seen by IWN women (including Likud women) as an upheaval in the feminist struggle for equality. The IWN, despite its political diversity, viewed the 1992 elections as a feminist turnabout for women's rights, stating that "1993 was one of the busiest in the nine-year history of the IWN. A group of energetic women members in the Knesset and a number of young feminists (both women and men) in government offices, a change for the better in the amount and quality of media attention devoted to women and women-related issues, unprecedented hope for peace—or at least a decline in hostilities—which could release resources hitherto dedicated to defense and military needs to be applied to domestic issues—all combine with IWN's current undeniable status as Israel's major advocacy group on women's issues to create a climate conducive to developing and advocating policy, legislation and administrative action designed to ameliorate the status of women in Israel" (*Networking* 1994, 1).

The global origins of feminism in Israel is disclosed in the fact that the Hebrew word for feminism is *feminism*. There is no local word; it is not an indigenous idea, yet it has become part of local politics. Cosmo-local feminism in Israel, however, is not monolithic; it displays different understandings of justice. For some women in groups such as the IWN feminism is divisible from justice to Palestinians, seeking partial justice (for women); they take on feminist ideas and at the same time hold right-wing ideologies that deny justice to Palestinians. For women peace groups the politics of gender and peace are linked by the principle of justice for both women and Palestinians. Yet women who hold different cosmo-local constructions of feminism come together in certain contexts to promote equality for women in Israel's political life.

Feminism is used locally to give the turnabout of the 1992 election a gendered meaning—one in which women from the Right end of the spectrum and from the Left can be active on a new Knesset committee for gender equality: "In the October edition of *Networking* we announced the formation of a Knesset caucus on women's issues. Now comes even more momentous news: For the first time in its 44-year history, Israel's parliament has established an official Knesset committee on equality between the sexes. Though this is not one of the Knesset's statutory committees, this is actually beneficial: since Knesset members are each limited to membership in only two statutory committees, they were free to add the new committee to their previous commitments. The committee is headed by M. K. Yael Dayan (Labor), who after a two-year term will be succeeded by Limor Livnat (Likud). The deputy chairwoman is Tamar Gozansky (Hadash). Six subcommittees will deal respectively with work and economics; education and advertising; domestic violence; human rights, personal status and representation; Arab women; gay and lesbian rights. Perhaps the most encouraging even exciting aspect of the committee's establishment was the discussion which preceded the Knesset's confirmation vote. Both women and men rose to express their support, proudly referring to themselves as feminists and lauding the (albeit belated) move to amend the Knesset's sins of omission. Those of us who have experienced years of scornful dismissal of the concept and its relevance to Israeli society felt true gratification at this evidence that 'feminism' is no longer a dirty word" (*Networking* 1993, 3). Feminism (cosmo-local) was transformed in the Knesset meeting from mere women's talk to a fact on the ground, a political act at the national level.

If, as Strathern (1990) cautions, anthropologists should not take on trust the idea of a global village, they also cannot make assumptions about the ways in which locals make use of imported global products. Imported feminism has its own local versions. It is deployed in different ways by women peace activists (indivisible from universal justice) and groups such as the IWN (addressed to justice for women). Women peace activists employ feminism to create solidarity across nations; it has been used by Palestinian women from the Occupied Territories and by Israeli-Jewish and Israeli-Palestinian women in times of political crisis. Women's public events, such as the Tel Aviv 1990 conference, revealed the limits of feminism (even for mizrahi women who identify themselves as feminists) to provide the ground for sororal unity between ashkenazi and mizrahi women.

The relationship of women peace activists to Western feminism displays locals' desire to stay authentic, despite the importing of ideas, and to have a sense of power by being not only receivers of goods but exporters as well. Imported feminism serves to show not only the fact of the growing global culture in its innumerable manifestations from popular culture to political ideas; it also illustrates how feminism as a global product acquires local features (IWN, women's peace groups).

Locals and the Gifts of the Global Context

Locals may want to emulate or partake of the global context, but at the same time they also wish to maintain an indigenous identity; that is, there is an equal wish to be unique and different from global products. The power of the globe is obvious to locals, to Israelis and to Palestinians (Bailkin 1993; S. Fischer 1993–94). This power elicits a local desire for balance, for placing some local substance in the centers of global power. Locals are aware that economics, culture, and politics are no longer contained within convenient and familiar borders and that the postcolonial, postsocialist world, if anything, has intensified this relationship. Because the global economy, culture, and politics often loom larger, more powerful, and because global power is often represented by the West, locals are simultaneously attracted to and anxious about it.

There is a wish to emulate, incorporate, consume, and use the best of the global, but alongside this wish is an anxiety that, realizing it, may mean the loss of the locals' authenticity. Israelis and Palestinians—who began to negotiate publicly not at home, not even in the Middle East—recognize the political power of global spaces. In the wider political context of the Middle East conflict, in which women peace activism is firmly anchored, it is impossible for Israelis and Palestinians to fail to see the intertwining of the local and the global and the significance of the latter on the former. Accordingly, women peace activists go to Brussels to talk to Palestinian women in a conference organized by Belgian citizens. Holding official talks between Israelis and Palestinians and a number of countries in the Middle East means traveling to Madrid, Oslo, or Washington.

The global and local are linked by a process in which insubstantial gesture (talk, inaction, silence) is transformed into substance (action, speaking) and is considered as "making politics." Collectives and individuals can be engaged in the process of making politics. Dayan and Chazan's meeting with the PLO after the 1992 elections displays the one way in which women not only were at the forefront of this turnabout but also used the global setting to transform a local ideology of "talk to the PLO" into a political fact. It took place globally, but it was carried back home for local consumption and inscribed locally the direction of the turnabout and the scope of upheaval in 1992. Similarly, the earlier women's peace conference in Brussels in 1989, while a contested issue between ashkenazi and mizrahi women, indicates the usefulness of the global setting for local concerns: Israeli women wanted to meet with women from the Palestinian diaspora. Diaspora Jews wanted to engage in a local matter, the Israeli-Palestinian conflict, and used the global space to allow women to transform a local position of peace and coexistence into a public event in Brussels. The global event became the birthplace of Reshet, a new local women's organization that sets out to make public space for the fact of coexistence by promoting meetings with Palestinian women.

Our Sisters' Promised Land: Solidarity and Coexistence as Political Substance

The terms *sisters* and *Promised Land* that I use in the title of this book are easily recognized, real entities. *Sister* is a kinship term, and the *Promised Land* is a geographic space in the Middle East. Yet both terms also mark political entities no less real in the import they carry. The term *sisters* takes on a meaning beyond the customary kinship, one of consanguinity (blood) and affinity (marriage). For women peace activists *sisters* has also taken on a political substance: what makes it real is solidarity. Just as blood (sisters) and marriage (sisters-in-law) provide the substance for the kinship term, solidarity provides the substance for political sisters. The web of political sisters can stretch from local places to global spaces and between people of different nations on the global periphery. When Hedwig Raskob greets the Israeli Women in Black as "Dear Sisters in Black," she gives the substance of solidarity to the term *sisters* that now defines a web of transnational relationships from Israel to Europe. A similar solidarity substance transforms the conventional kinship term into a political relationship, as when a Palestinian man from Hebron uses the word *sisters* when he writes to the Women in Black at Nahshon intersection in Israel. Solidarity transforms kinship terms of sisters (and brothers) into a political transnational relationship between Israeli and Palestinian women peace activists. The survival of sisters as political solidarity in the Israeli-Palestinian context depends on further acts and facts and is linked to the concept of a Promised Land.

In the Middle East the Promised Land, a geographic space, takes on political meanings. Political conflict dominated Israeli-Palestinian relations in this space until 1993. It was several years before the signing of the peace agreement in Washington, however, that women peace activists began to envision a new Promised Land. Coexistence was the political substance for their vision, which called for two states for two nations living side by side in peace. That vision began to be realized officially as a political act in a public event in Washington, D.C. The signing of the agreement gave further international legitimation to the women's local political acts; it gave official substance (coexistence) of a Promised Land to both nations.

In September 1993 it seemed that a Promised Land was created by official leaders as a political fact. Prime Minister Rabin forged a new space of peace and coexistence: "We, like you, are people. People who want to build a home, to plant a tree, to love, to live side by side with you in dignity." Chairman Arafat participated by reimagining the Promised Land as space now infused with hope: "Our two people are awaiting today this historic hope, and they want to give peace a real chance." Justice also becomes a substance for this new Promised Land, as Arafat said: "My people are hoping that this agreement which we are signing today will usher in an age of peaceful coexistence and equal rights." Foreign Minister Peres spoke explicitly of a new beginning and of children to make it a Promised Land for the region: "This should be another genesis. We have to build a new commonwealth on our old soil—a Middle East of the people and a Middle East for the children." President Clinton evoked ancient kinship to forge contemporary solidarity of this land: "The children of Abraham, the descendants of Isaac and Ishmael, have embarked together on a bold journey."

There Is No Epilogue

The talks that accompanied the signing of the agreement between Israelis and Palestinians gave a Promised Land its first official (local and global) substance. Women's peace goals seemed almost fulfilled as a peace process took over. Yet women's peace activism reveals that political facts must be constantly infused with substance or they can quickly turn into mere talk. Two of the women's goals—ending the occupation and having two states for two nations—have not materialized in the peace process to give the Promised Land its necessary substance for coexistence. This book, which tells about women's peace activism, therefore does not have an epilogue, or closure. From the women's perspective the question in the region is: Will there be enough (or any) political substance to keep coexistence as a fact on the ground?

Anchored in Israel's political life, women's peace activism highlights the center's political position. From the women's perspective the Labor government's peace process excludes what the women see as crucial: justice for Palestinians. Thus, they consider the peace process as a limited agreement (over Gaza and Jericho first), and they oppose the state's support of the settlers in the Occupied Territories. Moreover, in the precarious line between talk and facts, stage 2 of the agreement with Palestinians has been suspended. The agreement called for an Israeli military withdrawal from Palestinian towns and cities in the West Bank in 1994. The withdrawal would have meant a significant political act giving substance to peace. A year later, however, Israel has not yet withdrawn its army from the Occupied Territories, tipping the balance toward mere talk.

Women's peace activism also highlights the ways in which links between local governments and global politics can produce or reduce acts for a Promised Land of coexistence. A peace process in the Middle East in 1993 seemed to have a proper place in the discourse on a new global era and a caring international community. The United States, as I noted, played a critical role in supporting the notion of a changed world order; local leaders used it as a model to propose drastic political changes at home. Yet in the mid-1990s discourse on the globe is rapidly changing, matching the swift political change that took place in the 104th Congress in Washington. The media, which in 1993 talked about a new world order, now asks: "Global concerns? Not in Congress. In Congress the world fades away" (*New York Times,* January 15, 1995). The new Republican Congress is bound to have implications for the Middle East. It is not just a matter of a discourse about the globe but of political acts regarding global issues. What is important for issues such as an already threatened peace process in the Middle East is that "the real action in Congress these days is not a crafting of a larger global vision" and that the "Contract with America" does not include "the global agenda: peacekeeping, population control, international environmental programs and refugee relief." The change in a discourse on a global agenda is manifest not in mere talk but also in a political fact: that the Foreign Relations Committee is no longer a desired political activity on Capitol Hill. In fact, after the November 1995 election "the rush was away from the committee" (ibid.).

The locals in the Middle East are ready to use political changes in the United States for local purposes. For the Likud Party in Israel the new Congress offers an opportunity to oppose peace. Center and margins, as women's peace activism demonstrates, have two drastically different political agendas. The center strives for stability and consensus, while the margins contest and destabilize. When the Likud was in power in Israel it insisted on consensus and on government officials' exclusive right to speak for the state. But now, as an opposition party, the Likud feels free to destabilize the center of power and to derail the peace process. The Likud opposes returning any land to Palestinians on the West Bank and the Gaza Strip and to Syria on the Golan Heights. But peace with Syria cannot take place without a return of land. The Labor government wants American troops to monitor the Golan Heights as part of a peace agreement with Syria, but the Likud, which opposes the plan, may find allies in the new Congress who are reluctant to spend money on peacekeeping. New political facts in the United States may affect the degree to which the Promised Land as envisioned by women's peace activism will turn into mere talk or will be infused with further acts that give substance to peace.

Conclusion: The Margins Illuminating Politics

An Ethnography on the Margins as a Source
of Political Knowledge

Ethnographic projects such as this book on women's peace activism in Israel involve two stages. They begin with fieldwork, the gathering of material away from home, over "there"; the projects expand into the writing phase, which usually takes place "here," when anthropologists return home. Yet, as Strathern (1990) notes, ethnographies about locals (there) do address theoretical issues here. Anthropologists acknowledge that here and there are linked: theories that are at the forefront of the discipline inform thinking about fieldwork; the latter produces new theories and provokes new questions. Merely to acknowledge this theories/fieldwork process, however, fails to convey the nature of an extraordinary experience that stretches between the beginning of fieldwork there and the writing here. For me the most remarkable aspect in this ethnographic experience was that, the more I learned about women's peace activism, the more I found out about Israel's political life; the more familiar I became with the women's protest, the more knowledgeable I became about the center of political power.

When I began my fieldwork in Israel I was interested in the intersection of gender and political protest; I had in mind a project on the margins. Women's peace groups, however, brought to light what constitutes politics in Israel. Their peace protest revealed significant political features such as public events, the collective, and the difference between mere talk and facts and acts. Women's peace activism exposed simmering political issues, such as discrimination, hidden racism, inequalities, injustice, which the center (Likud or Labor) wanted to ignore, deny, or mask. The margins, thus, emerged as a source of political insights about the center.

There are numerous studies on marginalized groups and minorities in Western scholarship. The intention in much of it, however, is to tell the stories of these groups. This was my original plan as well. Not too many people are interested in women's peace activism in Israel, I reasoned, and, when coexistence with Palestinians becomes a reality, a fact on the ground, no one would remember the women. I wanted to participate in Israeli revisionist studies on the margins, which, as I noted, include accounts by and about mizrahi Jews and Israeli Palestinians, who for a long time were absent from public culture. I could also add to a growing body of literature on women and peace that aims to provide women's perspectives.

In this rich literature, thus, the political center is seen in its relation (dominant, oppressive, excluding) to minorities. While recognizing a traditional silence regarding minorities, and the silencing of marginalized groups, studies seldom regard such groups as having political wisdom or as providing illuminations about the political elite. Groups on the margins are rarely seen as having something important to say about any issue outside themselves. Women's peace activism, however, challenges such assumptions; it offers critical political insights into the transition from conflict to coexistence between Israelis and Palestinians. Women's public events, thus, did not allow me to write a book on the margins that would ignore the women's political illuminations; their acts of protest in 1990 foreshadowed the official agreement between Israel and the PLO in 1993. Their objection to the Labor government's (partial) peace position in 1993 predicted ongoing simmerings among Palestinians.

Locals (There) Comment on Academic Discourse (Here)

Anthropologists still ask if and how the material from specific local contexts is related to issues here at home. Mindful of leaping into useless universals, some may argue that anthropologists should avoid such questions. But, as I noted earlier, the local-global relationship no longer allows for simply leaving the analysis at the local level. Locals, as Israeli women's discourse on feminism demonstrates, comment on what academics produce here.

After the second part of my project, in the United States in 1993, the material on women's peace activism there (in Israel) commented, so to speak, on a specific academic discourse here. It happened when peace between Israel and the Palestinians was greeted by a surprise similar to the one that followed the collapse of the Soviet Union. A discourse on surprise at global political events appeared in scholarly literature; academics here commented on how no one could have known about events there. Fieldwork in Israel, challenges this academic discourse on surprise; more specifically, it questions whether the surprise is as self-evident as its proponents claim.

The Israeli material offers us (academics here) an opportunity to reconsider the discourse on surprise by reexamining the place of groups on the margins in our political analyses.

A Discourse on Surprise

Scholars and intellectuals claim that the collapse of the Soviet Union happened suddenly, with little warning, and overnight. It was seen as unpredictable, like a hurricane, and scholars used images of natural disasters to describe the surprise. Francisco Weffort said: "The event of the last three years hit the left like an earthquake. The collapse of socialism that began in 1989 surprised everyone. It was like a bolt of lightning from a blue sky" (1992, 90). The surprise was so vast that it became an academic embarrassment. As Susan Buck-Morss notes, "Not only atlases but scholarly work of every sort were suddenly dated" (1994, 16). The question is, however: Why are major political events greeted with astonishment in the West? The fact of the surprise is undisputed: "While experts and scholars were busy predicting more of the same, the Cold War system imploded" (11). Yet, rather than ask how it is possible that we (experts and scholars in the West) didn't know what was going on, the surprise is often seen as self-evident and obvious: How could we possibly have known?

The view that only surprise could greet such dramatic political changes is evident in a statement made by Jacques Derrida, one of France's leading intellectuals: "Ever since the fifties, for instance, people have known what was wrong with the totalitarianisms of the East, and how it was bound to lead to eventual collapse: for my generation it was our daily bread. . . . What could not be anticipated was the rhythm, the speed, the date: for example, that of the fall of the Berlin wall. In 1986–87, no one in the entire world could have had even the vaguest idea of it" (1994, 34).

Derrida's view is both accurate and misleading. Political experts have paid attention to the center of power in the East; hence, the material at their disposal revealed only what the political elite wanted to tell. Given the focus on the center, the West was indeed taken by surprise. But, as women peace activists in Israel demonstrate, scholars could have known more had they paid attention to simmerings on the margins of political life. Derrida's observation, thus, that in 1986–87 not a soul in the entire world could have known what was to come, is misleading. The simmerings on the margins in the former Soviet Union were ignored by all kinds of political experts who did not believe that the margins have any valuable insights.

Derrida claims that he and other intellectuals knew what was wrong with the totalitarianisms of the East. But, important as Western intellectuals' knowledge may be, it does not stand for, speak for, nor replace the knowledge of locals who lived in these regimes. As Buck-Morss notes, "If daily life in the East gave signals of impending collapse, its tremors were sensed more accurately by average citizens than by intellectual elites" (1994, 11). The lived experience of ordinary citizens on the margins and of those who have resisted the center in various ways have been mostly absent from Western political discourse on the East. Busy focusing on the centers of socialist regimes (which often included the cultural elite), we did not hear the people on the margins who could have, even in the Soviet Union, offered a different version from the official story.

This inattention to the margins cannot be attributed to having no access to the locals in totalitarian regimes. The material in this book suggests that inattention to the margins takes place in democracies such as Israel as well. There were no barriers to reach women peace activists in Israel; much of their political simmerings took place in public. Derrida indeed speaks of the significance of acts of public protest: "Never to give up on the Enlightenment, which also means, on *public* demonstrations of such discriminations (and this is less easy than you might think)" (1994, 34). Yet those who, like women peace activists, did not give up, who protested in public, could hardly find an audience among political experts, scholars, journalists, and others.

The issue, therefore, is not that the margins are hidden or inaccessible. The issue is that traditional political theories focus on organized politics, ruling political parties, and official stories. Numbers often seem to determine who is seen to have knowledge of political life or any political insights. Small groups are seen as having their own stories to tell, but these are stories only about themselves and not about the rest of political life. Thus, groups on the margins do not appear interesting in larger political discussions, either because of their (small) size or because of their extreme political views. Political theories that dominate Western social science do not consider groups on the margins to have political insights beyond their own specific agendas. Scholarly objection to those who do pay attention to groups on the margins can be seen in Veljko Vujacic's review of Walter Laqueur's book *Black Hundred: The Rise of the Extreme Right in Russia:*

"When it comes to the contemporary Russian Right, however, Laqueur is sometimes off the mark. Perhaps the greatest problem here is the difficulty, even for specialists, of distinguishing the truly important from the less significant. To take just one example, while Laqueur realizes the marginality of groups like 'Pamiat,' he nevertheless devotes a whole chapter to the internal politics of this extremist group" (1994, 713).

A focus on numbers and/or ideologies (finding marginalized groups too small to matter and/or too extreme), however, misses the fact that the simmerings among those at the margins, like women's peace activism, offer political illuminations that governments want to deny or ignore. During the Likud government, as I noted, women's activism indicated a vibrant support for peace in Israel that the government denied. In the current Labor government women's activism indicates a simmering concern about justice to Palestinians that must include an end to the occupation and two states for two people; so far the Labor government has tried to ignore both in the peace process. The more the women have protested, the clearer it has become that the government's position on coexistence with Palestinians is quite limited: it is wedded to security and not to justice. Women's protest provides insights into the links between the Labor government and the Gush Emunim settlers; security serves as the ground on which they stand together. Women's activism reveals the gap (of justice) that still divides the Israeli government, in the mid-1990s, from Palestinians. The women's insistence since 1992 on justice for Palestinians predicted the political simmerings that would accompany partial justice and a limited peace process (continued occupation and an Israeli resistance to a Palestinian state). In public events in 1993 women peace activists stated that a limited peace process offered by the Labor government invites violent acts by frustrated Palestinians; they warned that this in turn would bring about frustrations in Israel that could bring the Likud back to power and dim the prospects for coexistence with Palestinians. The Palestinians' political simmerings make more sense if one pays attention to women's peace activism than it does if one focuses on the government only and on its official version of the peace process.

Margins and Center Are Indivisible but Unequal

Groups such as women's peace activists in Israel illuminate political life precisely because center and margins are indivisible; the women's protest underscores the fact that simmerings on the margins are inseparable from

major political events. While center and margins are marked by power differences, both are part and parcel of the same sociopolitical fabric and in this
sense are indivisible. This (sociopolitical) indivisibility is made even more
obvious precisely in struggles, protests, and oppositions in which both center and margins make up different, but indivisible, parts of this fabric. Indivisibility, however, should not be confused with sameness; sociopolitical
indivisibility is not about similarity. It is in fact the agenda of the political
elite to disguise the fact that center and margins are inseparable but different
(unequal) and, instead, to insist on a fiction that they are divisible (the margins lack political wisdom) but similar (assimilable culturally). As mizrahi
women have noted, their (mizrahi) political insights on the Middle East are
dismissed by the political elite in Israel as separate (rooted in emotions
rather than rational politics), but at a stroke they are also invited to assimilate under a sameness banner of consensus and one nation.

Simmerings on the Margins There and a Debate
on Multiculturalism Here

The political elite's invention of a divisible/sameness relation between center and margins is meant to suppress or ignore social simmerings (of inequality) on the margins. The denial of groups' grievances in Israel is accompanied by a production of cultural sameness that excludes Israeli Palestinians
(as minorities) and invites mizrahim to assimilate. When the center insists
on sameness, of sharing a culture, it aims not merely to ignore cultural differences but also to deny social inequality that goes against the rhetoric of
equality in democratic societies. Moreover, the Israeli case suggests that a
gesture of making space for "difference," as in the case of giving mizrahim
some (belated) recognition in a folklorized version of their culture, as "tradition" is seen by mizrahim as further denial of their lived experience. They
see a gap between their daily lives (exclusions, hidden racism) and what
they have been told about their identities (no culture/wrong culture) and
about themselves. If homelessness, as some women have noted, has a
mizrahi face, the homeless are being told that they have no one to blame but
themselves.

The construction of the relationship between center and margins as
divisible (the margins lack political wisdom) but the same (culturally assimilable) in Israel raises some further questions about academics here. If a "surprise" discourse among intellectuals is a product of considering marginal

groups as separate from the center of power, is it accompanied by (deliberate or innocent) obscuring of social simmerings on the margins? If one listens to our scholarly debate on multiculturalism with a mizrahi ear, does the debate itself ignore the margins' claims while seeming to pay attention to them? I would like to insert into our debate on multiculturalism what, as readers will recall, mizrahi women on the margins over there say. Placing the conference in Tel Aviv "Peace and Identities in Israeli Society: The Place of Mizrahi Women in Political Activities" in the scholarly debate here suggests, as I will note, that multiculturalism on mainly white campuses is more a gesture of mere talk about equality than a fact on the ground. Mizrahi women would probably say that programs (African and African American, Latino\a and Latin American) designed to redress the exclusions of cultures are long overdue but insufficient in colleges and universities that are predominantly white. They would argue, as they did in the Tel Aviv conference, that something else has to take place within the dominant (in their case the ashkenazi) community. Mizrahi women would be quick to locate the barriers that stand between groups on the margins and the multicultural enterprise. The barrier stems, among other things, from a gap between the curriculum in the classroom and lived experience on campus. The very use of the word *multiculturalism* disguises hierarchy (the privilege of a Western curriculum) as it premises equality in using the prefix *multi*, creating the impression that all cultures are more or less equal participants. The word *difference* also allows for a certain ambiguity that disguises the fact (on the ground) of inequality or, worse, what mizrahi women would call hidden (or overt) racism.

I draw attention to two major issues in the simmerings of mizrahim, their own rage and ashkenazi denial; both were raised time and again by mizrahi women (and men). They talk about their rage at the gaps that they encounter between mere talk ("Where is there discrimination?") and facts on the ground (racism). Mizrahi women have called on ashkenazi women to come to grips with the facts of exclusions and hidden racism. They express rage at the gap between the rhetoric of equality and their lived experience; this gap is seen by mizrahi women as a serious hindrance to solidarities based on gender and peace. The questions thus are: What is the place of rage in the West-centered discourse on multiculturalism, and is there a presence (or absence) of a clear articulation in this debate of a white voice that explores its exclusions and racism (as a white issue) in the way that mizrahi women (and men) would like to see ashkenazim do?

An American debate on multiculturalism includes three major approaches to the traditional (Western) core curriculum: protecting it (traditionalists), expanding it (liberals), and transgressing it (postmodernists). All of them are West-centered positions, though only the traditionalists would identify themselves as such. They are all West-centered because the focus of their debate is still on traditional texts as the center of the intellectual enterprise and the ways in which it represents academic power and privilege. Traditionalists want to protect it (and their privilege and power), liberals agree to be more inclusive (share some privilege), and postmodernists ridicule the latter yet constantly contest the traditional curriculum (no one can escape its power, thus subversions), while they disengage, as Rorty claims, from "real actions and events in the political sphere," where the simmerings of the margins take place (1991, 489). They thus stay more involved with West-centered texts (which they subvert) than they do with the simmerings on the margins.

Scholars holding different positions (traditionalists, liberals, postmodernists) offer some insights on their own and their colleagues' positions. Simonson and Walker, for example, argue that those who most vocally oppose multiculturalism in academics (traditionalists) "think that most of what constitutes contemporary American and world culture was immaculately conceived by a few men in Greece, around 900 B.C., came to its full expression in Europe a few centuries later, and began to decline around the middle of the nineteenth century" (1988, x). Postmodernists, says Rorty, "are creating a left that spends much more time thinking about undergraduate curriculum than it does thinking about structural unemployment or health insurance or tax bases." In mizrahi terms postmodernists engage in mere talk when they claim that "academics stick to what they do best—trashing the work of previous academics, improving new professional jargon, building up networks among young scholars in order to change the self-image of academic disciplines." In one guise or another, according to Rorty, postmodernists ignore political simmerings on the margins and instead "redefine politics so that the campuses are where the real political is" (1991, 490).

Supporters of multiculturalism invoke various benefits, including knowledge (overcoming our ignorance) and ethical conduct (institutional respect for others). Simonson and Walker argue that those who oppose multiculturalism offer a narrow, parochial, or ethnocentric view of culture that is un-American, because, "when one in four Americans are people of color, none of us can afford to remain ignorant of the heritage and culture of any part of our population" (1988, xi). In her introduction to Charles Taylor's *Multiculturalism: Examining the Politics of Recognition* Gutmann notes that in the 1990s "Public institutions, including government agencies, schools, and liberal arts colleges and universities, have come under severe criticism these days for failing to recognize or respect the particular cultural identities of citizens" (1994, 3). Not to include particular cultures in the curriculum, she says, indicates "lack of respect for members of these groups, or disregard for part of their cultural identities" (18).

There is no agreement in the debate about multiculturalism on what constitutes politics. Traditionalists deny that there is anything political in their resistance to changes in the curriculum, claiming that it is merely a question of excellence (according to the Western canon) objectively judged. Liberals question the premise of objective judgment of quality as a Western bias and see political gains in expanding the canon to include the rest of the world. Scholars such as Rorty call attention to the gap between "academic politics" (mere talk) and the real world of facts of oppression.

For some people on the margins here, oppression is lodged in daily lived experience. In a talk in 1963 to American teachers James Baldwin begins, as mizrahi women would say, with facts on the ground, with a gap between the rhetoric of equality and acts of social racism and cultural exclusions (no culture/wrong culture). The black man, says Baldwin, "pledges allegiance to that flag which guarantees 'liberty and justice for all.' He is part of the country in which anyone can become president, and so forth. But on the other hand he is also assured by his country and his countrymen that he has never contributed anything to civilization—that his past is nothing more than a record of humiliations gladly endured. He is assumed by the republic that he, his father, his mother, and his ancestors were happy, shiftless, water-melon-eating darkies" (1988, 4).

Mizrahim, as I noted earlier, are familiar with the local Israeli version of the fiction of watermelon, which aimed to cast them as ignorant people who have "no culture." Yet mizrahim found out that they had to keep retelling their real story against persistent variations of the watermelon fiction. Similarly, Baldwin had to tell us what we should have known then and what we still need to know now: "I was never any of those things I was told I was. I was not, for example, happy. I never touched a watermelon for all kinds of reasons that had been invented by white people" (ibid., 8). Social restrictions (work, residence, recreation) and cultural (educational) exclusions are the black child's lived experience, and "there are very few things he can do about it. He can more or less accept it with an absolutely inarticulate and dangerous rage inside—all the more dangerous because it is never expressed" (6). We (academics and others who participate in the debate) could point out that Baldwin wrote these observations in 1963, and we might be tempted to argue that much has changed in the last three decades on mainly white campuses in America. But what are the facts on the ground of lived experience of students on campuses? Just how much do changes in the curriculum reflect the ways in which the "real world" is in fact part and parcel of campus life? In their introduction to *Multicultural Literacy* Simonson and Walker separate life on campus from the real world: "The issues of what our culture is and how it can be taught have not been settled. They have not been settled in the academic world nor in the everyday world in which we live and work" (1988, xiii). But there is no such separation on campuses between the academic world and the everyday world. Faculty work on campus, and students live and work on campus, which is our/their everyday life. How multicultural, or inclusive, is this life? In 1995 *Newsweek* participated in the country's debate on higher education and illuminated facts on the ground of the real world right at the heart of campuses. It told readers that "majority-white institutions like Northwestern can be stressful. Many blacks choose majority-black schools instead. And the Northwestern campus is no one's vision of interracial collegiality. Blacks and whites eat at separate tables and lead separate social lives, as they do in most big schools" (April 3, 1995, 31). Yes, students may sit in the same room taking a "multicultural" class, but outside the classroom black and white students lead separate social lives. The (necessary and belated) changes in the curriculum fail to transform mere talk about equality, inclusions, and respect into a political fact of campus life.

From a mizrahi perspective this gap between a multicultural curriculum and the fact of segregated social lives is linked to the nature of the project of multiculturalism. Is it intended for what mizrahi women called "an ashkenazi self-examination," or is it a project in self-enhancement (let us learn something about the exotic people)? There is an American resonance to this distinction that mizrahi women have located. Unlike scholars who support multiculturalism for the sake of self-enhancement—that is, knowing more or exhibiting a more respectful position by recognizing other cultures—people on the margins, like Baldwin, talk about the need for whites' self-examination. Only taking this first necessary step allows for the next step of self-enhancement. The benefit of expanding the curriculum for white people is, according to Baldwin, that they will deal truthfully with their (real) own history: "The reason is that if you are compelled to lie about one aspect of anybody's history, you must lie about it all. If you have to lie about my real role here, if you have to pretend that I hoed all that cotton just because I loved you, then you have done something to yourself. You are mad." This first step of self-examination is critical because: "If I am not what I've been told I am, then it means that you're not what you thought you were either!" (1988, 8).

Do gestures of cultural inclusions of self-enhancement conceal facts of social injustice on the ground? Mizrahi women argue that proposing cultural inclusions ("tradition" in Israel) without confronting the simmerings flies in the face of rules for proper social conduct; such rules require that the latter precedes the former. Baldwin similarly argues that without self-examination by white America there can be no meaningful multiculturalism. Mizrahi women resented gestures of inclusion (to be active in peace groups) in Israel, which they saw as deceptive talk meant to get their political support. Like mizrahi women, Baldwin insists that for the center to work with the margins (engage in multicultural projects) it must first listen to them: "A great price is demanded to liberate all those silent people so that they can breathe for the first time and tell you what they think of you" (1988, 9). Mizrahi women consider cultural inclusions that sidestep any self-examination as attempts to silence the fact of the social marginality of mizrahim and of hidden racism in Israeli society.

When scholars on university campuses participate, as Rorty (1991) notes, in a discourse of multiculturalism, of "celebrating difference," do they also participate in masking the simmerings of minority groups? Does a multicultural curriculum, seen against the Israeli material, offer a space for difference while at the same time ignoring daily lived experiences?

An Israeli discourse over there invites us academics here to consider mizrahi women's argument that celebrating cultural inclusions before confronting the simmerings of minorities (and self-examination by the center) in the United States is a transgression of social rules. If we on university campuses think that locals have something political to tell us, we have to rethink differences as not just a matter of the curriculum but of political realities that are part of minorities' daily campus experiences; we need to consider not just different cultural traditions but also power differentials that mizrahi women and Palestinian women in Israel have identified and found to be discriminatory and silencing.

The inattention to the margins among scholars and political elites raises another disturbing question about the agendas of both groups. While the intellectual community is diverse in its relation to political elites, it is clear that for scholars to ignore the margins in political analyses is to invite discourses on surprise. Similarly, to ignore self-examination and leap to self-enhancement perpetuates mere talk about inclusion. Attending to the margins (changing the curriculum) is not enough. A scholarly focus on marginalized groups (women, the working class, ethnic minorities, etc.) is not just a question of more studies celebrating silenced groups. When we attend to the margins, we should expect to find not only more about this or that particular group; we should expect to find out more about political life generally. When we pay attention to the simmerings on the margins, we should assume that we will find out more about the center. Center and margins are indivisible. Women's peace activism in Israel invites us to expect new political insight coming from the margins.

Notes

Introduction

1. See Gabriel 1992.

2. In Rabin's explanation of the Gaza-Jericho Agreement to the Israeli Knesset on May 11, 1994, there is no mention of justice to Palestinians. The agreement, according to Rabin, took place "out of a desire to free ourselves from managing the lives of the Palestinians, and from endangering IDF [Israeli Defense Force] soldiers in Gaza. This was our foremost concern" (Rabin 1994, 9).

3. A 1989 document inviting women locally and internationally to a conference of Women Go for Peace, in Jerusalem, states: "We, women of different perspectives and from various feminist and peace groups, have come together to form the 'Women and Peace' Movement." The document issues a call to women to act for three major goals: "We call on you to join us in this Women's Day for Peace: to stop the Occupation; for peace negotiations with the PLO; for two states for two peoples."

4. "In his essay 'Israel among the Nation,' . . . introduction to the 1952 Israel Government Yearbook, Ben Gurion, overlooking the fact that 12.5 percent of Israel's population was Arab, writes that the new State of Israel 'was set up in a desert land,' and that after the Arabs fled the country, 'it was virtually emptied of its former owners'" (Peretz 1991, 87).

5. Some Israeli scholars see the 1967 Six Day War as a turning point that placed Palestinian claim to the land at the center of public debates. "Our right to the land, our relationship to the Palestinians, terrorism, PLO, settlements, settlers and the Intifada—are at the heart of public debates in Israel since 1967" (Avineri 1992, 31).

6. In explaining the Gaza-Jericho Agreement, Rabin said to the Knesset that "the negotiations on Gaza-Jericho experienced many difficulties, mainly relating to security and Israel's insistence on arrangements that will allow it to exercise its responsibility over external security, the security of Israelis and the security of Israeli communities—about which we stood firm: No community will be uprooted" (Rabin 1994, 8). While using the word *security* several times in a single sentence, Rabin also utilizes the term *Israeli communities* as a euphemism for Jewish settlements in the Occupied Territories. Rabin glosses over the fact of continued government support for the settlements (Shahak 1994), which the United States government strongly opposed during the Likud government. By calling them "Israeli communities," Rabin gives the settlements an aura of support that it does not have in the general

241

population. Golan (1994) argues that a number of surveys indicate what she calls a creeping dovishness in Israel.

7. See also Shahak (1994) on what he describes as the Labor government's use of the notion of security to support settlers' acts of terrorizing Palestinians in the Occupied Territories.

8. There is a cultural "juxtaposition of the hero of words and arguments with the hero of action [and] a fundamental contrast between . . . ineffectual verbosity and inaction and . . . practical, heroic activism" (Zerubavel 1991, 196) that is manifested in public events.

9. Thus, when settlers in the West Bank, the Gaza Strip, and the Golan Heights were worried that agreements made at the Madrid Peace Conference in 1992 could mean dismantling settlements, they organized mass demonstrations, not in the settlements but on the streets of Israeli towns. To protest in the latter is more than drawing public attention; it also signified the indivisibility of the territories from the state. The settlers stopped demonstrating soon after mounting their efforts, however, because they realized very early that Yitzhak Shamir, who was prime minister at the time of the Likud right-wing government, had no intention of going beyond mere talk. A year later, in 1993, with a new left-wing government in power, the settlers resumed their demonstrations at the very seat of government: in the streets of Jerusalem (*Yediot Ahronot,* May 21, 1993). As peace talks proceeded in Washington between Israelis and Palestinians, the settlers feared that these talks might actually be transformed into political facts that would alter the status of the settlements; in June 1993 some activists on the extreme Right were warning that they will counter action of compromise with Palestinians with action against the Israeli government. They would fire, they said, with the intention to kill, at Israeli soldiers when they came to evacuate the settlements. One of the leaders of an extreme Right group, who evoked the Holocaust to delegitimate the Israeli government, cast soldiers who obeyed orders in the role of traitors, and justified settlers' rebellion, said: "In war there are no friends, no brothers. Let it be clear that no government in Israel has a right to return territories of *Eretz Yisrael,* the land of Israel. Soldiers should disobey such orders. Any soldier who will not do so is in our eyes like the *Kapo,* those who collaborated with the Nazis—and deserves death. We will fight for every inch of the land of *Eretz Yisrael* including Gaza" (ibid., June 11, 1993).

10. See *Challenge,* no. 27 (1994): 36.

11. In Hebrew, *mishelanu* and *anshei shlomenu.*

12. Simone de Beauvoir (1988) argues that women's failure to change their subordinate position is rooted in the absence of a "we" category. Women's peace activism in Israel indicates that there is more complexity and political power to women's "we" than de Beauvoir's statement suggests.

13. A number of scholars note the proliferation of protest movements in Israel (Aronoff 1989) as they discuss the indigenous qualities of the "politics of provocation" (Wolfsfeld 1988) and examine some historical Jewish antecedents of public protest, thus linking past and present (Lehman-Wilzig 1992). Various major political landmarks in Israel signal a shifting of boundaries between margins and the center and the growing activity of protest groups. These include the Likud taking over the government from the Labor Party in 1977, the Lebanon War in 1982, the onset of the Intifada in 1987, and the Labor Party's return to power in 1992.

14. Women from the extreme Right to the far Left, women in kibbutzim (communal settlements) and in cities, secular and religious, are increasingly inclined to repudiate women's marginalization in political life. On women's recent voices in kibbutzim, see Zamir (1992–93).

15. She said, "We never imagined in the 1970s that we would have to fight all over again for the same rights in the 1990s. There is not a single issue on the status of women that is not rooted in struggles." She called on the participants to reject women's marginalization in organized politics, in the workplace, and in family laws. *Naamat's* recent turnabout has spread beyond the issue of gender equality.

16. "Israeli women are less likely to be politically mobilized than men" (Wolfsfeld 1988, 42)—"but far more intriguing is the fact that when Israeli women are active, they are most likely to be Dissidents . . . this is the one category of activists where women achieve political parity with men" (67).

Chapter 1

Yerushalem dedicated this poem to a meeting between women peace activists from Israel and Palestinian women from the Occupied Territories.

1. Every time I went to the vigil I had to make a choice between demonstrating and taking ethnographic notes, taping and photography. When I joined the women I wore black; experience with violence (I was physically attacked by men from the opposition, and my camera and tape recorder were almost destroyed) taught me that when I acted publicly as an ethnographer I should not wear black.

2. Israeli political analysts describe the fragility of the peace process in terms of threats to derail it by groups on both sides. After the kidnapping of the Israeli soldier in October 1994, Barnea wrote in *Yediot Ahronot* that "the agreement is hostage in the hands of its opponents: Arafat is fettered by enemies of the agreement on his side, and Rabin is fettered by security needs of the settlers. If he redeploys the army he will abandon their security. If he resettles them he abandons Eretz Yisrael, the land of Israel" (Barnea 1994).

3. Because of this serious disagreement, the rivalry between the two par-

ties has implications for the peace process. Recent surveys, in September 1994, "show the prime minister running neck-and-neck with the Likud's leader, Binyamin Netanyahu, whom he has led by a wide margin until now." It is interesting to note that the surveys indicate strong support for the peace process, 65 percent said that was going "well" to "very well," and 34 percent thought that it was going "badly" (Hillel Halkin, *Forward,* September 23, 1994).

4. After the signing of the agreement with Jordan in the Arava in October 1994, Ariel Sharon, one of the Likud leaders, wrote in *Yediot Ahronot* (October 28, 1994) why he refused to participate in the ceremony and outlined his objections to the actions of the Labor government, which include relinquishing what he considers sacred Jewish land and the possibility of recognizing the right of Palestinian refugees to return to the West Bank and the Gaza Strip.

5. See Gal-Or 1991.

6. While most of the women in the vigil do not follow traditional Jewish practices, they are culturally familiar with them. A story in Jewish folklore highlights the import of women's mourning for the collective and the significance of black as a sign of mourning for women. It recounts that the prophet Jeremiah saw a woman in black sitting at the top of Mount Zion in Jerusalem. He went over to find out the reason for her grief and to comfort her. When he realized that her grief was not personal but that she was the Mother of Zion mourning for the nation, Jeremiah went down on his knees and blessed her (Zmora 1964). Grief for the collective is also the theme of the ninth day of the month of Av, in the Jewish calendar, which is a day of fasting and mourning for national tragedies. The Fast of Esther, *Taanit Ester,* on the thirteenth of the month of Av, while in support of Queen Esther, is related to her plea to the Persian king to save the Jews. The Women in Black, like the Mother of Zion and the mourners of the Ninth of Av and on the Fast of Esther, mourn for the collective.

7. That tradition is expressed in "a famed Talmudic statement [that] equates the worth of an individual life with that of a whole world" (Yudelson 1986, 23).

8. Emotion as an analytic category has drawn both interest and criticism in anthropology. Some consider the discussion of emotions as outside the bounds of the discipline (Rosaldo 1989), implying a division of labor between anthropology and psychology. Recently, however, anthropologists such as Catherine Lutz and Lila Abu-Lughod have called attention to the social features of emotions and particularly to "the role of emotional discourse in social interaction," to the "construal of emotion as about social life rather than internal states," and to "the close involvement of emotion talk with issues of sociality and power" (1990, 1).

9. Elsewhere I have discussed this tradition of associating women with emotions (Gabriel 1992). See also Coole 1988.

10. The claim to equal rights and the grounds on which women made the claim are expressed in Hannah Trager's account: "A young woman spoke up: 'Now is the time that we the daughters of this settlement, *moshava*, will insist on our right to participate equally in public affairs. We take part in building a new society in Eretz Yisrael, a society in which we should all be free. But is this society going to be built on equality between women and men? Did we not just like the men make our contribution in founding this settlement? Did not our mothers suffer as did our fathers, did they not know the same hardship and dangers? And we the daughters, did we not take on any job at home or in the fields? Did we not weed the vineyards under the blazing sun? Did we not gather the harvest, did we not milk the cows? And did we not do anything that we could in times of sickness and in trouble? Therefore, let us all go together. Not men against women, but men with women.' 'You should know (another woman turned to the men) that in the next public meeting we plan to bring up the question of our vote. We expect your support'" ([1923] 1984, 133).

11. Women's struggle to become equal citizens is noted by Sarah Azaryahu, who worked to advance the status of women in the *Yishuv* days. She offers a historical comment on the genesis of a hiatus between noble promises to women and harsh social reality: "In 1897, at the dawn of the political Zionist movement, Theodore Herzl declared that there would be equality for the daughters of Israel . . . the fact is that the political liberation movement of the Jewish people was founded upon the principle of equality. The Zionist woman had good reason to assume that when her turn came to immigrate to Israel, thereby fulfilling a lifelong ambition, she would be able to work and to create in a society in which she had full and equal rights in all spheres of activity. Reality, however, was a slap in the face. Upon arrival in Palestine, women were faced with the necessity of beginning the struggle for political and civil rights and this at a time when they had been certain that this issue had already been resolved" ([1948] 1980, 1, 2).

12. The highest percentages of female participation in parliaments are found in Norway, 32.4 percent; Finland, 32.5 percent; and Sweden, 32.5 percent.

13. As Wolfsfeld notes, "Israeli children learn . . . that politics is a predominantly male concern" (1988, 42). His view is that "even those women who do want to participate find it difficult to take part in institutional action. . . . The political parties may recruit from a variety of social classes, but it seems that they prefer men" (1988, 67).

14. Amira Dotan, the head of Israel's Women's Corps, who was promoted in 1988 to the rank of brigadier-general, the first woman to hold this high

rank, talked about implementing changes. She spoke of her "intent on moving a significant percentage of female soldiers out of conventional clerical jobs where most pass their two years of obligatory military service to tasks at the cutting edge of new technologies hitherto occupied almost exclusively by male soldiers" (1991, 139). While the general said she believed that women have the physical and psychological qualities required for combat, she did not plan to push for a change in that direction. To support her decision not do so she, like many Israelis, drew on Jewish tradition. She said: "We cannot ignore our heritage. There is a special role for the Jewish woman as mother and the center of the family" (140).

15. This status has been reproduced in various areas, such as the workplace, through regulations and laws designated "to protect women as women" (Karp 1989, 9).

16. Chazan notes that "there are now more known incidents of domestic violence and more shelters for battered wives" (1989, 12).

17. The project's name means, in Hebrew, a "female human being," a counterpart term to *Ben Adam,* the masculine word for a human being, which is commonly used in reference to both genders in a similar way that *man* or *mankind,* for example, are used in English. In colloquial Hebrew the term *Ben Adam* (masc.) is used as a compliment and implies being a good person.

Chapter 2

1. Shani reminded the readers that the PLO had issued a statement dated November 15, 1988, in which the Palestinian National Council recognized Israel indirectly by accepting various United Nations resolutions. In December of 1988, in his UN speech in Geneva, Yassir Arafat declared that the PLO has recognized Israel and has turned away from terrorism. "In a press conference after his speech, Arafat spoke of 'the right of all the parties in the Middle East conflict to exist in peace and security, and these parties include the Palestinian state, Israel, and other neighboring countries'" (Shani Publications 1990, 10).

2. Not only women peace activists were critical of the Likud government's position regarding Palestinian nation-ness. On September 9, 1990, during the Gulf Crisis, Yaakov Shimoni wrote in *Haaretz:* "In the last two generations, Arab-Palestinian nationalism has undergone a change in an increased emphasis on its Palestinian nature and goals. . . . In the last few years, and today, the Arab Palestinian identifies as both and the national political party is both pan-Arab and Arab Palestinian specifically. . . . King Hussein [of Jordan] has been stating for a number of years that he does not speak for the Palestinians, that he will not negotiate on the future of the ter-

ritories without the Palestinians, and that he supports the creation of an Arab-Palestinian state." Shimoni warns Israelis: "We should not delude ourselves by theorizing the nature of the Arab-Palestinian nationalism, and the useless supposition that it is merely pan-Arab, or only ethnic or just local: It is simultaneously pan-Arab and Arab Palestinian."

3. Buber remarks that Herzl's initial position was "'neither against Palestine nor for Argentina'; but it is clear from the distribution of the words 'against' and 'for' in this sentence that he tended more towards America at this time" (1973, 131). Buber discerns a change in Herzl's position in the publication of *The Jewish State,* which emphasized Palestine as a place with emotional ties for Jews that will therefore mobilize a national project. Herzl compared two attempts to resettle Jews and concluded in favor of the Palestine experience. For him it has become clear that "'What Baron Hirsch failed to achieve in Argentina is succeeding in Palestine. Why? Because 'national Judaism' is fertilizing the old soil'" (133). Herzl realized that attachment to a specific land, not just any land, was a crucial element to nation-states; though he understood its significance, he may not have known the serious ramifications that the "old soil" would have in the future state; as I note in this book, religious meanings would be attached to *land* in ways that would make land and nation indivisible for some Israelis.

4. Herzl considered the Dreyfus trial in France a turning point in his life, an event that revealed to him in full force the terror that Jews faced in European countries. As Bein notes, "In that fateful mòment, when he heard the howling of the mob outside the gates of the *Ecole Militaire,* the realization flashed upon Herzl that the anti-semitism was deep-rooted in the heart of people" ([1986] 1988, 34). Herzl was shocked into political action by the French reaction to the Dreyfus affair, which "embodies the desire of the vast majority of the French to condemn a Jew, and to condemn all Jews. Death to the Jews! howled the mob. . . . Where? In France. In republican, modern civilized France, a hundred years after the declaration of the Rights of Man. The French people, or at any rate the greater part of the French people, does not want to extend the rights of man to Jews. The edict of the great Revolution had been revoked" (ibid., 34).

5. Herzl came away from his eyewitness experience as a journalist in Paris convinced, as he wrote in his notes, that "the situation will not change for the better, but rather for the worse. . . . There is only one way out: into the Promised Land" (ibid., 35). Witnessing the mob reaction in Paris to the Dreyfus affair had prompted Herzl "to stand by his Jewishness; the ghastly spectacle of that winter morning must have shaken him to the depths of his being. It was as if the ground had been cut away from under his feet. In this sense Herzl could say later that the Dreyfus affair had made him a Zionist" (ibid., 35). As Herzl himself stated: "I picked up once again the torn thread

of the tradition of our people. I lead it into the Promised Land" (Herzl [1986] 1988, 39). But, as a number of scholars note, while for Herzl the Promised Land meant sovereignty for the nation, its exact location was at first undetermined. A safe place for the nation-state was paramount for Herzl, but Zion for him was not instantly a "natural" homeland; it was constructed over time as the natural and logical place for Jews. He argued that land itself was unimportant, whereas state, anywhere, was: "it is true that the Jewish State is conceived as a peculiarly modern structure on unspecified territory. But a State is formed, not by pieces of land, but rather by a number of men united under sovereign rule" (ibid., 137).

6. Scholars, natives, and others use the terms *Israeli Palestinian* and *Israeli Arab* interchangeably.

7. As Amal outlines the women's peace protest of the occupation, she, like Jewish Israelis, used a biblical phrase as she notes that the international community has "heard our cry." The Hebrew phrase *shamoo et tzaakatenu* echoes the biblical phrase in Exodus 3:7, which says that God has heard the cry of suffering of the Children of Israel, *veet tzaakatem shamati*. Ancient slavery and contemporary inequalities thus are placed in a single narrative. The Israelites' suffering in Egypt, the Palestinian suffering in the Intifada, and women's peace activism are told in one local text.

8. See Grossman 1992.

9. The failure or futility of the efforts to claim that the population on the West Bank and the Gaza Strip is nationless was brought home to Israelis with the onset of the Intifada. Much of women's peace activities and alliance with Palestinian women and their readiness to cross national boundaries was prompted or recharged by this event (Chazan 1991). Yehoshafat Harkabi, a former chief of Israeli military intelligence, describes the beginning of the Intifada: "In December 1987, riots broke out in Gaza and in the West Bank. These erupted spontaneously, without PLO instigation or direction, and are often referred to as the 'Intifada.' The uprising expressed the Palestinians' humiliation and indignation over the Israeli domination and, although predictable, came as a shock to the Israeli authorities and public" (1989, x). The Intifada, as some scholars note, jolted Israelis into facing one of their sentimental myths, that the state could be a benign occupier. "The Intifada laid to rest the idea that it is possible to sustain a forced occupation at a low economic and moral price" (Horowitz and Lissak 1990, 88). "The need to contain the Intifada sharpened the political polarization between doves and hawks in Israeli society" (89) and mobilized women to enter the politics of the Israeli-Palestinian conflict. It sharpened political awareness within the Left and, as Sarit noted, heightened women's awareness of the suffering of another nation.

Chapter 3

1. The religious Jewish community in Israel consists of Zionists, non-Zionists, and anti-Zionists. Both Oz Veshalom/Netivot Shalom and Gush Emunim belong to the religious Zionist community.

2. The meaning of Torah is broader than a reference to Pentateuch; it is a way of life that includes Scripture and Rabbinic law.

3. Lazarus-Yafeh argues that "there can be little doubt of the fact that fundamentalism today is a worldwide phenomenon, on the fringes of all three monotheistic religions (including the Catholic church) and perhaps in non-monotheistic religions as well" (1993, 43).

4. Friedman argues that "the concept of fundamentalism originally evolved within the framework of the history of Christianity, [and] cannot always be used in the same way with reference to non-Christian religions such as Judaism or Islam." He offers, however, a broad definition of fundamentalism as a "religious outlook shared by a group of believers who base their belief on an ideal religious-political reality that has existed in the past or is expected to emerge in the future. Such realities are described in great detail in the religious literature. And the fundamentalist believer is obliged to use whatever religious and political means are necessary to actualize these realities in the here and now" (1993, 148).

5. "From a strict halakhic viewpoint, there is no justification for the argument against territorial compromise, if compromise would indeed seriously enhance the peace process in the Middle East and thus the prospect of saving lives" (Tal 1986, 37).

6. In their opposition to Gush Emunim's understanding of God and Torah, religious women share an ideological position with men in Oz Veshalom/Netivot Shalom such as Simon, who argues: "Under no circumstances must one accept the view of Gush Emunim as stemming unequivocally from the Torah" (Simon 1986, 22). Women and men also share an understanding of the relationship between the Promised Land and ethical conduct and the idea that "the Master of the universe intended the land of Israel for the people of Israel, but only in conjunction with the severe admonition that our real hold on the land is conditional on our behavior. There is a need for this warning, for clinging to the dangerous delusion that God will be on our side unconditionally, by virtue of our Covenant with Him, may lead us to sin. In light of this, it seems appropriate that the educators of Israel should always couple that verse of Psalms CXI:6—'He has shewed His people the power of His works, that He may give them the heritage of the nations'—with the verse immediately following: 'The works of His hands are truth and justice; all His commandments are trustworthy.' God's power is not exerted in an arbitrary or amoral manner, and He does not give His

people the heritage of the nations, except in accordance with truth and justice. It follows that we are commanded not only to believe in the sovereignty of the Creator, but also to take care that the realization of our right to the land will be compatible with truth and justice" (23). Despite the masculine language used to describe God, women and men in the religious Left reclaim an image of God as a God of "truth and justice" and see the relationship between the Jewish people and the divine as conditional on their ethical behavior within and between communities.

7. Enfolded in Glass's (1986) statement is a notion that human beings are created in God's image and that Jews who act unethically in God's name commit the gravest sin: *Chillul HaShem,* the desecration of God's name. Ethical Jewish conduct includes concepts of justice, peace, and mercy; these are in sharp contrast to what the religious Left views as Gush Emunim's unethical conduct in which, armed with Uzis, they act on the basis of "might makes right" instead of "right makes might."

8. While both Likud and Labor included religious parties in their governments, some secular Israelis had high hopes after the 1992 election, which Labor won in what Israelis called an "upheaval" after fifteen years of the Likud government. Gidon Samet broadens the term *upheaval* not only as a shift from Right to Left but also a promising change regarding the secularizing of public culture. He wrote in *Haaretz* on June 26: "The real meaning of upheaval, *mahapach,* is beyond the mathematics of the elections. Its significant meaning is a change in the political behavior and a striving to overturn the ways that governments have been formed in the past. . . . Such behavior would give the upheaval its appropriate color. . . . Rabin can withstand the demands of religious parties." Shortly after the 1992 election, on June 30, Gabi Nitzan wrote in *Hadashot:* "We are facing today a historic opportunity: a government without religious politicians . . . we have become prisoners of a world view that says that we cannot live without the dictatorship of fundamentalist clerks . . . who have taken on the monopoly on belief and spirit and persecute every citizen from birth, through marriage and unto burial." The option for Labor, as people like Samet and Nitzan saw it, was to leave the religious parties out of the government, which also would mean to include the Israeli-Palestinian members of Knesset in the Labor government. The party, however, was unwilling to do it. Rabin made the choices according to what he thought was most useful to his own political plans. In hindsight it may have been easier for him to sign a peace agreement with the Palestinians with religious Jews in his government, even though they did not vote for the agreement; Rabin won a slim majority precisely because the Palestinian members of parliament did vote for it. In some ways Labor and its partner, Meretz, had to choose between the rock of religious concessions and the hard place of including people from another nation in their govern-

ment. Their choice reveals that among ultraorthodox (some of whom are not Zionists) and Palestinian members of Knesset, Labor (and the more left-wing Meretz accepted it) preferred Jewish non-Zionists and made a statement about the indivisibility of state and nation in the Knesset politics. Yet secular Jews, whether they agreed with Rabin or not on his choice, were concerned about the outcome of government that includes ultraorthodox political parties.

Chapter 4

1. The large majority of mizrahi Jews who came to Israel in the 1950s from North Africa and the Middle East are also known as *Edot Hamizrach* (Oriental communities). They are referred to as Sephardim (descendants of Spanish Jews) and as Orientals (Swirski 1989). *Mizrah* in Hebrew means "East," and *Middle East* is referred to as *Mizrah Tichon*. The close association in Hebrew between *Mizrahim* (Oriental Jews) and the region Mizrah Tichon is not merely linguistically obvious but has, as this conference reveals, significant implications for the discourse on differences. The division between mizrahim (Orientals) and ashkenazim is one of the major social divisions in Israeli society today. *Ashkenaz* is the traditional Hebrew term for Germany and refers to Jews from Western communities. (See also Horowitz and Lissak 1990; Dominguez 1989; Swirski 1989).

2. In 1990 a different view was offered by Rivka Bar Yosef, an Israeli sociologist: "Some things are resolving themselves. Take, for example, what is called the ethnic conflict, which only a few years ago was thought to be the gap between Sephardim and non-Sephardim. This conflict has not disappeared, but it's smoothing out. The Sephardim have a high rate of mobility, and many of them have entered politics. If you look at the Knesset, you probably cannot recognize them, but among the outstanding Knesset members, not the back-benchers, there are Iraqis, Moroccans, Tunisians: some of the very well-to-do and very newly well-to-do are Sephardim. So while there still is poverty among them . . . there is also a high rate of intermarriage. This is a problem that is resolving itself, while others are now boiling" (Bar Yosef 1990, 526).

3. Gibel-Azoulay said in the *Tikkun* peace conference in Jerusalem: "Moral myopia is also what makes it possible for some Israelis represented here, and writing for American publications like *Tikkun* and on the Op-Ed of the *NY Times*, to show compassion for the plight of Arab Palestinians but having no patience for the concerns of Arab Jews. . . . Those of you familiar with American political movements of the sixties, will remember the New Left's failure to attract working-class white, black, Latino and ethnic support" (1991, 2).

4. In Israel's annual statistical yearbook, published by the Israel Bureau of Statistics, only the third generation of Israeli born are no longer identified by the families' country of origin (Dominguez 1989; Swirski 1989).

5. The issues of the cultural divide and hidden racism that women in the conference exposed were expressed by Eran Riklis, an Israeli director who made a film, *Zohar,* that describes the life and untimely death of a popular mizrahi singer, Zohar Argov. Riklis noted that "there is still a typical ashkenazi audience between the ages of 25 and 35 who will not come to see the film. . . . This is an audience that has a barrier when the story is about a mizrahi hero. There is today in this country a much more sophisticated and hidden racism . . . a few days ago I spoke to my accountant, an ashkenazi, who did not see the film. 'Don't be mad at me,' he said, 'but that is not for me, all these *franks* (a derogatory term for mizrahim) and Zohar Argov" (*Yediot Ahronot,* November 19, 1993).

6. Swirski believes that mizrahim have internalized ashkenazi perceptions. "This ideology has permeated the ranks of the Orientals themselves, and many of them . . . have come to believe that Ashkenazim are in fact intellectually superior and therefore merit a higher social position. This is especially true for many of the Orientals who have entered the state apparatus—as politicians, educators, social workers, and community organizers—and who tend to talk about 'them,' that is, their Oriental constituents, in terms not unlike those used by Ashkenazim" (Swirski 1989, 28).

7. "According to the 1983 Census, 70% of the first-and-second generation Israelis residing in development towns are Orientals. . . . Those Ashkenazim who do live in the development towns often live in separate neighborhoods. . . . In the big cities—Tel Aviv, Haifa, Jerusalem and Beer Sheva—the same ecological differentiation is found: in Tel Aviv we find the classical north-south division; in Haifa the division is between the upper and lower levels of the Carmel Mountain; in Jerusalem the main division is also reminiscent of the north-south one" (ibid., 22).

8. The issue of ashkenazi arrogance that came up in the Tel Aviv conference resonates the words of mizrahim a year later in the 1991 *Tikkun* conference. The *Jerusalem Post* (June 28, 1991) reported that Yossi Yona, a Hebrew University philosophy professor and a Sephardi peace activist who participated in the conference, was feeling particularly bitter after listening to member of Knesset Dedi Zucker (Citizen's Right Movement): "Zucker said in an interview before his speech, 'I do not accept the view that we have to have a special message to the Sephardim.'" The newspaper also informed its readers that "one Sephardi activist, who spoke on condition of anonymity, called Zucker's comment 'typical establishment arrogance.'"

9. Batya Goor writes about Ofakim, a predominantly mizrahi development town, and specifically of a mizrahi wound, which she claims is

expressed in a sense of inferiority. Goor offers an ashkenazi perspective and says that when mizrahi immigrants came to Israel "they aspired to be assimilated in a culture in which they could assimilate in one generation"; they have lost their own cultural certainty, which resulted in a "cultural gap" (1990, 61). In their wish to assimilate in what was seen as progress and by giving up their own cultural world, a wound was opened. But Goor talks of mizrahi "silent agreement, of their lowering of the heads before the superiority of the old-time structure expressed in daily small things. Customs that were hidden, prayer styles and melodies that were silent" (126). Goor sees the mizrahi immigrants' response as passive: "The passivity that marked the beginning of the process has continued, despite socio-economic changes" (146).

10. Culture may, however, become a bone of contention once the Palestinian question is settled. "Peace may open Israel to Arab culture and may make relevant the Oriental Jews' cultural affinity with the Arabs. Israel's cultural orientation may become a real issue that would divide Oriental and Ashkenasik Jews" (Smooha 1993, 321).

Chapter 5

1. The Cairo agreement hammered out details left unspecified in Oslo.

2. The written announcement of the conference said: "Five years of the Intifada; a change in the Israeli government, "peace talks"—yet the bloodshed continues. It seems more and more that the current political process is not leading to a just solution. We Women and Peace coalition, know that as long as the occupation, violation of human rights, violence, and killing continues, the protest must not die. We must foster a political culture of peace to ensure peaceful existence for all peoples in the region. On Friday, January 8, 1993, a national conference is being held in Beit Agron, Jerusalem, with the participation of Israeli and Palestinian women from Israel and the Occupied Territories. From 13:00–14:00 we will join the national demonstration of Women in Black marking five years of that organization's protest, in French Square, Jerusalem. Everyone is invited! Women in Black, of the past and present, from all over the country, women from groups working for peace and women's rights, women who think that the time has come to work for peace."

3. Ruth Behar describes Esperanza, a Mexican woman, who dauntlessly invites herself to be of the nation. In her own transgressive way Esperanza "is writing herself back into national epic history . . . refusing to be seduced into femininity, she is cutting out a new window from which to view, and enter, a male narrative that seems to be sealed off to her gaze" (1993, 315). In telling Esperanza's story, Behar reinscribes her political act to a transna-

tional audience so that this Mexican woman's "uninvited" imaginings move from a local to the global context. In the Israeli local context women's peace activists have invited themselves, before and after the 1992 elections, to imagine nation-ness that includes justice for Palestinians.

4. Eban noted the concealment of the fact that "the government of Israel is now negotiating with the PLO while disguising this fact in terms flimsier than the fig leaves in the ancient Garden of Eden" (*Yediot Ahronot,* July 9, 1993).

Chapter 6

1. Ruggie 1994.

2. Kaplan 1994.

3. The awareness of the political significance of the link between local women and global vigils is revealed in a local Israeli call to Women in Black worldwide: "We would like to publish the locations of the many Women in Black vigils throughout the world. If you participate in a Women in Black vigil (not just a peace dialogue or organization), please write to us and let us know" (*Women in Black National Newsletter,* no. 6 [Fall 1993]: 1).

4. For those who do not know about the local/global Women in Black, *Ms.,* an American feminist magazine, brings vigils such as the one in Belgrade to global attention: a "group of longtime women's rights activists decided to make the antiwar campaign more high profile. They established themselves as 'Women in Black'—joining scores of women in the Middle East, Europe, and elsewhere who, under the same name, have advocated for peace" (Sekulic 1994, 18–19). In this version Women in Black appear as an international pacifist phenomenon taking on local issues.

Bibliography

Abu-Amr, Ziad. 1993. "Hamas: A Historical and Political Background." *Journal of Palestinian Studies* 22, no. 4: 5–19.

Alternative Directory of Progressive Groups and Institutions in Israel and the Occupied Territories. 1991. Jerusalem: Alternative Information Center.

Anderson, Benedict. [1983] 1990. *Imagined Communities: Reflections on the Origin and Spread of Nationalism.* London: Verso.

Antonovski, Aaron. 1969. "Discussion." *The Integration of Immigrants from Different Countries of Origin in Israel,* 88–89. Jerusalem: Magness Press.

Appadurai, Arjun. 1990. "Disjuncture and Difference in the Global Cultural Economy." *Public Culture* 2, no. 2: 1–24.

———. 1991. "Global Ethnoscapes: Notes and Queries for a Transnational Anthropology." In *Recapturing Anthropology: Working in the Present,* ed. Richard Fox, 191–210. Santa Fe: School of American Research Press.

Appadurai, Arjun, and Carol A. Breckenridge. 1988. "Why Public Culture?" *Public Culture* 1, no. 1: 5–9.

Arendt, Hannah. 1974. *Rahel Varnhagen: The Life of a Jewish Woman.* New York: Harcourt Brace Jovanovich.

Arlozorof-Goldberg, Gerda. 1926. "On the Women Workers' Conference." *Ha'Isha,* 16–20. In Hebrew.

Aronoff, Myron J. 1989. *Israeli Visions and Divisions: Cultural Change and Political Conflict.* Oxford: Transaction Publishers.

Aviad, Janet. 1986. "Religious Zionism Today." *Religious Zionism: Challenges and Choices,* 25–31. Jerusalem: Oz Veshalom Publications.

Avinery, Shlomo. 1992. "Comments on the Meaning of the Elections of the Israeli 13th Knesset." *Alpayim—A Multidisciplinary Publication for Contemporary Thought and Literature,* 6: 29–34. Tel Aviv: Am Oved. In Hebrew.

Azaryahu, Sarah. [1948] 1980. *The Union of Hebrew Women for Equal Rights in Eretz Yisrael.* Haifa: Woman's Aid Fund.

Baldwin, James. 1988. "A Talk to Teachers." In *Multicultural Literacy,* ed. Rick Simonson and Scott Walker, 3–12. Saint Paul: Graywolf Press.

Bar Meir, Oded. 1989. "Exposed to Curses and the Blazing Sun." *Davar,* October 19.

Barnea, Nahum. 1994. *Yediot Ahronot,* October 14.

Bar Yosef, Rivka. 1990. "An Israeli on Israel." *Partisan Review* 57, no. 4: 526–40.

Behar, Ruth. 1993. *Translated Women: Crossing the Border with Esperanza's Story.* Boston: Beacon Press.

Bein, Alex. [1986] 1988. "Biography." In *The Jewish State,* by Theodore Herzl, 21–66. New York: Dover Publications.

Ben, Ami. 1990. *Al Hamishmar,* October 23.

Ben David, Joseph. 1969. "Discussion." *The Integration of Immigrants from Different Countries of Origin in Israel,* 89–91. Jerusalem: Magness Press.

Ben-Eliezer, Uri. 1990. "From Bab El Wad to Santa Monica and Back." *Politika* (November): 13–17. In Hebrew.

Benziman, Uzi. 1989. "Gliding on the Teflon Walls." *Politika* (July): 38. In Hebrew.

Bernstein, Deborah. 1987. *The Struggle for Equality: Urban Women Workers in Prestate Israeli Society.* New York: Praeger.

Bialkin, Kenneth J. 1993. "Israel: Toward Becoming a Major Financial Center." *Midstream* 39, no. 9: 25–28.

Bowes, A. M. 1989. *Kibbutz Goshen: An Israel Commune.* Prospect Heights, Ill.: Waveland Press.

Bruner, Edward M., and Phyllis Gofain. 1984. "Dialogic Narration and the Paradoxes of Masada." In *Text, Play, and Story: The Construction and Reconstruction of Self and Society,* ed. Edward M. Bruner, 56–79. Proceedings of the 1983 American Ethnological Society annual meeting, Washington, D.C.

Buber, Martin. 1973. *On Zion: The History of an Idea.* New York: Schocken Books.

Buck-Morss, Susan. 1994. "Fashion in Ruins: History after the Cold War." *Radical Philosophy* 68:10–18.

Butternweck, Annelise. 1993. *Women in Black National Newsletter* 5, no. 9 (Spring), 5.

Cassell, Joan. 1989. *A Group Called Women: Sisterhood and Symbolism in the Feminist Movement.* Prospect Heights, Ill.: Waveland Press.

Chazan, Naomi. 1989. "The Israeli Woman—Myth and Reality." Interview. *New Outlook* (June–July), 2–3.

———. 1991. "Gender Equality? Not in a War Zone." *Israeli Democracy* 3, no. 2: 4–8.

Cohen, Ruth. 1993. "Women in Black Step Down." *Challenge* 4, no. 6: 11.

Cohen, Stan. 1993. "More Vigilant than Ever." *Challenge* 4, no. 6: 16–17.

Cohn, B. S., and N. B. Dirks. 1988. "Beyond the Fringe: The Nation State, Colonialism, and the Technologies of Power." *Journal of Historical Sociology* 1:224–29.

Coole, Diana H. 1988. *Women in Political Theory: From Ancient Misogyny to Contemporary Feminism.* Hertfordshire: Harvester Wheatsheaf.

Cornu, Francis. 1991. "La fin du rêve de Saddam Hussein." *Le Monde,* 19 January.

Cowell, Alan. 1991. "Shattered Illusions in an Angry Jordan." *International Herald Tribune,* January 18.

Dayan, Arye. 1989. "Making History." *Kol Hair,* April 19.

De Beauvoir, Simone. [1949] 1988. *The Second Sex.* London: Pan Books.

Derrida, Jacques. 1994. "The Deconstruction of Actuality." Interview. *Radical Philosophy* 68:28–41.

Deutch, Yvonne. 1992–93. "The Women and Peace Coalition in Haifa." *Women in Black National Newsletter* 4, no. 3 (Winter), 2.

Dominguez, Virginia R. 1989. *People as Subject, People as Object: Selfhood and Peoplehood in Contemporary Israel.* Madison: University of Wisconsin Press.

Dotan, Amira. 1991. "Israel's First Female General." In *Calling the Equality Bluff: Women in Israel,* ed. Barbara Swirski and Marilyn P. Safir, 139–41. New York: Pergamon Press.

El Or, Tamar. 1992. *Educated and Ignorant: On Ultra-Orthodox Women and Their World.* Tel Aviv: Am Oved. In Hebrew.

Espanioly, Nabila. 1991. "Palestinian Women in Israel Respond to the Intifada." In *Calling the Equality Bluff: Women in Israel,* ed. Barbara Swirski and Marilyn P. Safir, 147–51. New York: Pergamon Press.

Fischer, Michael M. J. 1986. "Ethnicity and the Post-Modern Arts of Memory." In *Writing Culture: The Poetics and Politics of Ethnography,* ed. James Clifford and George E. Marcus, 194–233. Berkeley: University of California Press.

Fischer, Stanley. 1993–94. "Building Palestinian Prosperity." *Foreign Policy* 93 (Winter): 60–75.

Fox, Richard G. 1990. *Nationalist Ideologies and the Production of National Culture.* Washington, D.C.: American Anthropological Association.

Freud, Sigmund. 1969. *A General Introduction to Psychoanalysis.* New York: Pocket Books.

Friedman, Ariela, Ruth Shrift, and Dafna Izraeli. 1982. *The Double Bind: Women in Israel.* Tel Aviv: Hakibutz Hameuchad. In Hebrew.

Friedman, Menachem. 1993. "Jewish Zealots: Conservative versus Innovative." In *Jewish Fundamentalism in Comparative Perspective: Religion, Ideology, and the Crisis of Modernity,* ed. Laurence J. Silberstein, 148–63. New York: New York University Press.

Gabriel, Ayala H. 1992. "Living with Medea and Thinking after Freud: Greek Drama, Gender and Concealments." *Cultural Anthropology* 7:346–74.

Gabriel, Ayala H., and Orit Ziv. 1973. "Identity and Community among Bucharian Jews in Jerusalem." MS.

Galili, Lily. 1989. "Women in Black Have Learned Self-Defense Techniques." *Haaretz,* September 10. In Hebrew.

Gal-Or, Naomi. 1990. *The Jewish Underground: Our Terrorism.* Tel Aviv: Hakibutz Hameuchad. In Hebrew.

Gefen, Dorit. 1990. *Al Hamishmar,* October 23.

Gibel-Azoulay, Katya. 1993. "The Politics of 'The Politics of Representation': Cultural Capital, Ethnicity, and Israeli Women." Paper presented at the Department of Anthropology, University of Rochester, April 30.

————. 1991. Paper presented at the *Tikkun* Conference in Jerusalem, June 6.

Gillath, Nurit. 1991. "Women against War: Parents against Silence." In *Calling the Equality Bluff: Women in Israel,* ed. Barbara Swirski and Marilyn P. Safir, 142–46. New York: Pergamon Press.

Glass, David. 1986. "Might Makes Right: Travesty of Torah." *Oz Veshalom: Religious Zionists for Strength and Peace* 7–8 (Summer–Fall): 45–47.

Glazer, Nahum N. 1973. Foreword to *On Zion: The History of an Idea,* by Martin Buber. New York: Schocken Books.

Glick, Shimon M. 1986. "Tempering Hubris with Humility." *Oz Veshalom: Religious Zionists for Strength and Peace* 7–8 (Summer–Fall): 43–44.

Goitein, S. D. 1974. *Jews and Arabs.* 3d ed. New York: Schocken.

Golan, Galia. 1994. "A Palestinian State from an Israeli Point of View." *Middle East Policy* 3, no. 1: 56–59.

Goor, Batya. 1990. *Next to Hunger Road.* Jerusalem: Keter. In Hebrew.

Gopin, Marc. 1986. "Seeking Peace: In the Footsteps of Aaron." *Oz Veshalom: Religious Zionists for Strength and Peace* 7–8 (Summer–Fall): 62–63.

Grossman, David. 1992. *Present Absentees.* Tel Aviv: Hakibutz Hameuchad. In Hebrew.

————. 1990. *Yediot Ahronot,* August 24.

Gupta, Akhil. 1992. "The Song of the Nonaligned World: Transnational Identities and the Reinscription of Space in Late Capitalism." *Cultural Anthropology* 7:63–79.

Gupta, Akhil, and James Ferguson. 1992. "Beyond 'Culture': Space, Identity, and the Politics of Difference." *Cultural Anthropology* 7:6–24.

Gutmann, Amy. 1994. Introduction to *Multiculturalism: Examining the Politics of Recognition,* ed. Amy Gutmann, 3–24. Princeton, N.J.: Princeton University Press.

Handler, Richard. 1991. "Who Owns the Past? History, Cultural Property, and the Logic of Possessive Individualism." In *The Politics of Culture,* ed. Brett Williams. Washington, D.C.: Smithsonian Institution Press.

Hannerz, Ulf. 1992. *Cultural Complexity: Studies in the Social Organization of Meaning.* New York: Columbia University Press.

Harkabi, Yehoshafat. 1988. *Facing Reality: Lessons from Jeremiah, the*

Destruction of the Second Temple, and Bar Kochva's Rebellion. Jerusalem: Van Leer Jerusalem Foundation. In Hebrew.

————. 1986. *Fateful Decisions.* Tel Aviv: Am Oved. In Hebrew.

————. 1989. *Israel's Fateful Hour.* New York: Harper and Row.

Hassan, Manar. 1991. "Growing Up Female and Palestinian in Israel." In *Calling the Equality Bluff: Women in Israel,* ed. Barbara Swirski and Marilyn P. Safir, 152–61. New York: Pergamon Press.

Herzl, Theodore. [1986] 1988. *The Jewish State.* New York: Dover Publications.

Horowitz, Dan, and Moshe Lissak. 1990. *Trouble in Utopia: The Overburdened Polity of Israel.* Tel Aviv: Am Oved. In Hebrew.

Ibrahim, Youseff M. 1993. *New York Times,* September 12.

Isha L'Isha Daf Maida. 1990. (November–December). In Hebrew.

Jaquette, Jane, ed. 1989. *The Women's Movement in Latin America: Feminism and the Transition to Democracy.* Boston: Unwin Hyman.

Kaplan, Caren. 1987. "Deterritorializations: The Rewriting of Home and Exile in Western Feminist Discourse." *Cultural Critique* 6:187–99.

————. 1994. "'A World without Boundaries': Transnational Feminist Complicities and Resistances." Paper presented at the Department of Anthropology, the University of Rochester, March 2.

Karp, Judith. 1989. "The Legal Status of Women in Israel Today," 8–11. *Israeli Democracy* (Summer).

Keshet, Silvi. 1989. "To Run Over." *Yediot Ahronot,* February 2.

Kimerling, Baruch. 1992. "Al Daat Hamkom." *Alpayim—A Multidisciplinary Publication for Contemporary Thought and Literature,* 6:57–68. Tel Aviv: Am Oved. In Hebrew.

Kourvetaris, Y. A., and B. A. Dobratz. 1987. *A Profile of Modern Greece in Search of Identity.* Oxford: Clarendon Press.

Kristeva, Julia. 1991. *Strangers to Ourselves.* New York: Columbia University Press.

Landau, Yehezkel. 1986. Introduction to *Religious Zionism: Challenges and Choices,* 1–4. Jerusalem: Oz Veshalom Publications.

Lazarus-Yafeh, Hava. 1993. "Contemporary Fundamentalism: Judaism, Christianity, Islam." In *Jewish Fundamentalism in Comparative Perspective: Religion, Ideology and the Crisis of Modernity,* ed. Laurence J. Silberstein, 42–55. New York: New York University Press.

Lehman-Wilzig, Sam. 1992. *Public Protest in Israel: 1949–1992.* Ramat Gan: Bar Ilan University. In Hebrew.

Lieblich, Amia. 1988. *Tin Soldiers on Jerusalem Beach.* Tel Aviv: Schocken. In Hebrew.

Liebman, Charles S. 1993. "Religion and Democracy in Israel." *Israel Democracy under Stress,* 255–72. Boulder: Lynne Rienner Publishers.

Lustick, Ian S. 1993. "Jewish Fundamentalism and the Israeli-Palestinian Impasse." In *Jewish Fundamentalism in Comparative Perspective: Religion, Ideology and the Crisis of Modernity*, ed. Laurence J. Silberstein, 104–16. New York: New York University Press.

Lutz, Catherine A., and Lila Abu-Lughod. 1990. *Language and the Politics of Emotion*. Cambridge: Cambridge University Press.

Macdonald, Sharon, Pat Holden, and Shirley Ardner. 1987. *Images of Women in Peace and War: A Cross-Cultural and Historical Perspective*. Madison: University of Wisconsin Press.

Morris, Benny. 1991. *The Birth of the Palestinian Refugee Problem, 1947–1949*. Tel Aviv: Am Oved. In Hebrew.

Networking for Women: A Quarterly Publication of the Israel Women's Network. 1993. Vol. 6, no. 1: 3.

———. 1994. Vol. 7, no. 1: 1.

Newsweek. 1995. April 3.

Okin, Susan Moller. 1989. *Justice, Gender and the Family*. New York: Basic Books.

Ortner, Sherry. 1974. "Is Female to Male as Nature Is to Culture?" In *Woman, Culture, and Society*, ed. Michelle Zimbalist Rosaldo and Louise Lamphere, 67–88. Stanford, Calif.: Stanford University Press.

Oz, Amos. 1983. *A Journey in Israel*. Tel Aviv: Am Oved. In Hebrew.

Parker, Andrew, Mary Russo, Doris Sommer, and Patricia Yaeger. 1992. *Nationalism and Sexualities*. New York: Routledge.

Peres, Shimon. 1993. "Making Peace with Our Neighbors and Ourselves." *Tikkun* 8, no. 6 (November–December): 57.

Peres, Yohanan. 1969. "Ethnic Identity and Interethnic Relations in Israel." In *The Integration of Immigrants from Different Countries of Origin in Israel*. Jerusalem: Magness Press.

Peretz, Don. 1991. "Early State Policy towards the Arab Population." In *New Perspectives on Israeli History: The Early Years of the State*, ed. Laurence J. Silberstein, 42–56. New York: New York University Press.

Pratt, Mary Louise. 1990. "Women, Literature, and National Brotherhood." In *Women, Culture, and Politics in Latin America*, ed. Emilie Bergmann, Janet Greenberg, Gwen Kirkpatrick, Francine Masiello, Francesca Miller, Marta Morello-Frosch, Kathleen Newman, and Mary Louise Pratt, 48–73. Berkeley: University of California Press.

Rabin, Yitzhak. 1992. "Address to the Knesset." Israeli Government Press Office; *Jerusalem Post*, July 14. Reprinted in *Near East Report*. 1992. July 20. 4–5.

———. 1994. "An Explanation of the Gaza-Jericho Agreement." *Presidents and Prime Ministers* 3, no. 4: 8–10.

Rekhess, Elie. 1991. "Initial Israeli Policy Guidelines toward the Arab

Minority, 1948–1949." In *New Perspectives on Israeli History: The Early Years of the State,* ed. Laurence J. Silberstein, 42–56. New York: New York University Press.

Rorty, Richard. 1991. "Intellectuals in Politics: Too Far In? Too Far Out?" *Dissent* (Fall): 483–90.

Rosaldo, Renato. 1989. *Culture and Truth: The Remaking of Social Analysis.* Boston: Beacon Press.

———. 1988. "Ideology, Place, and People without Culture." *Cultural Anthropology* 3, no. 1: 77–87.

Rosenblum, Illith. 1993. "Like So Many Cassandras." *Women in Black National Newsletter* 6 (Fall): 5.

Ruddick, Sara. 1989. *Maternal Thinking: Toward a Politics of Peace.* Boston: Beacon Press.

Ruggie, John Gerard. 1994. "Third Try at World Order?" *Political Science Quarterly* 109, no. 4: 553–70.

Sekulic, Isidora. 1994. "Inside Serbia: The War at Home." *Ms.* 4, no. 5: 18–19.

Sela, Michal. 1989. *Jerusalem Post,* May 28.

Selah, Avraham. 1991. "Was, in Fact, the State of Israel Conceived in Sin?" *Haaretz,* October 4 and 11.

Sered Starr, Susan. 1992. *Women as Spiritual Experts: The Religious Lives of Elderly Jewish Women in Jerusalem.* Oxford: Oxford University Press.

Serri, Bracha. 1990. *Red Heifer.* Tel Aviv: Breirto. In Hebrew.

Shahak, Israel. 1994. "The Religious Settlers: Instruments of Israeli Domination." *Middle East Policy* 3, no. 1: 44–55.

Shani. 1990. "The Israeli-Palestinian Conflict: Questions and Answers." A Shani publication.

Sharfman, Daphna. 1988. *Women and Politics.* Haifa: Tamar Publications. In Hebrew.

Shiran, Vicki. 1991. "Feminist Identity vs. Oriental Identity." In *Calling the Equality Bluff: Women In Israel,* ed. Barbara Swirski and Marilyn P. Safir, 303–11. New York: Pergamon.

Shreiber, Mechtilde. 1993. "German Women: The Many Roads to Peace." *Women in Black National Newsletter* 6 (Fall): 12.

Sichrovsky, Peter. 1991. *Abraham's Children.* New York: Pantheon Books.

Simon, Uriel. 1986. "Religion, Morality and Politics." *Religious Zionism: Challenges and Choices,* 16–24. Jerusalem: Oz Veshalom Publications.

Simonson, Rick, and Scott Walker. 1988. Introduction to *Multicultural Literacy,* ed. Rick Simonson and Scott Walker, x–xv. Saint Paul: Graywolf Press.

Smooha, Sammy. 1993. "Class, Ethnic, and National Cleavages and Democracy in Israel." In *Israeli Democracy under Stress,* ed. Ehud Sprinzak and Larry Diamond, 293–308. Boulder: Lynne Rienner Publishers.

Snitow, Ann. 1989. "A Gender Diary." In *Rocking the Ship of State: Toward a Feminist Peace Politics,* ed. Adrienne Harris, 35–74. Boulder: Westview Press.

Sprinzak, Ehud. 1993. "The Politics, Institutions, and Culture of Gush Emunim." In *Jewish Fundamentalism in Comparative Perspective: Religion, Ideology and the Crisis of Modernity,* ed. Laurence J. Silberstein, 117–47. New York: New York University Press.

Steinsaltz, Adin. 1980. *The Thirteen Petalled Rose: A Discourse on the Essence of Jewish Existence and Belief.* New York: Basic Books.

Strathern, Marilyn. 1988. *The Gender of the Gift.* Berkeley: University of California Press.

———. 1990. "Out of Context: The Persuasive Fictions of Anthropology." In *Modernist Anthropology: From Fieldwork to Text,* ed. March Manganaro, 80–132. Princeton, N.J.: Princeton University Press.

———. 1981. "Self-Interest and the Social Good: Some Implications of Hagen Gender Imagery." In *Sexual Meanings: The Cultural Construction of Gender and Sexuality,* ed. Sherry Ortner and Harriet Whitehead, 166–91. Cambridge: Cambridge University Press.

Swirski, Barbara. 1989. *Daughters of Eve, Daughters of Lilith: On Women in Israel.* Givatayim: The Second Sex. In Hebrew.

Swirski, Shlomo. 1989. *Israel: The Oriental Majority.* London: Zed Books.

Tal, Uriel. 1986. "Historical and Metahistorical Self-Views in Religious Zionism." *Religious Zionism: Challenges and Choices,* 5–15. Jerusalem: Oz Veshalom Publications.

Teveth, Shabtai. 1985. *Ben Gurion and the Palestinian Arabs.* Tel Aviv: Schocken. In Hebrew.

Trager, Hannah. [1923] 1984. "The Women's Right to Vote." *Stories of Women of the First Alyia,* 132–35. Tel Aviv: Zahal.

Verdery, Katherine. 1991. "The Production and Defense of 'The Rumanian Nation,' 1900 to World War II." In *National Ideologies and the Production of National Cultures,* ed. Richard Fox, 81–111. Washington, D.C.: American Anthropological Association.

Vujacic, Veljko. 1994. "Laqueur, *Black Hundred: The Rise of the Extreme Right in Russia." Political Science Quarterly* 109, no. 4: 713–14.

Weber, Max. 1948. "Politics as a Vocation." In *From Max Weber: Essays in Sociology,* ed. and trans. H. H. Gerth and C. W. Mills. London: Routledge.

Weffort, Francisco C. 1992. "The Future of Socialism." *Journal of Democracy* 3, no. 3: 90–91.

Wolfsfeld, Gadi. 1988. *The Politics of Provocation: Participation and Protest in Israel.* Albany: State University of New York Press.

"*Women in Black* Statement." 1990. Pamphlet. Jerusalem, May.

Yaniv, Avner. 1993. "A Question of Survival: The Military and Politics under Siege." In *National Security and Democracy in Israel,* ed. Avner Yaniv, 89–104. Boulder: Lynne Rienner Publishers.

Yudelson, Larry. 1986. "Raising a Religious Voice for Compromise on the West Bank." *Religious Zionism: Challenges and Choices,* 5–15. Jerusalem: Oz Veshalom Publications.

Zajovic, Stasa. 1993. "Women in Black in Belgrade, Yugoslavia." *Women in Black National Newsletter,* no. 5 (Spring).

Zamir, Aviva. 1992–93. "The Status of Kibbutz Women." *Kibbutz Trends* 8, no. 13 (Winter): 54–56. In Hebrew.

Zerubavel, Yael. 1991. "New Beginning, Old Past: The Collective Memory of Pioneering in Israeli Culture." In *New Perspectives on Israeli History: The Early Years of the State,* ed. Laurence J. Silberstein, 193–215. New York: New York University Press.

Zmora, Israel, ed. 1964. *Women of the Bible.* Tel Aviv: Dvir. In Hebrew.

Glossary of Hebrew Terms

aflaya: discrimination

aliya: wave of immigration

almana: widow

am echad: one people

am Yisrael: people of Israel

anshei shlomenu: one of us

arumot: naked (feminine, plural)

ashkenazim: Jews of European descent

beezrat hashem: God-willing

beshem hashem: in the name of God

bikur hizdahut: solidarity visit

Brit Shalom: Covenant of Peace

boreh olam: Creator of the Universe

chariga: deviant (feminine, singular)

chasrei diyur: homeless

Chillul Ha Shem: desecration of the Holy Name (blasphemy)

Dai Lakibush: End the Occupation

datiim: religious people

domeh: resemble, be alike (masculine, singular)

domim: resemble, be alike (masculine, plural)

du kiyum: coexistence

dvar Torah: homily

edah: holy community

edot hamizrach: Eastern/Oriental Jewish communities

eretz Yisrael: land of Israel

ezrat nashim: women's space in the synagogue

galut: exile

ger-toshav: stranger-resident

gizanut smuya: hidden racism

Gush Emunim: Block of the Faithful

gvul: boundary, border, limit

haam haphalstini: Palestinian nation

hafrada: separation

Halakha: Jewish law

halutzim: pioneers

haredim: ultra-orthodox Jews

har habayit: Temple Mount

Ha Shem: God (The Name)

historia hadasha: revisionist history

hitnachalut: settlement

Kaddish: mourning prayer

kaliker: physical wreck (Yiddish)

kanaim: zealots

kapo: Nazi collaborators

kibbutzim: communal settlements (plural of kibbutz)

Kol hamtzil nefesh keilu hitzil olam umloo: To save one life is to save the whole world

Knesset: Israel's parliament

maavak: a struggle, a conflict

mahapach: upheaval, turnabout

mechitza: the divide between women and men in the synagogue

mefutah: developed

menukarot: alienated (feminine, plural)

minyan: the quorum of ten necessary for public prayer

mishelanu: one of us

mitnahel: settler (masculine, singular)

mitzvot: divinely commanded acts

mizrah: east

mizrah tichon: Middle East

mizrahim: Jews of Middle Eastern descent

mizug galuyot: ingathering of exiles

morat ruach: displeasure

moshava: settlement

moshavim: communal villages

motza adati: ethnic origin

Nashim Beshahor: Women in Black

nashim datiyot lemaan shalom: Religious Women for Peace

Nashim Veshalom: Women and Peace Movement

protekzia: protectionism, connections, favoritism

rak diburim: mere talk

Reshet: Women's Network for the Advancement of Peace

ribono shel olam: Lord of the Universe (for God's sake)

rofeh aravi: Arab doctor

Shabbat: Sabbath

sabra: native-born Israeli

shamoo et tzaakatenu: they heard our cry

Shani: Israel Women's Alliance against the Occupation

shavar et hakelim: broke the rules

shehorim: black people

shoa: Holocaust

shomrot mitzvot: women who follow halakhic life

shtachim gdolim veyekarim: large and precious territories

smol: Left

talmidim gizanim: racist students

Torah: Pentateuch, the Hebrew Bible, Jewish tradition

traifa: nonkosher food

uvdot bashetach: facts on the ground

veet tzaakatem shamati: I heard their cry

yefei nefesh: beautiful souls

yemot hamashiech: the coming of the messiah (miracle)

Yesh Gvul: There Is a Limit

Yishuv: prestate settlement of Israel (1880–1947)

zaam: rage

ze hamakom: this is the place

ze hazman: this is the time

Index

turnabout and, 175, 177; women peace activists and, 1, 3, 6, 46–47, 62, 68, 174

Mere talk: about international community, 213–14; political action and, 11–12, 47; about peace, 13, 98, 172, 177, 207; about equality, 35, 138, 149; deportation exposes peace agreements as, 186, 188, 208; about multicultural equality, 235–38, 240; peace agreements and, 203; political acts revert to, 207–9, 214, 225–27; public events and, 212

Meretz Party: advocates' talks with PLO, 190–91, 199–202; deportation and, 188, 199–200; justice and, 183, 202; mizrahim and, 161; turnabout and, 171–75, 178, 194, 250–51n.8. *See also* Labor government

Merom, Hagay, 189

Messianic movements, 100, 102–3, 106, 108, 111, 113. *See also* Fundamentalism; Gush Emunim

Military administration of Palestinians, 57, 64

Miliary service, 30, 38, 82–84

Ministry of Education and Culture, 142–43

Mizrahim, 133–70, 251–53nn. 1–10; definition of, 16, 20; discrimination against, 41; public culture and, 124; multiculturalism and, 234–40

Moledet, 23, 85

Morasha (development town), 151

Morris, Benny, 8, 9, 57

Mothers Against Silence, 5

Mourning customs, 27–32, 244n.6–7

Ms., 254n.4

Multiculturalism, 17, 234–39

Muslim Brotherhood, 85. *See also* Fundamentalism

Naamat, 15, 16, 40

Namir, Orah, 181

Nashim Beshahor. *See* Women in Black

Nashim Veshalom. *See* Women and Peace coalition

Nation-ness: as cultural construct, 51; Gush Emunim and, 104, 107; Jewish, 49, 50, 52, 59, 68–69, 71, 79, 176, 183; justice and, 183–86, 189, 201–2, 205, 208; legitimization of, 50, 55–56, 80, 91; Palestinian, 43–47, 49, 50, 58, 63, 79, 91, 107, 181, 196; turnabout and, 176, 177–86; Zionism and, 69, 183–86

Navon, Yitzhak, 173

Near East Report, 198

Neeman, Yuval, 182

Netanyahu, Binyamin, 197, 244n.3

Netivot (development town), 151–52

Netivot Shalom, 97, 98

Neturei Karta, 103

Networking, 221, 222

Newsweek, 238

New York Times, 226

Nitzan, Gabi, 250n.8

Ofakim (development town), 151, 152, 168, 252–53n.9

Occupation: denial of, 181–82; exposes peace process as mere talk, 207–8; human rights violations and, 41, 182, 196; under Left government, 39, 95, 181–84, 197; life under, 88–89; military service in, 82–83; power differentials and, 192; Right supports, 24; silence and, 205; vigils oppose,

Palestinian nation, 199, 213;
women peace activists and, 5, 21,
44, 46; meet with, 173–76, 179,
180, 181, 223
Politika, 168
Pratt, Mary Louise, 185
Production of politics, 11–13. *See
also* Public events
Promised Land, 50, 53–55, 59, 69,
70, 224–27, 247–48n.5, 249n.6.
See also Homeland; Land
Public culture (Israeli), 122–24;
between religious and secular
Jews, 125–31, 250n.8; divided
between mizrahim and ash-
kenazim, 133–70, 230
Public events: affirm coexistence,
89; construct sororal solidarity,
95; establish political facts,
11–17, 29, 47, 167, 207–9, 212,
214; rabbanit Levinger, 98, 99,
100, 102, 126; reveal limits of
feminism, 222; vigils as, 25, 41;
women's, create transnational
space, 44–46, 90, 193

Rabin, Yitzhak, 1, 4, 9, 13, 16,
171–86, 190, 194–95, 197–98,
201–2, 205, 207, 212–23, 225,
242nn. 2, 6, 243n.2, 250n.8
Racism, 52–54, 66–68, 138–39, 235.
See also Discrimination; Mizrahim
Ramallah, solidarity visit to, 44–48,
50, 60, 88, 89, 90
Ramon, Haim, 175, 179
Rashi, 111
Raskob, Hedwig, 215, 224
Rekhes, Elie, 56, 58
Religious Jewish community, 105,
249n.1
Religious women: for peace, 137,
249n.6. *See also* Women's peace
conferences, Jerusalem

Reshet, 5, 91, 123, 133, 138–41,
219, 224. *See also* Women's peace
conferences, Tel Aviv
Revolt against Rome, 103
Right, the: deportation and, 187,
188; Greater Israel and, 12, 177,
179, 185, 192; in Knesset, 203;
mizrahim and, 159–63; opposes
Palestinian nation-ness, 21, 45,
48; opposes peace process, 3, 4;
Rabin and, 201; rage and, 175,
179; religious, 69, 97–114; transfer and, 62, 195; turnabout and,
172–75; women and, 30, 221. *See
also* Gush Emunim; Likud government; Likud Party
Right, ultra: counter-demonstrations
to peace vigils and, 23–25, 28;
Gush Emunim and, 99; mizrahim
and, 160; as opposition to peace,
2, 3, 175, 242n.9; rage and, 29–32;
Tchiya, 176, 182; threaten democ-
racy, 71; transfer and, 80–81, 195;
Zionism and, 68
Riklis, Eran, 252n.5
Rorty, Richard, 236, 237, 239
Rosaldo, Renato, 141, 185, 244n.8
Rosenblum, Illith, 181–82
Rosenfeld, Maya, 182
Russo, Mary, 95

Sabbath, 19, 27, 69, 122, 123. *See
also* Shabbat
Samet, Gidon, 250n.8
Sarid, Yossi, 173, 190, 191
Schreiber, Mechthild, 217
Security, 9; coexistence and, 45, 59,
74, 88, 89, 90, 139, 204, 233; lack
of, for Palestinians, 93; Right and,
111; separate from Occupied Territories, 179–80, 184; threatened
by Palestinian state, 79
Sela, Michal, 140–41